SRI LANKA: VOICES FROM A WAR ZONE

Sri Lanka

Voices from a War Zone

NIRUPAMA SUBRAMANIAN

PENGUIN
VIKING

VIKING

Published by the Penguin Group

Penguin Books India Pvt. Ltd, 11 Community Centre, Panchsheel Park, New Delhi 110 017, India

Penguin Group (USA) Inc., 375 Hudson Street, New York, New York 10014, USA

Penguin Group (Canada), 10 Alcorn Avenue, Toronto, Ontario, Canada M4V 3B2 (a division of Pearson Penguin Canada Inc.)

Penguin Books Ltd, 80 Strand, London WC2R 0RL, England

Penguin Ireland, 25 St Stephen's Green, Dublin 2, Ireland (a division of Penguin Books Ltd)

Penguin Group (Australia), 250 Camberwell Road, Camberwell, Victoria 3124, Australia (a division of Pearson Australia Group Pty Ltd)

Penguin Group (NZ), cnr Airborne and Rosedale Roads, Albany, Auckland 1310, New Zealand (a division of Pearson New Zealand Ltd)

Penguin Group (South Africa) (Pty) Ltd, 24 Sturdee Avenue, Rosebank, Johannesburg 2196, South Africa

Penguin Books Ltd, Registered Offices: 80 Strand, London WC2R 0RL, England

First published in Viking by Penguin Books India 2005

The extracts on pp.182–183 and 195 have been reproduced from *When Memory Dies*, by A. Sivanandan, by kind permission of the author.

Typeset in Sabon by Mantra Virtual Services, New Delhi
Printed at Chaman Offset Printers, Delhi

This book is a belated gift to my parents for their fiftieth wedding anniversary, and for their love, support and encouragement to me.

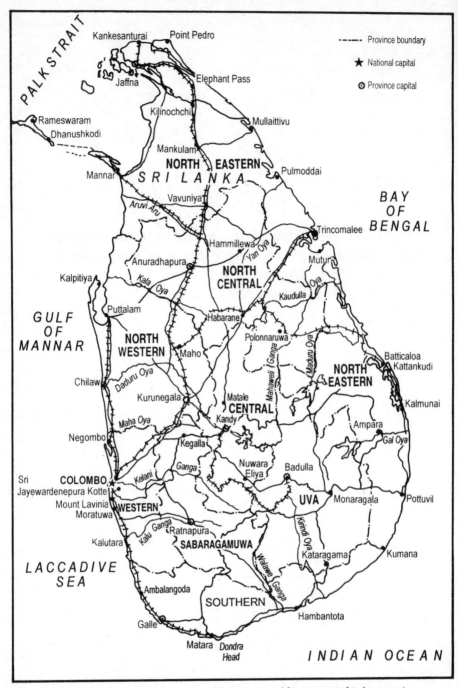

The international boundaries of the map on this page are neither purported to be correct nor authenticated by the Survey of India.

Contents

Acknowledgements

For my knowledge and understanding of Sri Lanka, I thank all the people who gave me their time, and shared their stories and insights with me. They indulged me with their patience and tolerance. Their numbers are countless. Some are in this book but many are not. I am grateful to each one of them.

I particularly value the assistance of the members of the Tamil parties that I was in touch with during my time in Sri Lanka: Dharmalingam Sithadthan of the People's Liberation Organisation of Tamil Eelam (PLOTE); Varatharaja Perumal, T. Sritharan and Suresh Premachandran of the Eelam People's Revolutionary Liberation Front (EPRLF); Douglas Devananda, S.Thavarasa and R. Vigneswaran of the Eelam People's Democratic Party; V. Anandasangaree, Joseph Pararajasingham and R. Sampanthan of the Tamil United Liberation Front (TULF); M.K. Shivajilingam of the Tamil Eelam Liberation Organisation (TELO); and Shankar Rajee of the Eelam Revolutionary Organisation of Students (EROS).

Rajan Hoole, Radhika Coomaraswamy, Loganathan Ketheeshwaran, Nanda Godage, Bradman Weerakoon, Pakiasothy Saravanamuttu, Rohan Edirisinghe, Jehan Perera, Jayadeva Uyangoda, Betram Bastiampillai, Sunimal Perera were always ready to help me with their analyses and views about Sri Lanka's fast-paced developments.

I owe special thanks and a belated apology to Air Marshal Harry Goonetilleke. On my first visit to Sri Lanka in April 1995, I intruded into his home for his analysis of the military situation, not caring that he was in mourning for his son, killed two days earlier when the Tigers shot down the military transporter in which he was flying to Jaffna. I still squirm when I think about it.

Thanks also to Ananda Chittampalam, a storehouse of information that I could tap at any time of day or night.

Several journalists in Colombo and elsewhere in Sri Lanka were always helpful—Karunakaran of United News of India, Sivaganesan and Nilam of *Thinakkural* in Colombo, Vithyatharan and Kuganathan of *Uthayan* in Jaffna, P. Maniccavasagar and Vivekaraja in Vavuniya, Victor Ivan of *Ravaya*, Waruna Karunatileke of Reuters TV, Shan Thavaraja and Thurairatinam in Batticaloa, Sinha Ratnatunga, Anthony David and Iqbal Athas at the *Sunday Times*, Lasantha Wickremetunge of the *Sunday Leader*.

The Nadesan Centre for Human Rights Through Law proved to be an invaluable resource with its well-catalogued books and newspaper clippings. My thanks to Suriya Wickremesinghe and the staff at the Centre. A special thank you to P. Thambirajah, chief librarian at the International Centre for Ethnic Studies (ICES), one of the first people I met in Sri Lanka. He was always helpful, gave me useful tips on what to read, loaned me books from the excellent library at the ICES and let me keep them for longer than he should have.

I can never forget the generous hospitality of Kumari Jayewardene, Sithie Tiruchelvam, Neloufer de Mel and Ramani Muttetuwagama. I cherish the lively banter and spirited exchanges at the dining table at each of their homes. I returned from those occasions infected by their energy and enthusiasm.

My wanderings across Sri Lanka would not have been half as interesting without the easy companionship of Marwaan Macan-Markar, Suzy Price, Kathy Klugman, Jane Ogge and Flora Botsford.

To Medha and Sondur, Sanjala and Sandeep, Bindiya and Yakesh, Patrick and Indranee, Jayshree and Trips, Juliet and Prakash, Shireesh and David, thank you for being there always.

I cannot thank Siri and Hiranthi Fernando and Siema Kundra enough. They opened their doors and their hearts to me and tolerated me when I treated their homes and their friends like mine. They went out of their way to help me. Siema was the epitome of patience, generosity and hospitality when I camped at her home writing parts of the book.

I began writing this book in February 2003, six months after I started my Nieman Fellowship at Harvard University. The fellowship ended in June 2003 and I had to return to my job at the *Hindu* after nearly a year away from work. I thank the editor-in-chief of the *Hindu*, N. Ram, for giving me a few more months off to complete the book. I also thank the newspaper's editor, N. Ravi, and the executive editor, Malini Parthasarathy, for allowing me to apply for the Nieman Fellowship in 2002, and to N. Ravi for his generous letter supporting my application.

Several people read through the manuscript or parts of it. My writing class at the Nieman Foundation read the first draft of the chapter on child soldiers. Their suggestions were invaluable and helped shape the book. Sue Valentine gave me valuable information on the Pass Laws of South Africa, which has put in perspective the chapter on Sri Lanka's Pass Laws. Siema Kundra, Vinay Kamath and Swarna Rajagopal were good enough to read through some chapters and suggest important corrections. I am indebted to M.R. Narayan Swamy, the author of two excellent books on Sri Lanka, for not only reading through the entire manuscript and suggesting changes, but also for being the first to plant in my head the idea of writing this book. I thank Kamini Mahadevan, formerly of Penguin, for saying 'yes' to this book without hesitation. My editor at Penguin, Nandini Mehta, was a constant source of encouragement.

This book would have been impossible without two people. Rose Moss, whose fiction-writing class at the Nieman Foundation I attended, was inspirational. I took courage to start working on the book mainly due to her prodding. She taught me the importance of using words to 'show' rather than 'tell'. Rose went through two drafts of every chapter, guiding me on both form and content. Her enthusiasm for the book was a tremendous confidence booster. I could not have done this without her.

Scott McDonald, formerly the Reuters bureau chief in Colombo, now posted in London, is the other person without whom this book would not have taken shape. With so much happening in Sri

Lanka, he was always busy, but he readily undertook the painstaking job of editing every chapter and then went through it all a second time. He set me deadlines and relentlessly pushed me, by email, SMS and telephone, to stick to them. Most importantly, he questioned several of my assumptions about Sri Lanka. I owe him a deep debt of gratitude.

Introduction

In 1994, Sri Lanka was in the throes of momentous political changes. The country was trying to shake off its old skin, over which war and violence had formed a multilayered crust. Chandrika Kumaratunga, a member of the Bandaranaike political dynasty, swept into power that year as the leader of a new coalition called the People's Alliance (PA). She was elected president on her promise to end the strife that had devastated Sri Lanka since the early 1980s.

The task was not easy. In the island's north-east, the Liberation Tigers of Tamil Eelam (LTTE), a guerilla organization with the capabilities of a conventional army and a reputation for terrorism using suicide bombers, had been waging a relentless war against the Sri Lankan state since 1983. Its goal was to carve out a separate state in the north-east for the country's minority Tamils, historically oppressed by the Sinhalese majority.

The rest of the country was recovering from a bout of savage violence arising from an armed insurrection by the Janatha Vimukthi Peramuna (JVP), or the People's Liberation Front, from 1989 until the end of 1990. The JVP was a party founded on Marxist principles that grew by fanning the flames of nationalism among the Sinhalese. The trigger for the insurrection had come with the 1987 Indo-Sri Lanka Accord aimed at resolving Sri Lanka's Tamil question. Indian troops were sent to Sri Lanka to help impose this Accord.

The Sri Lankan government came down heavily on the insurrection. The violence unleashed by both the JVP and the government killed an estimated 40,000 young men and women. The violence had affected Kumaratunga personally. Her husband

Vijaya, a popular film actor-turned-politician, was gunned down, in 1989, by suspected insurrectionists, apparently for supporting the Accord. It was not her first personal experience of assassination. In 1959, her father, Solomon West Ridgeway Dias Bandaranaike, was shot dead two years after his election as prime minister of Sri Lanka.

In 1994, people believed Kumaratunga was uniquely placed to heal the wounds of both Tamil and Sinhalese and gave her a massive mandate in the presidential election. Within weeks of taking up office, true to her promise, Kumaratunga offered the Tigers a ceasefire and talks on a political solution that would resolve Tamil grievances without breaking up the country.

In April 1995, my editors at *India Today*—I was then the news magazine's Madras (now Chennai)-based correspondent—asked me to travel to Sri Lanka to write about the three-month-old ceasefire and the prospects it held for permanent peace in Sri Lanka. By then, Sri Lanka was no longer a big story for the Indian media. Indian involvement had ended messily in 1990. Soon after arriving in 1987, the Indian Peace Keeping Force (IPKF)—the official name for the 100,000-strong contingent of Indian soldiers—was drawn into a war with the Tigers who had at first accepted the Indo-Sri Lanka Accord but later opposed it. Over a thousand Indian soldiers were killed and nearly 3000 wounded in action in Sri Lanka.

Despite the losses, the Indian army had kept the Tigers on the run. In 1989, desperate for a breather, the Tigers turned to the Sri Lankan government with an offer for talks. The condition was that the Indians had to leave. The Sri Lankan government, under fire from the JVP for the Accord, and facing widespread Sinhalese opposition to it and to the presence of Indian troops on Sri Lankan territory, made the expedient decision of taking up the offer made by the Tigers. When the Sri Lankan government asked India to withdraw its troops to enable talks with the Tigers, the Indian government, under attack at home for sending Indian soldiers into someone else's war, agreed.

Within months of the departure of Indian troops in March 1990, the Tigers were back at war with the Sri Lankan government.

India watched with aloof interest. With Indian troops no longer involved, the Indian media too lost interest. Kumaratunga rekindled some of that interest. Under her, it seemed Sri Lanka might finally find a happy ending to its tragic story.

For India, there was another point of interest. The man with whom Kumaratunga was talking peace—the leader of the Tigers, Velupillai Prabhakaran—was at the top of the long list of Tigers and their sympathizers accused in the assassination in May 1991 of Rajiv Gandhi, prime minister of India between 1984 and 1989, and the principal architect of the Indo-Sri Lanka Accord.

But the story of imminent peace changed dramatically even before I began my assignment. On 19 April 1995, the day before I was due to fly to the Sri Lankan capital, Colombo, the Tigers broke the ceasefire by bombing two Sri Lankan navy ships. The country was plunged into another war, its third since 1987. This time, the fighting would last six years. It would be Sri Lanka's longest and most fiercely fought war.

After that visit, I shuttled to Sri Lanka several times for *India Today*, until eventually moving to Colombo to be based there as the correspondent for the *Indian Express* newspaper in November 1996, and from May 2000 for the *Hindu* newspaper. In all, I covered Sri Lanka for seven years, a period that coincided with the end of one peace process and the beginning of another. When I finally left in June 2002, the wheel had turned full circle. Kumaratunga's government had been voted out. She still remained president, re-elected for a second six-year term in 1999. But the United National Party (UNP) she had defeated in 1994 was back in government. Its leader, Ranil Wickremesinghe, was the prime minister, having led his party to victory in the December 2001 parliamentary elections on the promise to end the war with the Tigers, just as Kumaratunga had done seven years before. In February 2002, the new government signed a ceasefire with the Tigers. Peace talks between the two sides began later that year.

This book is about those seven years in Sri Lanka. War is the dominant theme of this book as it was through those seven years. Specifically, it is the story of those years from the point of view of the people most affected by the events of that time—the people of Sri Lanka.

In his book *War is a Force that Gives Us Meaning*, the veteran *New York Times* war correspondent Chris Hedges speaks of most war coverage as not adequately portraying the horrors of war. He talks of the 'seduction of the machine of war, all-powerful, all-absorbing'. Perhaps it was the government censorship of war coverage in Sri Lanka, perhaps it was my diffidence about breaking those rules. The fact is I did not get anywhere close to the actual fighting. I now believe that to have helped me get a better perspective on the conflict. In order to compensate for what I saw then as a huge gap in my reporting, I travelled incessantly to those parts of the north-east to which journalists had access, and in southern Sri Lanka.

That is how I met the people in this book: soldiers and their widows; army deserters; the families of the disappeared; mothers of child soldiers; children who escaped from training camps; people displaced by the war; people living amidst war; a government official whose job demanded walking the fine line between the government and the Tigers; the only psychiatrist in Sri Lanka's north-east; a counter-insurgent; a child monk; women training to work as housemaids in rich homes abroad; the distraught father of a woman who was killed in a suicide bombing; people who thought they had escaped the war but realized they had become virtual prisoners in their refugee camps.

In years to come, historians will doubtless deal with the period in their own way. But orthodox histories usually look at events from above, painting broad brush strokes that do not take into account the lives of ordinary people who are affected by those events, and how, in turn, they influence the march of history. As a reporter who witnessed those turbulent years, I found the narratives of the Sri Lankans who lived through them crucial for an understanding of the way in which events have taken shape in the country since the mid-1990s right up to the present.

The little histories in this book tell the story of families, communities, towns and cities shattered and permanently scarred by the war. They also tell the parallel story of a leader elected with a massive mandate who had a progressive vision for a modern Sri Lanka, but who was trapped in a war so intense that she was unable to live up to her promise of peace. The people in this book and millions of others like them, crushed psychologically and physically by the war, resorted to the only weapon they had. They used their vote to defeat her party in the parliamentary election of 2001.

I am writing this at a time when the February 2002 ceasefire between the government and the Tigers has lasted nearly three years, the longest time there has been no fighting in the twenty-year-old conflict. By itself, this is a big achievement. But the ceasefire is not peace, which continues to remain elusive. The two sides held six rounds of talks from September 2002 until April 2003 but those negotiations were not about a permanent solution to the conflict. After the UNP's cohabitation government with Kumaratunga unravelled in late 2003, another election in April 2004 brought Kumaratunga's party back to power. This time it is in alliance with the JVP, now no longer insurrectionist as it was in the 1980s, but a party that has built its present strength through the ballot and an ideology that is a mix of socialism and Sinhala nationalism—pro-poor and pro-Sinhalese.

As Kumaratunga and her new government struggle to restart the stalled negotiations with the Tigers, many questions have as yet no answers: How far will the JVP, which is against federalism and devolution, allow Kumaratunga to travel in her efforts to make peace with the Tigers? But before that, are we sure that a federal solution is what the Tigers really want? Have they given up their goal of a separate state?

But the main question now is this: how long can the ceasefire hold, especially if the peace process does not resume soon?

At the end of December 2004, a tsunami rolled across the Indian Ocean from the epicentre of an earthquake under the seas off Sumatra in Indonesia, hitting several countries in the region. Sri Lanka was the worst affected after Indonesia. The scale of the tragedy that this disaster set off was far worse than anything Sri Lanka has witnessed during the years of war. The war killed 60,000 people in twenty years. Nature's fury killed over 40,000 people, all in twenty minutes, wiping out entire villages in the north-east and in southern Sri Lanka. The tidal waves did not discriminate between Sinhalese, Tamil and Muslim, making the conflict seem remote and irrelevant. But the hope that this might be the chance for all sides to bury the conflict faded quickly, with the Tigers bickering with the government over control of relief operations in the north-east. Indeed, the tragedy provided another opportunity to emphasize the lines of conflict.

Most of the men, women and children in this book do not know one another, but they are joined by the common thread of war. I met them and wrote about them in one form or another as I covered the conflict in Sri Lanka. They made me look at it through several and different eyes. Each of their experiences is unique, but the message from each is identical: there is no such thing as a just war, and there are no military solutions.

Certain is Death for the Born

When Kadirgamar Velupillai Somasundaram spotted his daughter's blue car at the Galadari Hotel, his hopes of seeing her alive again sank. Parking was always tight in Fort, Colombo's business hub, so whenever Vasumathy Somasundaram had work there, she parked at the hotel and walked the short distance to the business district. On the morning of 31 January 1996, she had to collect a cheque from the Central Bank.

All day, her father hoped she had put it off for another day because behind the hotel, the Central Bank, Sri Lanka's financial and economic nerve centre, lay in smouldering ruins.

At 10 a.m. that day, just when Vasumathy would have been there, Tamil Tiger suicide bombers drove a truck packed with explosives into the nine-storeyed building. Of the front of the building nothing was left except charred rubble. The blast shook all of Colombo, destroyed several other buildings across from the bank and killed seventy people in the bank and on the street outside. One thousand people were injured.

'But I was still positive, I still had some hope,' Somasundaram said. He told the parking attendant he would come back for the car later and thought he would check the hospitals first. 'She could have got hurt and someone would have taken her to hospital, that is what I thought.'

But Somasundaram was in no condition to face the hospitals. 'I was in so much shock, I came back home. My son, my daughter-in-law, two of my friends, they were the ones who went to all the hospitals.' At one hospital, a doctor who knew the family said she had seen someone who looked like Vasumathy being wheeled in. The doctor was mistaken.

'For two days, we waited. No news,' Somasundaram recalled. On the third morning, rescue teams found his daughter's burnt body under a concrete slab in the rubble of the bank. The family identified the body from the label on the shirt Vasumathy was wearing when she had left home, a scar on the abdomen from an operation, and a distinctive toe on her left foot.

'We still have the car,' he said, pointing to the garage where it stood. 'That was her first car.'

*

I arrived in Colombo as the Sri Lanka-based correspondent for the *Indian Express* just three months before the first anniversary of the bombing. On 31 January 1997, I saw page after page in the *Daily News* filled with first death anniversary messages for people killed in the Central Bank blast from their families, friends and co-workers. From among the single column photographs that accompanied each remembrance message, one face leapt out.

'Vasumathy Somasundaram, 1958–96,' the message said. 'Fondly remembered by her family and friends.' The picture showed a woman in a white sari, head held high, her gaze determined. Two verses from the Bhagavad Gita accompanied the picture:

Weapons cleave the Atman not,
Fire burns It not,
Water moistens It not,
Wind dries It not.

Indeed, certain is death for the born,
And certain is birth for the dead;
Therefore, over the inevitable,
You should not grieve.

From then on, I noticed the photograph with the same two verses

in the newspaper twice a year, once on the anniversary of the
bombing and every October, on her birthday. Each time I wondered
who this woman might have been. From the name I could make
out she was Tamil. The verses from the Gita told me she was—like
most Sri Lankan Tamils—a Hindu. But I was curious to know
more. Had she been an employee at the bank? Had she been
married? Did she have children? The address was in the insert, so
I knew where the house was. But it was only when I began writing
this book that I went to meet her family.

Vasumathy had lived with her parents off Flower Road, a
neighbourhood in Colombo Seven, the capital's upscale district. I
knocked at their door with some apprehension. More than seven
years had passed since her death. After all these years, would they
want to relive their tragedy with a stranger? But Vasumathy's father
ushered me in as if I was an old friend.

Somasundaram was seventy-seven years old and, like most Sri
Lankan men when at home, he was barefoot and dressed in a
checked sarong and a shirt.

'I don't mind talking about it at all. Talking helps me. If we
don't tell our stories, who will?' he asked, his tall frame hunched
in an armchair. The low centre table in the living room was cluttered
with newspapers, magazines and several Hindu religious books.

He said his wife Sriranjani had died recently, two years after
being paralysed by a stroke. Somasundaram attributed the stroke
to the shock of Vasumathy's sudden death.

'I somehow coped with the loss. But my wife really suffered,'
he said.

He described how Ammah, as he referred to his wife—a healthy
woman till the day of the bomb blast—first stopped speaking,
progressively lost her memory and then had the stroke. From the
time the bomb went off, Sriranjani retreated into a shell, showing
no reaction through all the phone calls and the panic-stricken
activity in the house, not even when Somasundaram broke the
news of Vasumathy's death to her.

'No tears, she said nothing,' Somasundaram said.

'On the funeral day, we were all standing around the coffin. It came to us sealed; we could not see the body. My wife came into the room and asked, "Where is Vasumathy?" You see, her mind refused to accept she was dead.'

During our entire conversation, Somasundaram broke down only once, while speaking about his wife.

'I really miss her,' he said.

In his mind, Somasundaram had kept a meticulous diary of the events on the day of the Central Bank blast, as it is now known, and of the days that followed. Now, as he spoke, he closed his eyes as if he was looking in that diary. He was at home, upstairs in his office, when he heard the explosion. Another bomb, he thought. There had been so many in Colombo of late.

'But the sound was so loud, I knew it was a big one, but where, I did not know.'

The windows shook and rattled like they were going to fall out, so the blast had to be somewhere close.

Some time later, his niece called to say the explosion had been at the Central Bank, 5 km away.

'I screamed out for God when I heard that,' he said.

He knew of Vasumathy's plan to go to the bank and so began making frantic calls to trace her. Defeated, at about 3 p.m., he set off for the Galadari Hotel.

Vasumathy was to fly to Sydney three days later. Like many well-off Sri Lankans who had contingency plans to leave the country if the situation worsened, Vasumathy had permanent resident status in Australia.

'But she was not going for good. She wanted to study and get a degree so that her job prospects would improve,' Somasundaram said.

On that day, Vasumathy was running last-minute errands.

'I told her I could go later to the bank and get the money, but she said, "Appah, I want to clear my desk before I leave,"' Somasundaram said.

'Thirty-two thousand rupees. Was it worth it?'

*

Even before the attack on the Central Bank, Sri Lanka's capital had become a battleground away from the main conflict zone in the island's Tamil-dominated north-east where, since 1983, the LTTE, or Tamil Tigers, had been fighting the Sri Lankan military to establish an independent Tamil state called Eelam. Every now and then, they would bring the war 250 km south to Colombo.

Since 1986,[1] the city had been the scene of several terrorist attacks by Tamil militants, suicide bombings and a string of political assassinations. The Tigers had killed Cabinet ministers and military brass in Colombo. They had even blasted the military command office. In 1993, a suicide bomber killed President Ranasinghe Premadasa while he was walking in a May Day parade. And in October 1994, the Tigers intervened in the presidential election by killing one of the two main candidates, Gamini Dissanayake of the UNP,[2] the party that had ruled the country for seventeen years until then. Chandrika Kumaratunga, leader of the Sri Lanka Freedom Party (SLFP), and a member of the Bandaranaike political dynasty, was Dissanayake's main opponent.[3]

Kumaratunga had promised during her election campaign to bring peace back to Sri Lanka. Her party, in a coalition (PA) with smaller parties, had already won the parliamentary election two months earlier and Kumaratunga had taken office as the prime minister of Sri Lanka. Even though the office had limited powers— under the country's 1978 constitution, the president, elected separately, is the head of government—Kumaratunga immediately opened peace negotiations with the Tigers. She evidently anticipated victory in the November presidential election. All over the country, there was clearly a wave in her favour.

In the north-east, the Tigers canvassed for Kumaratunga. In order not to disrupt her good equation with the Tigers—which she would need to continue the peace process after becoming president—Kumaratunga demurred from condemning the Tigers for killing her rival a few days before the presidential election. The Tamils voted for her.

Among the Sinhalese too, Kumaratunga was the most popular candidate. The grieving UNP put up Dissanayake's widow,

Sirimavo, as a last-minute replacement for him, hoping she would win on sympathy. But that did not work. An accomplished lawyer but a political novice, Sirimavo did not stand a chance. The country had seen too much bloodshed since 1983: first the worsening conflict in the north-east; then, from 1988 to 1990, an armed insurgency in southern Sri Lanka by the JVP, or People's Liberation Front. The JVP had gone on a killing spree, decapitating its opponents, burning them on tyre pyres or just shooting them down. Kumaratunga blamed the JVP for killing her husband, Vijaya, a popular film star-turned-politician who had floated his own party, for his support of the Indo-Sri Lanka Accord. The government's reaction was to meet violence with violence. Thousands of people disappeared in the south, never to be seen again. Given a carte blanche by the government, security forces hunted down and killed the JVP leadership. All that time, the UNP had been in charge. Sri Lanka was in the mood for change. People wanted to give Kumaratunga the opportunity to deliver on her promise, and they did.

After being sworn in as president, the all-powerful executive head of the country, Kumaratunga accelerated her efforts to bring about peace. Her first step was a unilateral ceasefire with the Tigers, which the Tigers reciprocated.

But Kumaratunga lost favour with the Tigers within six months of becoming president. In April 1995, citing bad faith on the part of Kumaratunga, the Tigers ended the ceasefire and pulled out of the peace talks. They announced their withdrawal by blasting two Sri Lankan navy ships berthed in the high-security naval harbour in Trincomalee, in north-eastern Sri Lanka. Fighting erupted immediately in the north-east. But more than that, the war came to Colombo in a way Sri Lanka had not experienced before.

*

I was with *India Today* news magazine in July 1995 when I went to Sri Lanka on an assignment. I remember being in a photo studio on Galle Road near Colombo's seaside when I heard over the shop's radio that a bomb had gone off at Independence Square. I ran out and hopped into a three-wheeler taxi to get to the blast site. New to the city, I did not know its topography. A short ride later, I saw crowds of agitated people walking hurriedly, all in the same direction. They were obviously fleeing the blast, I thought. The trishaw driver refused to go any further, so I got off and began walking against the flow of people to reach the Square. Ten minutes later, I was still walking and seemed no closer to my destination. Finally, I asked a man for help.

'Oh, you are going in the opposite direction. Just follow all these people, that's where everyone is going,' he said.

Independence Square is a small park in Colombo Seven. In the early morning and evenings, power walkers go round and round the centrepiece of this garden, a raised pavilion with carved stone pillars and pitched roof that are typical of Sri Lankan architecture. In the daytime, the garden is deserted, but there is always a crowd at a government office opposite the pavilion. That morning, a Tamil Tiger suicide bomber pretending to be a coconut vendor blew himself up outside the government building. He killed twenty-four people. Many more were hurt.

When I finally reached the Square, tense soldiers and policemen—sweat pouring down their faces, fingers on the triggers of their automatic rifles—were shouting, trying to keep people away from the taped-off area where the severed head of the suicide bomber still lay. His victims' bodies were laid out on the grass nearby. Patches of blood on the road showed where they had fallen. Coconuts and pieces of human flesh lay strewn all around. Pushed back a hundred feet or so by the troopers, people stood in semicircular rows, like an audience at a Roman amphitheatre watching a grisly spectacle. Some had climbed the pavilion for a better view.

Everyone looked bewildered. Many people were crying. It was the first time the Tigers had struck in Colombo after the short-lived peace process. Over the next few months and years, a series of suicide attacks by the Tigers would leave people in the capital feeling even more overwhelmed and powerless to stop the violence.

When the ceasefire broke, President Kumaratunga had declared that she would fight the Tigers and weaken them so much that they would have no option but to come back to negotiations. She also drew up a political package designed to give Tamils a bigger role in running their affairs than they had ever had in independent Sri Lanka. It was more than any Sinhala leader had done for the Tamils.

The political package, essentially a new constitution for Sri Lanka, had to be approved by parliament. Meanwhile, Kumaratunga would set out to win the war against the Tigers. Journalists like myself described this as the president's 'two-pronged strategy'—a military plan against the Tigers, and a political plan for the Tamils. Kumaratunga called it 'war for peace'.

The Tigers responded by striking terror in Colombo. They virtually laid siege to the Sri Lankan capital, which rapidly began to resemble a war zone. On each successive visit to Sri Lanka through 1995, I noticed more checkpoints and barricades in the city. Roads on which the president and her Cabinet ministers lived became no-go areas for the public. Schools shut down. Public places like cinemas and shopping malls were deserted.

With black humour, a Sri Lankan journalist friend said he was going to start a bomb-site tour of Colombo for visiting international journalists.

A noted Sri Lankan artist, Chandragupta Thenuwara, would later capture the mood of the time in an art form he named 'barrelism' after the oil barrels painted in camouflage colours that soldiers used to block roads. Barrels became the theme of all his paintings. One of his exhibits was a 'barrel map' of Colombo showing all the roads blocked with drums. In the small garden of his studio, he worked on installations with real barrels.

But the barrels could not keep the Tigers out. Government troops took control of Jaffna peninsula in December 1995. Two months later, the Tigers hit back in Colombo at the Central Bank.

*

President Kumaratunga was determined not to allow a repeat of 1983, when the killing of thirteen soldiers in Jaffna by the Tigers had provoked immediate riots and an organized anti-Tamil pogrom in Colombo. There are conflicting estimates of the number of Tamils killed in those riots, but everyone agrees the event was a turning point in the conflict. The UNP government of the time—the one that Kumaratunga defeated in 1994—had done little to stop the killing and looting. The riots brought the Tigers rich dividends, driving a wedge between Sinhalese and Tamil and becoming a powerful justification for Tamil militancy and the armed struggle.

With each suicide attack in Colombo by the Tamil Tigers, Tamils living in the capital feared they might once again become targets of mob violence. But following every attack, Kumaratunga asked people to stay calm and instructed her administration to maintain the peace. It was crucial to her plan of winning over the Tamils and sidelining the Tigers.

But the backlash against Tamils came in other ways. Of the 2.2 million people who live in Colombo, slightly over 12 per cent are Tamil.[4] Many of them have lived in the capital for generations. Others had moved there in recent years to escape the conflict in the north-east, confident that 1983 would not happen again. It did not. But when the Tamil Tigers targeted the capital, Tamils in Colombo were the first to feel the heat of the new security measures the police and army put in place. So severe were these security measures that Tamils who had voted for Kumaratunga less than a year before, began looking at her as enemy number one. The Tigers had effectively checkmated Kumaratunga's plan to win over Tamils.

One of the measures the government implemented at that time was police registration of Tamils. On paper, Sinhalese were also included in this scheme, but in practice, the lines of people waiting outside police stations to register themselves consisted entirely of Tamils.

Tamils who had recently arrived in Colombo from other parts of Sri Lanka—especially people displaced in the renewed fighting in the north—suffered the most because they had no permanent address in the capital. Anyone with Tamil visitors from outside

Colombo staying overnight had to register them at the nearest police station. House owners were reluctant to rent to Tamils because it could get them in trouble with the police. In working-class neighbourhoods like Pettah and Kotahena where scores of small hotels provided cheap accommodation to Tamils from outside the capital, the hotel owners had to update the police on new lodgers every day. The police made registration as difficult as possible.

Selvarajah Aadavan, a young Tamil human rights activist, spent most of his time those days getting Tamils released from police detention.

'Every police station was its own kingdom. There was no unified procedure. At some stations, Tamils had to provide recent photographs. Some stations wanted the landlord's signature on the registration form. At others, they would register the person only for a week or a month,' he said.

'In Kotahena, for instance, the police station declared that it would not register more than twenty-five people a day,' Aadavan said. A Tamil without registration could be arrested and so, people would queue up early to be among those twenty-five. At Koswatta, a Colombo suburb, Tamils were fingerprinted. The whole scheme spawned a market for touts and brokers who had lines to the police and could get the registration done quickly for a fee and thus save Tamils public humiliation.

Working with police lists, soldiers mounted cordon-and-search operations in Tamil areas like Pettah and Kotahena and in middle-class Tamil suburbs like Wellawatte and Dehiwela. Most were night-time operations. Soldiers would block the top and bottom of every lane in a neighbourhood and search house to house, demanding IDs and registration papers from old and young, men and women. Those without documents were taken to police stations. Many were released a day later after being put through a background check by police or military intelligence. But if they were arrested on a Friday, they could expect to be held until the following Monday because intelligence agencies did not work weekends.

'Of what use is carrying the national identity card when despite the card they are kept on the streets for many hours on suspicion during checkings?' asked the *Veerakesari*, a Tamil newspaper. The newspaper reported 1000 arrests in the first few days of October 1995.

Amnesty International said thousands of Tamil people were held in Colombo and in north-east Sri Lanka, solely on the basis of their ethnic identity.[5] The large majority of those arrested were released within forty-eight hours, but others were held for months without charge or trial. At the end of the year there were an estimated 600 detainees under the Emergency Regulations or Prevention of Terrorism Act (PTA).[6]

The government's panic did much to spread paranoia among Sinhalese about Tamils. Defence officials encouraged vigilantism. The police urged citizens to report any suspicious activity in their neighbourhood. Overzealous Sinhalese flooded police emergency lines with tip-offs about suspicious Tamils, most of them wrong.

Aadavan, who used to live in Batticaloa in the north-east before coming to Colombo in 1995, experienced this first-hand. Policemen and soldiers visited his home several times, and on three occasions, carried out a full search.

'Not ordinary searches. They turned the house upside down. Pulled out everything. Each time, it took us three or four days just to put things back in place,' he said. 'They would barge in and say, we know who you are. Where did you go in a trishaw yesterday? Who gave you money to buy a bike?'

Once, a policeman who had been to Aadavan's home during a previous search, showed him a letter. Written in Sinhalese, the letter reported 'suspicious activities' at Aadavan's address. 'The policeman was apologetic. He said to me, "When we get such a letter, we cannot ignore it."'

The irony, Aadavan said, was that he lived in hiding from the Tigers because he was among the few Tamils who dared speak against them. It had put his life in danger. He had come to Colombo because it was more difficult for the Tigers to track him down in a big city than in Batticaloa.

But with every attack, the security measures for Tamils only got worse. In the aftermath of the bombing of the World Trade Center in New York, people accused US security agencies of racial profiling. But this had been happening in Sri Lanka long before that. Every Tamil was a suspected 'kotiya', the Sinhalese word for tiger.

This is what a writer to the Letters column in the *Island* newspaper had to say in response to Tamil protests over such treatment:

> They accuse the forces of unlawful arrests of the Tamils. How do they want the security forces to prevent terrorist attacks? By asking, are you a Tiger? And if the answer is in the negative, allow them to go?
>
> Come on, you gentlemen . . . should know better. If all Tamils are good, then who are the Tigers? They are also the Tamils of the north. How are the forces to know [who is a Tiger and who is not]? So you catch them for us or tell us who the bad guys are and the forces will arrest them and bring peace to the nation . . .

I was caught in the 'Tamil equals Tamil Tigers' equation many times. My last name marks me as Tamil, which I am. There are sixty million Tamils in India and before I came to Sri Lanka, that name had never posed a problem.

After a suicide bomb attack behind a five-star hotel where I was staying in November 1995, soldiers barged into the hotel and demanded access to the guest register. They searched three rooms. All three had people with Tamil surnames staying in them. I was one of them. I later learnt that even before the suicide bombing, my name, combined with the press releases the Tigers sent me at the hotel business centre, had made me a prime terrorist suspect. It turned out that a hotel employee had even stolen a map of Jaffna from my room and passed it on to military intelligence as evidence of my links with the Tigers. Kumaratunga's administration never accepted that professional journalism meant keeping contacts with all sides.

At checkpoints, soldiers would thoughtfully turn my laminated government-issued press ID between their fingers and slowly murmur 'Subramanian' a couple of times to themselves before asking me, 'Tamil?' I always avoided the question and gave out only my nationality. 'Indian,' was my stock response. Usually, I was waved through on the strength of that and the serious-looking card with the government seal, but on one occasion, neither worked.

'We know all Tamils forge documents,' the policeman told me when I showed him my Indian passport.

He put me and the *India Today* photographer G. Krishnaswamy, also a Tamil from India, in his jeep and took us to the police station where we were asked to give detailed statements about our movements for the two weeks we had been in the country. He let us go three hours later after a Sri Lankan journalist called the police station and vouched for us.

Much later, when I was based in Colombo working for the *Indian Express*, a dozen armed soldiers carried out a raid at my home-office one afternoon in 1998, pouncing on press releases from the Tigers as evidence that I was a terrorist. The major who led the search chanced upon a photograph of me and the BBC correspondent Flora Botsford taken in Tiger-controlled Batticaloa in the east. We were posing under the signboard of a Tiger courthouse.

'Ah, so you went to Tamil Eelam,' the major said.

'We call it Batticaloa,' I said.

*

With the help of a few others, Aadavan put together a Citizens' Committee in Colombo to bring back some sanity to security procedures. But, he said, his efforts ended in 'failure'. After a period of hectic lobbying, he managed to persuade some prominent Sinhalese human rights activists to join the committee, but because they were high-profile people, they had other commitments and the committee soon became a grouping of Tamils.

'The police just would not take Tamils seriously, so we could not carry out any liaison work with them. The committee just faded out,' Aadavan said.

In 1994, Tamil voters had weighed in heavily behind Kumaratunga in the presidential election. Her slogan during the election was peace, and after eleven years of being in a continuous war, Tamils were looking for deliverance. Kumaratunga promised that. Just on the basis of that promise, she shot to levels of popularity among Tamils that no other Sinhalese leader had known.

When the Tigers walked out of the peace talks in April 1995, Tamils were still willing to give Kumaratunga the benefit of doubt. But trust in her changed to hostility within months when the government began treating all Tamils like terrorists.

I have young Tamil friends in Colombo. One of them is a lawyer, another a businessman. Each time we met, the conversation would veer around to how Kumaratunga was the worst leader Tamils had had to deal with in the history of independent Sri Lanka. The previous government, the one that Kumaratunga defeated in 1994, had stood by with arms folded during the 1983 riots. But to my friends, the humiliation that Kumaratunga's government was heaping on Tamils was as bad if not worse.

'Prabhakaran [the leader of the Tigers] is the only man who can show these people what's what. We Tamils need someone like him,' both would say.

Like Aadavan, there were many Tamils who did not subscribe to the Tigers' politics of terrorism but found themselves painted as Tigers—or Tiger supporters.

*

Like many well-off Tamils, the Somasundarams had moved to Colombo from Batticaloa in the early 1960s so that their two children could be educated in the country's best schools. When the political conflict between the Sinhalese and Tamils escalated into a war between the government and various militant groups, Batticaloa was among the worst affected places in the north-east. The Somasundarams thought they had escaped from it by being in Colombo.

'We thought we were lucky to be living away from the ground situation in the north-east. But it is our tragedy that we had to get caught in the war anyhow, in Colombo of all places,' Somasundaram said.

Somasundaram found it unbelievable that the explosives-packed truck that caused his daughter's death had passed through the city's checkpoints undetected. 'It went around the entire city three times,' he said, ticking off the places that the truck had crossed as its driver bided his time before driving it into the Central Bank. 'Those security fellows . . . donkeys.'

But for all the suffering that the security measures had caused the Tamils, Somasundaram blamed the Tigers.

'I am just not able to sympathize with the Tigers, whatever their cause might be,' he said.

Then he showed me a letter he had received from someone who, like me, had noticed the anniversary remembrances for his daughter in the papers. There was no name on it. The single sheet of typewritten paper was folded many times over and stuffed in a cheap brown envelope with the address also typewritten.

This is what the anonymous letter said:

To the family and friends of Vasumathy Somasundaram.

I have been wanting to write this small note to you, from the year 1997, but only now have I got around to doing it.

I sincerely feel sorry for you all that you lost your daughter. However, I am extremely glad to note that you regard her death as 'inevitable and that you should not grieve'. Is this because your God Prabhakaran killed her? I suppose he has the right to take anybody's life, isn't it?

If this is so, I can't understand why you Tamils (also known as under-cover Eelamists) protest when the Forces destroy the terrorists in the North and East. Then too, you should say that 'Death is inevitable and that no one should grieve'.

In its own perverse way, the letter brought up the question of crime and punishment. Demanding accountability, as the letter writer wanted Somasundaram to do, is still a distant dream in Sri Lanka, whether it is from the government or the Tigers. Somasundaram knew his anger at the Tigers was futile. Instead, he said, he blamed himself.

'Every day, I wake up and the first thing I see is my daughter's photograph. Every day, for the last seven years, I stand in front of that photograph and apologize to her for two things,' he said.

He holds himself indirectly responsible for his daughter's death by not allowing her to pursue a college education abroad earlier and for pushing her instead into an arranged marriage that lasted just six months.

'She would have been somewhere else now had I allowed her to go abroad for higher studies. And I would be telling you a different story.'

Notes:

1.   The first-ever terrorist strike by Tamil militants in Colombo was on 3 May 1986, when a bomb exploded in an Air Lanka plane at the Katunayake International Airport on the outskirts of the city, killing seventeen people.

2.   A suicide bomber killed Gamini Dissanayake at a public meeting on the night of 23 October 1994, two weeks before the presidential election.

3.   Kumaratunga's father, Solomon West Ridgeway Dias Bandaranaike, was prime minister from 1956 to 1959, when he was assassinated. Her mother, Sirimavo, contested elections in 1960 and won on a sympathy wave to become the first woman elected prime minister in the world.

4.   *Statistical Pocketbook of Sri Lanka—2002*, Department of Census and Statistics, Ministry of Interior, Government of Sri Lanka.

5.   Amnesty International Annual Report 1996, covering the period January to December 1995.

6.   The PTA was originally enacted in 1979 for three years and made permanent in 1982. It provides for detention of the accused for up to eighteen months without trial and without access to lawyers or family members. The Act can be applied to a wide range of offences. It allows confessions made to the police to be admitted in court as evidence.

2

Exodus

Kumaravel Jagan[1] remembers people scurrying past his home that day. 'Hundreds. Thousands. You could not count them. They were going like ants, moving, moving, moving,' he said. Men and women, mostly on foot, some on bicycles, a few in cars. Some cradling babies, others pushing children and the elderly before them to walk faster. From the gate of his home, Jagan watched them all as they fled Jaffna that afternoon of 30 October 1995.

A car fitted with speakers had gone up and down his street a few hours before. 'The men in the car were announcing, "The enemy is at the door, we must leave at once to protect the honour of our women, the lives of our elders",' Jagan said.

'People believed that. I saw the fear on their faces. You can imagine how much fear when I tell you that the announcement was made at four-thirty or five in the afternoon, and by six, all those people were on the roads, leaving.'

They were taking whatever they could carry.

'Everyone carried plastic shopping bags in both hands. They were taking whatever they could fit in those little bags,' Jagan told me.

Only those with cars or money to hire taxis took suitcases.

Jagan was talking about the exodus from Jaffna peninsula in northern Sri Lanka. An estimated five hundred thousand fled Jaffna on that October day in 1995, one of the largest displacements of human beings in a single day anywhere in the world in recent years.

The men in the car ordering people to leave were cadres of the

Tamil Tigers, who until then had run Jaffna peninsula and a large swathe of Sri Lanka's northern mainland virtually as a separate state, independent from the rest of the country. The Sri Lankan army was now marching into the peninsula from the northern tip to re-establish state control over the region. The Tigers were retreating south into the mainland under their control but they wanted to leave behind an empty peninsula so that government rule over it would become meaningless.

I came across Jagan when I was trying to put together a picture of the exodus nearly eight years after it happened. There were no first-hand reports of this cataclysmic event in newspapers, no television shots and few eyewitness accounts because, at that time, the Sri Lankan government had banned journalists from covering the war or otherwise travelling to the north.

A mutual friend directed me to Jagan as a reliable eyewitness. He was one of the few hundred people in Jaffna who had not immediately joined the exodus. He had waited a few days weighing his choices before realizing he did not have any. Now he lived in a run-down part of Dehiwela, a suburb of Colombo. We were sitting in the fading light of day outside his modest home.

Before the exodus, Jagan used to run a profitable machine-making unit in Jaffna. Now, the fifty-five-year-old mechanical engineer did odd jobs in Colombo to support his wife and three teenaged children. He spoke calmly as he brought forth his memory of the events of that day, but he stroked his short grey beard furiously and continuously. He spoke in Tamil. Now and then, he ordered his wife to refill our steel glasses with sugary tea.

Jagan said that at first he decided to ignore the Tiger announcement ordering everyone to leave.

'There was all the machinery. I was not going to leave all that behind,' he said.

In any case, the road was packed. There was no room to move on it.

'Imagine a 15-foot-wide road. By nightfall, the road was so jammed with people, bikes, and the odd car here and there, believe me, there was virtually no movement. You could take no more than a couple of steps at a time.'

It poured that night.

'I heard that at least ten people died,' Jagan said. 'I knew one of them slightly. He had asthma. It must have been the exertion of pushing his motorcycle. Motorcycles are precious possessions in Jaffna. No way he could have left that behind. I heard he loaded a lot of his things on it. He had a seizure that night and died.'

The next morning, Jagan discovered that of the 150 families in his neighbourhood, only four others had ignored the announcement.

'They each had their special circumstances. One was a pawnbroker who did not know how to transport his jewels safely. One was an old couple. Then there was a mentally upset woman. And there was another family, it had some problems too—some mental problems.'

Jagan was forty-eight then. Except for the five years he spent at Peradeniya University in central Sri Lanka as a student in his twenties, Jagan had lived all his life in Jaffna. He had never seen it the way it looked the morning after the exodus.

'It was a graveyard.'

*

The Sri Lanka-born Canadian writer Michael Ondaatje describes the country of his birth as a 'pendant off the ear of India'.[2] Jaffna, the northernmost province of Sri Lanka, must then be the little link from which this pendant hangs.

For Sri Lanka's Tamils, who make up 11 per cent of the country's nineteen million population[3] and constitute its main ethnic minority, Jaffna is the heart of the homeland they want in Sri Lanka. Jaffna is both the peninsula and the name of its most important city. For the Tamil Tigers, Jaffna, the city, is the capital of Eelam, the independent state in the north-east for which they began waging a war against the Sri Lankan state in 1983. They believe that Tamils are not a minority but form a distinct nation, possessing a well-defined homeland and separated from the

Sinhalese by language. Over a million Tamils call Jaffna peninsula home, even though two decades of conflict have forced half this number to live abroad.

On the Sri Lankan map, Tamils will point to their homeland, or Eelam, as four districts in the northern mainland, together known as the Vanni, along with the two districts of Trincomalee and Batticaloa in the east, tapering down into the district of Ampara. But the Jaffna peninsula is where Eelam begins.

Before we go further, I should perhaps give a brief background about the Tamils of Sri Lanka and why some of them wanted to break away from this tiny island into an even tinier independent nation. Most people in Sri Lanka—81 per cent of them[4]—are Sinhalese, and most Sinhalese are Buddhist. When the British gave independence to Sri Lanka in 1948, the Tamil people wanted safeguards to protect their rights in the country's new democratic politics.

They were afraid of being swamped by the majority, a fear that came true when governments dominated by Sinhalese Buddhists made it clear that, for political reasons, they would do everything to protect the interests of the Sinhalese Buddhist people, even at the expense of the Tamils. Soon enough, the Tamils began to feel left out. Aggravating their resentment was the introduction of a language act in 1956 that made Sinhala the official language of Sri Lanka. Tamils felt even more cheated when the government, under pressure from the Opposition, hastily abandoned a plan to give them a measure of self-rule in the north-east.[5] A new constitution in 1972 in which Ceylon was renamed Sri Lanka and became a republic, removed the section safeguarding the rights of minorities which the 1948 constitution had contained.[6]

Fed up, Tamil politicians first issued a cry for an independent Eelam in 1976. Just then, young Tamil men in Jaffna had begun to form themselves into militant groups to vent their anger against the government's discriminatory policies, especially in education. Tamil politicians began to use the militants to increase their bargaining clout with the government. But before the politicians knew it, the militants had picked up the separatist ball and run away with it.

The first time I heard of the problems in Sri Lanka was in Delhi University where I was a student at the Delhi School of Economics. A few weeks after I joined my course in 1983, I came across a pamphlet on campus with gruesome pictures of Tamils killed in riots in the Sri Lankan capital that July. Tamil militants had killed thirteen soldiers in Jaffna. The government flew in their bodies to Colombo where mobs went on a rampage, killing Tamils and burning their homes and properties. The month is now known as Black July in Sri Lanka.

India had sixty million Tamils of its own in the southern state of Tamil Nadu and the riots in Colombo triggered off an outpouring of sympathy there for the Tamils in Sri Lanka. Tens of thousands of Tamils had fled Sri Lanka to take refuge in India. The Indian government, which was separately pursuing an agenda of dominance in the region, used the riots to intervene in Sri Lanka. Through the mid-1980s, India set up camps to train Tamil militants, who came in with the refugees, and gave them weapons to go back and fight the Sri Lankan government.

Of all the nascent Tamil guerilla groups that sprang up then, the LTTE tolerated no rivals, and after a series of wars with the other militant groups, emerged as the most powerful group battling the government.

By 1995, when Jagan witnessed the great exodus from Jaffna, the Tigers had been running a semi-independent Eelam in northern Sri Lanka for nearly five years. They had held out against the Sri Lankan army and ousted the Indian army, sent in by India in 1987 to help in the implementation of the Indo-Sri Lanka Accord.

The Accord was aimed at ending Tamil militancy and giving Tamils limited self-rule. It committed the Sri Lankan government to implementing a devolution plan that gave Tamils limited self-rule in the north-east.[7] It committed India to assisting the Sri Lankan government in the implementation. The job of the IPKF was to disarm the militants and maintain peace in the peninsula.

India had already made it clear to the militant groups, including the Tigers, that they must agree with the Accord. The militant groups handed in their weapons once the Accord was signed. But the Tigers did so with great reluctance and, as it turned out, not fully. Resentful at being arm-twisted by the Indians, the Tigers soon enough made clear that they were not bound by the Accord, which, they said, did not meet Tamil aspirations for an independent Eelam. The Indian soldiers soon found themselves drawn into a full-scale war with the Tigers.

Three years later, after losing over a thousand men in battle, and carrying three times that number wounded, India pulled out of Sri Lanka for a combination of reasons. In 1989, the Tigers offered to talk peace with the Sri Lankan government on the condition that the Indians left. The Tigers made the offer at a time when they were under considerable pressure from the Indian forces. The Sri Lankan government jumped at the offer by the Tigers for its own reasons. It was under pressure from the JVP and other Sinhalese nationalists not to implement the Accord and to throw out the Indians. India was the common enemy for both Tamil and Sinhalese extremists. At home too, the Indian government was facing pressure to withdraw, and finally it agreed to withdraw its troops. By the end of March 1990, the last Indian soldier had left Sri Lankan shores.

The Tigers at once moved into Jaffna peninsula from where they had been ejected by the Indians in 1987, and established control over it. They ruled over a quasi-country in the peninsula that extended to the Vanni. Seven hundred thousand Tamils had fled Sri Lanka through twelve years of war, but 500,000 still lived in the peninsula, ruled by the Tigers, even though it was almost a medieval existence compared to the rest of Sri Lanka.

The peninsula had no power supply and no telephones. The government did send up food supplies, but not 'sensitive items' like fuel and cement for fear that these would be siphoned off by the Tigers for military purposes. Chocolate and instant noodles were banned items as these were part of standard military food. The government sent up neither surgical equipment nor a number of life-saving drugs in order to deny these to LTTE cadres wounded in battle. The only cars in Jaffna were a few dozen Austins, leftovers from the first half of the twentieth century. But the Tigers had their ways of getting what they wanted, including sophisticated weapons, vehicles, fuel and medicines. Government officials who worked in Tiger-controlled areas got their salaries from Colombo but took their orders from the Tigers.

In 1995, Sri Lanka's newly elected president, Chandrika Kumaratunga, decided to wrest the peninsula from the Tigers and re-establish government rule there. She had failed in her attempt to make peace with the Tigers. The Tigers had withdrawn from a ceasefire in April that year and declared war on the government. Kumaratunga decided to hit back. In October 1995, Sri Lankan forces launched a military offensive code-named Riviresa, the Sinhalese word for sunshine, to capture Jaffna. The operation was unprecedented. Never before had the Sri Lankan forces attempted anything like it and no one thought they would succeed. The Tigers were expected to throw everything they had into the fight. Instead, after offering some resistance at the beginning, to everybody's surprise, the Tigers withdrew south into the Vanni mainland.

But they retaliated with the exodus, depriving the government of an all-out victory. It was Sri Lanka's biggest humanitarian crisis since the flight of refugees from Colombo following the anti-Tamil riots in the city in 1983.

*

Jagan said people had on their own begun moving out of the path of soldiers in early October. The Sri Lankan forces started the advance towards Jaffna town, the main headquarters of the Tigers in the peninsula and the capital of their de facto state, from Palaly, the north-western corner of the peninsula. In Palaly, the Sri Lankan military had managed to retain a lone base all through the years of conflict. As the soldiers moved south to Jaffna town, entire villages along the path of their advance emptied out.

'That is normal for our Jaffna people. Clear out for a while when the fighting comes your way, come back when it has moved on, or after one or the other side takes charge. The main thing is not to get caught in the crossfire,' Jagan said.

For administrative purposes, Jaffna peninsula is divided into three sections. The western part is called Valikamam and Jaffna town is in this section, at its southern tip. In the east, there are two sections, Thenmarachchi in the south and Vadamarachchi in the north. A lagoon runs east to west at the southern tip of the peninsula, with a single road bridge linking the two sides.

By the end of October, Jaffna town was full of displaced people from the northern areas of Valikamam. They were living in schools and temples, with friends and relatives, anywhere they could find shelter. All the while, the army was advancing further into the peninsula. Then, late in the afternoon of 30 October came the car with the loudspeakers:

> 'No one must take this announcement lightly. We are doing battle intensely and bravely with a demonic force. It will attack us from several directions. We too will respond likewise. Since we are going to resist every inch against a state drunk with racism, you people must evacuate for Thenmarachchi and Vadamarachchi this same night.'

Jagan said the announcers did not say they were Tigers. 'But we knew no one else would dare give such orders in Jaffna.'

Moreover, bands of Tigers were going from house to house asking people to leave, warning that the town would soon be engulfed in battle. As if on cue, said Jagan, two mortar shells and two artillery shells fell in the town area.

Jagan was sure the Tigers had fired the mortars to scare people into leaving.

'One mortar fell right behind my house,' he said.

I asked him how he could tell who had fired the mortars. Jagan told me to put it down to experience. Army shells make a different sound from the Tiger shells. 'Over the years, we Jaffna people have learnt to differentiate one from the other,' he said.

The Tigers gave people four hours to leave but the people began moving out in two. Most headed towards Chavakachcheri, the second-largest town in the peninsula after Jaffna, across the lagoon in the Thenmarachchi section of the peninsula. The 20 km between Jaffna and Chavakachcheri can usually be covered in about forty-five minutes to an hour by bus.

'That first day, it took people about twenty hours. It did not matter if you were walking, on your cycle or in a car. The roads were clogged. Those with cars had to abandon them,' Jagan said.

Within minutes of the announcement by the Tigers, rumours spread in Jaffna that soldiers were raping and looting in the areas they had brought under their control.

'People were scared into fleeing. Don't underestimate the Tamil fear of the Sinhalese,' Jagan said. The Sri Lankan army, which grew into a fighting force only after the rise of Tamil militancy, is almost entirely Sinhalese.

Jagan added that he was unwilling to bow so readily to the orders of the Tigers. He held out in Jaffna town for twelve days.

'I had forty-five employees. Except five, all of them left with their families on the first day,' he said.

Every other day, a group of Tigers visited him and told him to leave or suffer 'bad consequences'. All the while, Jagan had been emptying his house and workshop of all valuables, including a lathe machine and a transformer, and transporting them to a friend's place in Vadamarachchi.

'Once the roads cleared after the first forty-eight hours, we made six trips with my stuff,' he said.

His route took him past the towns of Navatkuli, Kaithady, Nunavil, Chavakachcheri, Meesalai and Kodikamam.

'People would be standing around the junctions, looking for somewhere to go. The whole way from Kaithady to Kodikamam, on both sides of the road, people had put up palmyra-leaf huts for shelter. That was the first time I saw a slum in Jaffna. In some places, the smell of excreta pervaded the air.'

While he was still in Jaffna, Jagan described how he saw people who had fled on the first day creeping back to town to collect their belongings.

'They had to get a pass from the Tigers to cross the bridge and come back. It was only a day pass. No one could stay overnight.'

Many people who had pets and had left them behind made repeated trips back home to ensure the animals did not starve to death.

'On the eleventh day, the Tigers called at my place once again. They said if I did not leave, they would blow me out of my house with a bomb,' Jagan said.

He left the next day in his tractor-trailer, with his wife and three children. They went to a friend's place in Alwaye, across the bridge, past Chavakachcheri, then all the way up the eastern section of the peninsula to Vadamarachchi.

*

On two earlier assignments in Sri Lanka that year for *India Today*, I had written about the breaking down of the ceasefire and Kumaratunga's spectacular offer of constitutional reforms to the Tamils. Now I was back in the country to report on the government's offensive in Jaffna.

I was not alone. A large contingent of international journalists had flown in to report on the drama unfolding in Jaffna. We discovered we were grounded in Colombo. Guided by the misplaced conviction that control over journalists was half the war won, Kumaratunga broke her campaign promise to help build a freer press and banned journalists from travelling to the north. The rule informally came into force immediately after peace talks broke down in April 1995. By the end of the year, it had become a well-established ban.

Thanks to the ban, the exodus from Jaffna must be one of the few humanitarian crises of its magnitude not documented by the press first-hand. We were completely cut off from what was happening up there. There was no question of even phoning someone because Jaffna had no telephones.

Cabinet ministers gave various paternalistic explanations for the ban: the Tigers were so clever they would entice journalists who went to the 'other side' or Tiger-controlled territory, with their propaganda; the government was only ensuring the safety of journalists; what if the Tigers kidnapped a foreign journalist and then set conditions for the release that the government could not meet?

Journalists could not even accompany Sri Lankan soldiers in the advance into the peninsula. All we did was follow the story from the press releases the ministry of defence and the Tigers sent us at our hotels in Colombo.

Here's a sample of the press releases:

> Government of Sri Lanka has noted the statement issued by a spokesman on behalf of the secretary-general of the United Nations expressing his concern at the reported displacement of the civilian population in northern Sri Lanka. The government of Sri Lanka reiterates its constant concern for the welfare of its citizens in the north and its desire to alleviate their suffering in the present situation. The government is confident that it can handle the question of humanitarian relief in cooperation with those agencies whose assistance the government might seek.[8]

And from the Tigers:

> The mass exodus of Tamils from Jaffna peninsula has dealt a severe blow and signalled a political defeat to the Chandrika administration. It has made meaningless the political objective behind the Jaffna invasion. The mass exodus has clearly demonstrated the collective resentment and opposition of the Tamil people towards the strategy of military takeover of Jaffna.[9]

'This is the first war I have covered from my hotel poolside,' one journalist said to me. It was only half a joke. He was the New Delhi-based correspondent for a well-known European magazine, and like me, had a looming deadline and a major human interest story but nothing on which to base his reporting except for the empty rhetoric of the press releases.

An international television crew flew in but packed up and left when they found they could get nowhere near the action. For visuals, journalists could choose from stock photos or footage shot by cameramen of the ministry of defence, usually of two brigadiers shaking hands as they linked up at one or another strategic point during the forty-eight-day operation.

The director of information in the government's media ministry, Ariya Rubasinghe, was a friendly man but his job was to carry out government orders. When confronted by journalists, he would throw up his hands and say, 'I can't do anything. These are the instructions I've got and I am implementing them.'

First-hand accounts of the exodus had to wait till the people who had experienced it somehow made their way out of the conflict zone. When we finally managed to meet some of these people, they were too overcome by the suddenness of their flight to speak coherently and requested that their names not be published or at least be changed. The sketchy accounts of the exodus that we wrote after these conversations simply failed to convey the magnitude of what they had been through.

*

Further down the road from Jagan's home in Jaffna, in the middle-class suburb of Chundukuli, Rajanayakam Vasantha[10] also held out until the Tigers ousted her from her home. I met her too in 2003, eight years after the event.

'At first, I had no intention of leaving,' she said.

Vasantha had moved to Jaffna following the anti-Tamil riots in central Sri Lanka in 1977. Her husband, Rajanayakam, a land surveyor, was nearly killed in those riots. Eight years later, he left Jaffna to take up a job in the Middle East, coming back only for short vacations. For moral support during the exodus, Vasantha had only her teenaged son and daughter, and the daughter of a family friend who was living with them. She had come out of hospital only days before the exodus after being diagnosed with suspected cancer.

As the exodus began, she turned her home into a rest house for

weary people as they fled from Valigaman towards Chavakachcheri.
Old people who wanted to rest their feet, young couples with
children, poor people, rich people, all sorts.

'Whoever came, we gave them whatever food we had, water. In
that sort of a situation, you don't start asking names and addresses,'
Vasantha said.

A woman even gave birth in her house.

'Before she could walk properly, she was out on the road again
with her newborn baby.'

Vasantha's son escorted the new mother on her journey to
Chavakachcheri. The Tigers did not allow the boy to return to
Jaffna and Vasantha would be reunited with him only several weeks
later.

With the worry of a missing son hanging over her, Vasantha
had also to deal with a group of Tigers who visited her home every
day, asking the people resting there to keep moving. Several days
later, when almost everyone had left Jaffna and people had stopped
streaming into her home, a group of ten Tigers arrived in a tractor.

'First I heard a gunshot,' Vasantha said.

Vasantha, now a resident of Colombo with a good cake-making
business, went over the sequence of events slowly as she looked
back over the years.

It was just before dusk, she said. She was at the back of the
house, feeding the cows and hens in the small dairy farm that she
operated out of her yard. When she hastened to the front, the
leader of the group said to her, 'Leave now, or we will shoot you.'

They fired a warning shot in the air to show they meant business.

'I said to him, "I don't mind, kill me,"' Vasantha said. 'Then
they saw the two girls [her daughter and her friend]. They accused
them of working as spies for the army and threatened to kill them
both.'

One of the Tigers strode up to the house next door. The owners
of the house had already left. But there was a couple from somewhere
else who had stopped at the empty house to rest.

'He shot the man in the leg and then put them both in the
tractor to take them away.'

After that, Vasantha and the two girls left the house and started walking. They took nothing, not even a plastic bag like the others. It was 14 November, and they were among the last to leave Jaffna.

'I felt so ill I could not stand straight, but we had to leave,' Vasantha said.

She used to be a schoolteacher. On the way, one of her former students saw her struggling to walk, sat her on his bicycle and gave her a ride to Chavakachcheri. The blessing was that in Chavakachcheri, Vasantha was reunited with her son. He had been living in a house with other displaced people. When she saw him, he was threading his bicycle through the crowds milling around the main junction at Chavakachcheri, looking for food and water.

*

Legend has it that a king who ruled over northern Sri Lanka gifted a sandy tract of land in the peninsula to a minstrel or panan, with whose playing of the yal—a one-stringed instrument—he was greatly impressed. Historians have traced the Tamil name for Jaffna, Yalpanam, to this legend.[11]

Medieval Sinhalese literature refers to the city as Yapapatuna. The 'Kokila Sandesaya', or the song of the cuckoo bird, is a Sinhalese poem that a Buddhist priest wrote in the mid-fifteenth century after Prince Sapumal, the son of a Sinhalese king, captured Jaffna from its Tamil ruler. This is how the poem described Jaffna:

Enter thou, Yapapatuna, graced with stately buildings
Emblazoned with golden flags;
Gems and stones shedding brilliant transplendent,
In charm and splendour vying with Vaishravana's city,
Alakamanda.[12]

When the Sri Lankan army entered Jaffna on 4 December 1995, they found only the shell of a city. Jaffna was a ghost town. There were just 400 people who had defied the Tigers and stayed back. They had taken refuge in schools, mainly elderly people who could not have walked the distance to Chavakachcheri.

There were no stately buildings left, only burnt-out structures from a war that was by then more than a decade old. The latest offensive by the army had contributed its own share to the damage. Abandoned homes along the path of the military advance took the brunt of the shelling. But the government remained buoyant.

'Some forces have already looked upon the liberation of Jaffna, Yapa Patuna of ancient fame, as a historical parallel to its re-taking by Prince Sapumal in the 15th century by vanquishing the forces of rebel chief Arya Chakravarthi,' the *Daily News*, a government-owned newspaper wrote in a front-page story.

*

From Chavakachcheri, the Tigers began herding people to march further south, this time into the mainland, the Vanni. They knew it would be only a matter of time before the Sri Lankan military decided to take the eastern divisions of the peninsula. Their aim was to empty the entire peninsula of its population before the army took control of it.

By the first week of November, the Tigers had moved their headquarters to Kilinochchi in the Vanni. The top rungs of the organization, including the leader, Velupillai Prabhakaran, had been the first to move there from Jaffna.

But forcing people to retreat into the Vanni was difficult. Compared to Jaffna, the Vanni had nothing. It was a backward, underdeveloped area, mostly scrub land.

'Together, let us till the red soil of the Vanni,' a press release from the Tigers said.

To the people of the urbanized peninsula, this was not an attractive proposition.

'When we reached Chavakachcheri,' recounted Vasantha, 'the homes of all our relatives were already full of people who had reached there before us. We finally found a place to stay in Point Pedro. The Tigers came around again, asking us to get ready to leave for the Vanni. We just refused to go.'

But more than 100,000 people went to the Vanni just to escape the overcrowded conditions in Chavakachcheri. The houses in Chava, as Tamils call it, were all overflowing, sometimes with up to seventy people. There was no food. The bakeries were working overtime. People stood in bread queues for up to five hours for just one loaf each. With the banks all shut down, they were also running out of money. Drinking water was in short supply. People were collecting rainwater in upturned umbrellas to drink.

The Tigers offered free boat trips over the Kilali lagoon, the strip of water between the peninsula and the mainland. The land route was blocked because the army had a large camp over the Elephant Pass isthmus.

Velupillai Sundaralingam, a retired government official, was among those who did the crossing. He was one of the people I met in the days immediately after the exodus.

'The main thing people were taking into the mainland was their bicycles. I took mine too. When I crossed over, there was one boat just full of bicycles, another boat with their owners. There were two other boats loaded with people. A motorboat tugged all four to the other side of the lagoon,' he said.

At the jetty on the mainland, Tiger cadres—men and women—were distributing tea and bread.

'That was a big relief. In Chavakachcheri, the bread queues were a mile long,' he said.

There was a free bus to Kilinochchi. Sundaralingam stayed in Kilinochchi only long enough to sell his bicycle for Rs 2500. For Rs 200, he managed to buy an 'exit pass' from the Tigers to leave the Vanni.

'I got the pass because I am well over the fighting age. They were not giving passes to anyone between the ages of fourteen and thirty.'

He caught the next bus to Omanthai, 70 km south of Kilinochchi, at the edge of the Vanni where Tigers and soldiers eyeball each other over a strip of no-man's land. After showing his exit pass to the Tigers at Omanthai, Sundaralingam crossed into Vavuniya, a government-administered town in northern Sri Lanka.

From there, he caught a train to Colombo. I met him as he stumbled out of the train at Colombo's Fort railway station where I was waiting for someone—anyone—on that train who had witnessed the Jaffna exodus. He had the look of a person who has suddenly emerged from a dark tunnel into bright sunlight.

*

By April 1996, the Sri Lankan forces had taken over the entire peninsula. The government invited people to return to their homes. By June, those who had resisted the Tigers' attempts to shift them to the Vanni and stayed on in Chavakachcheri began going back to their homes. By the end of the year, more than a 150,000 people were back in their homes in Valikamam.

The Columbia University-based Sri Lankan anthropologist, Valentine Daniel, has described the Tamil psyche as being rooted in the *ur* and *veetu*, the Tamil words for a place of belonging, and house.

Ur, Daniel says, is person-centric rather than a defined territory such as *kiramam*, village, or *desam*, country. All inhabitants of an *ur* are believed to share in the substance of the soil of that territory. As for *veetu*, to a Tamil, it is a living being. It grows, 'goes through a formative period comparable to childhood, matures and attains a stable nature, interacts in perceptible ways with its human occupants and with neighbouring houses and ultimately dies when it is abandoned'. Daniel's thesis is based on research in a village in Tamil Nadu in south India.[13]

Daya Somasundaram, a research psychiatrist at the University of Jaffna, who also treats patients of war trauma at the Jaffna Teaching Hospital, was one of those who witnessed and experienced the exodus of 1995, and he uses Daniel's research to explain how the exodus had affected people in the peninsula.

Somasundaram is the peninsula's only psychiatrist. Like several other Tamil doctors who had fled the peninsula, Somasundaram too could have emigrated to the West but he chose to stay on.

He told me that in the Sri Lankan Tamil context, *ur* had become meaningless long ago. People had been displaced so many times during the long period of war that they had now lost the connection to the *ur*. Then came the exodus, which broke the link with the *veetu*.

'The home is like the womb in many ways. When a person has to suddenly abandon it, he is cut off from the womb. When people came back to Jaffna, their relationship with their home was all gone. They did not care for their homes like they used to, they could not be bothered with even the smallest repair,' Somasundaram said.

Many of the people he met, both professionally and otherwise, believed their homes were haunted by evil spirits and they could not live in them happily any more, he said.

Somasundaram too fled his home in Udduvil, outside Jaffna town, during the exodus. With him were his pregnant wife and little son.

'I did not want to leave but there was so much panic that the army was coming, I felt like I was being carried away in a flood and I stopped resisting it,' he said.

Somasundaram's first instinct was to take refuge in Jaffna Hospital, which was a second home to him. He had hoped that the doctors there would defy attempts to evacuate the hospital and hold out as a pocket of resistance to what he described as an 'engineered' migration. But finally, the entire hospital was evacuated to Point Pedro in Thenmarachchi. Somasundaram went too.

Somasundaram later wrote introspectively about the episode in the international journal *Medicine, Conflict and Survival*:

Doctors tend to pride themselves as being neutral, above politics, doing a humanitarian task without taking sides. Often this goes to the extreme of not knowing what is going on around them, an ostrich-like denial, feigned or real ignorance, hoping that the situation will pass them by. However, by refusing to take hard decisions or clearly analysing the implications of the situation, which they have the capacity to do, the

doctors only postpone facing up to reality. By then it may have become
too late with no honourable way out. They may also avoid taking
leadership in critical junctures where society may expect them to do so,
saying that is not their duty.[14]

The Tigers had clearly pressured the doctors into leaving. The
hospital operated within the International Committee of the Red
Cross (ICRC) Safety Zone. Somasundaram wrote that even though
the Tigers said they would continue to honour the safety zone,
they also made clear they would turn all of Jaffna into a battleground
rather than allow anyone else to run the civil administration in the
peninsula. The Tigers also convinced the ICRC that as all the people
were leaving Jaffna, there would be no more work in the hospital.
Finally, the ICRC arranged for the evacuation of the doctors to its
hospital in Point Pedro in Vadamarachchi.

Somasundaram wrote that doctors working in Jaffna had always
avoided involvement in the important problems that confronted
the people of the peninsula and opted out of difficult decisions.
This was so even when the Tigers killed one of their colleagues,
Rajini Thiranagama, in 1989. In such a situation, the evacuation
of the hospital under pressure from the Tigers was only inevitable.

'By not voicing their concerns and taking the lead in a society
which respected their views, doctors failed in their moral duty to
their community. As a result, when events eventually overtook them
it would be already too late.'[15]

While speaking to me, Somasundaram drew a distinction
between the continuing migration from the peninsula due to the
conflict and the exodus. 'People have been leaving Jaffna all the
time since 1983 and even before. They go abroad to live, they go
to Colombo, they emigrate. They have done that all through the
war. But there was never any direct force on anyone to leave. The
exodus was different, just the scale of it, of 450,000 people forced
to leave, all at once, all together.'

When Somasundaram returned to his home the following year,
he said he experienced first-hand the break with the *veetu*.

'Part of my house was occupied by the army. We were sharing

our space with them. I felt the sanctity of my home had been violated. For me, the spirits haunting my house were the soldiers,' he said.

Somasundaram talked of how people were using the term 'professional refugees' to describe Tamils. 'It's very true. I have heard people say after the exodus that they will never again leave their homes. But they have a bag packed and sitting in one corner of the room, and are ready to leave at a moment's notice if they have to,' he said.

Somasundaram described the exodus as a 'turning point' for the people of Jaffna. 'Like BC and AD, people talk about before the exodus and after the exodus,' he said.

Over the years, most people in Jaffna had learnt to accept uncritically whatever the Tigers gave them because punishment for non-conformity could be swift and brutal. 'Did Tamils blame the Tigers for the exodus?' I asked Somasundaram.

Somasundaram said even when the Tigers no longer controlled the peninsula, people were cautious about blaming them for anything. In all talk of the forced evacuation, people erased the role of Tigers. Instead they said the exodus would never have taken place had the army not launched its Jaffna offensive.

'It just does not enter into people's conscious thinking to blame the Tigers for the exodus. It goes to show how people's memory can be changed through totalitarian control on history,' he said.

He described it as 'collective amnesia'. 'It is not done consciously. Deep down, people have learnt to put restrictions on their memory,' Somasundaram said.

Though the exodus was the biggest migration for the Tamils in their history, Somasundaram said no one in Jaffna remembered 30 October as a special day. At the time there was some anger against the Tigers, but gradually, he said, it was forgotten.

'But were a lot of lives not saved by the exodus, forced though it was?' I asked Somasundaram. He said he did not think the exodus was necessary to save lives.

'There were discussions going on between the army and the ICRC and the United Nations High Commissioner for Refugees

(UNHCR) on creating safety zones, no-war areas. If the Tigers had not forced the exodus, perhaps people in the path of the offensive would have left, like it has happened during earlier operations. But not everyone.'

*

'Please get me exactly right on this,' Jagan said.

It had grown dark, giant mosquitoes were feeding off me, and the stench from a nearby canal was overpowering, but Jagan had not finished yet with what he wanted to say.

In June 1996, he went back to Jaffna, where the army had established itself, to restart his life. But he found it difficult to adjust to the new masters of Jaffna. In 1998, Jagan moved to Colombo in search of opportunity. Now he was thinking of moving back to Jaffna again. He had lived a disrupted life for nearly a decade. But for all that, he blamed himself.

'This is our calibre, the calibre of the Tamil people, that we have allowed our national struggle to be appropriated by an organization that is fascist, an organization that tyrannizes its people.'

Jagan added, however, that he would never join the Sinhalese nationalist clamour for the Tigers to be defeated militarily.

'We have to accept that Tamil nationalism is now in the hands of the Tigers. The day the Sinhalese finish off the Tigers will also be the end for Tamil nationalism.'

So what option do the Tamil people have, I asked him. His reply was one of both resignation and determination.

'The Tigers have to be handled by us, the Tamils. We have allowed a tyrant to come up from among us. Now we have to throw him out. But we cannot do it till the Sinhalese stop treating the Tamils as their enemies. Look at it this way, we carry a double burden now. We have to fight Sinhalese racism and the tyranny of the Tigers, both together.'

Notes:

1. Name changed to protect identity.
2. Michael Ondaatje, *Running in the Family*, Toronto: McClelland and Stewart, 1982.
3. *Statistical Pocketbook—2002*, Department of Census and Statistics, Ministry of Interior, Government of Sri Lanka.
4. ibid.
5. The Bandaranaike–Chelvanayakam Pact of 1957. The prime minister, S.W.R.D. Bandaranaike and the leader of the Federal Party (FP) that represented the Tamils, S.J.V. Chelvanayakam, signed an agreement for limited devolution to the north-east through a system of regional councils. The regional councils would have powers over specific subjects including land and land development, colonization and education.
6. Section 29 of the 1948 constitution, drafted by Lord Soulbury, sought to protect minority rights by barring legislation that was discriminatory against any community or religion. The 1972 constitution removed this section. Chapter 3 of the 1972 constitution gave Buddhism the 'foremost place'.
7. Signed on 29 July 1987 by the prime minister of India, Rajiv Gandhi, and the president of Sri Lanka, J.R. Jayewardene. It was the culmination of four years of Indian involvement in Sri Lanka, beginning with the 1983 anti-Tamil riots in Colombo. Under the Accord, the government agreed to set up provincial councils that would have independent powers from the Centre in specific areas of governance. The Accord went part of the way in conceding that the north-east was a Tamil homeland, main demand of the Tamils, by agreeing to merge the northern and eastern provinces temporarily so that they functioned as one province and under one provincial council.
8. Government of Sri Lanka, press release, 4 November 1995.
9. Liberation Tigers of Tamil Eelam, press release, 2 November 1995.
10. Name changed to protect identity.
11. M.D. Raghavan, *Tamil Culture in Ceylon*, Colombo: Ceylon Printers Limited, 1971.
12. ibid.
13. Valentine Daniel, *Fluid Signs—Being a Person the Tamil Way*, University of California Press, 1984.

14. Daya Somasundaram, 'Abandoning Jaffna Hospital', *Medicine, Conflict and Survival*, Vol. 13, 1997, London: Frank Cass.
15. ibid.

3

The Shadow Line

Sri Lanka looks like a fat teardrop, and about two-thirds of the way up the teardrop, 250 km from Colombo, is Vavuniya, the gateway to the northern Sri Lankan Tamil mainland. Imagine a line going east to west from Vavuniya. The government rules south of the line, over what everyone calls the 'Sinhala south'. North of this imaginary line, including Vavuniya, is all Tamil.

Vavuniya is the first Tamil town on the A9, the highway going north from central Sri Lanka. Jaffna is the last. The government administers both towns. While Jaffna passed into government hands in 1995, Vavuniya has always been with the government, its main link to what lies sandwiched in between—the Tamil mainland comprising the four districts of Mannar, Kilinochchi, Mullaithivu and the rest of Vavuniya, excluding the town, that the Tigers control.

Vavuniya's location on the boundary of the conflict zone made it the natural destination for people fleeing the fighting in the north. For that reason, it was also a natural destination for journalists. With the government ban on travel to LTTE-controlled territory from 1995 to 2002, Vavuniya was the closest journalists could get to the conflict and the people affected by it, and during my stay in Sri Lanka, I found myself frequently on the road north to Vavuniya.

Even in the worst of times, Sri Lanka could be breathtakingly beautiful, an enchanting mix of ocean blue and forest green. The highway north is narrow and winding and the traffic on it thick with fume-belching vans and trucks, but the canopy of green on both sides is like a soothing balm. At Dambulla, a religious and cultural centre with a thriving vegetable wholesale market as well, the highway splits. One road goes north to Vavuniya and the other heads off towards Polonnaruwa, another cultural centre, where the historic ruins of an ancient Sinhalese Buddhist capital draw tourists and pilgrims.

The state of the two roads tells its own story, part cause and part consequence of a conflict that has created two countries within one. The road east to Polonnaruwa is laid out smooth as a carpet and is a pleasure to drive on. But the road north to Vavuniya, on the other hand, deteriorates rapidly with each passing mile. After Mihintale, another pilgrimage centre for Buddhists, the highway was at one time just loosely packed gravel. Except for the odd farmer on a motorcycle, army trucks and buses, and absurdly large white vehicles marked UN or ICRC—equipped with antenna reaching up to the sky—were the only traffic on this section of the highway. The further north the road went, the farther apart the villages got, until a sprawling military base announced the arrival of Vavuniya.

From 1995, hundreds of displaced Tamils streamed continuously into Vavuniya. Many came during the exodus from Jaffna at the end of October 1995, and when the war grew in scale the next year, the number of new arrivals grew exponentially. When I went in December 1996, at least 9000 freshly displaced people had fled to Vavuniya from Kilinochchi where fighting had erupted two months before. Faced with these unprecedented numbers, the government converted several schools in Vavuniya into massive refugee camps.

Then, because of government and military fears that there were so-called Tiger sleepers among the refugees ready to fan out into southern Sri Lanka to spread terror, the government began to implement a rigorous pass system in Vavuniya. In its scope, it was comparable to the infamous pass laws of apartheid South Africa.

*

'My name is Rajalingam Mahendran. I was in the Poonthoddam refugee camp.

'Whenever I wanted to go out of the camp, I had to get a pass from the police post at the camp.

'After a few weeks, I got a job in a communications shop near the camp. I went to the camp police post every day to get a pass so I could go to work. It could take up to three hours to get the pass because there were many people in the line. If I wanted to leave the camp at nine in the morning, I had to queue up from six.

'The pass was valid only for six hours. If you got delayed, the police would harass you. You would be questioned: "Where did you go? Who did you meet?"

'But after a while, because the policemen knew where I was working, they did not bother me if I was a little late.

'After a few months, we were able to get a one-month pass. With that we left the camp and found accommodation in the town.

'The way you got a one-month pass was like this: you had to find a permanent resident of the town who could vouch for you. Permanent resident means one listed in the 1992 voters' list. For an amount, that person would sponsor your pass.

'Not everyone managed to get a one-month pass. Some people would get only a two-week pass. At the end of every month, I had to renew the pass.

'For the renewal, you had to take a copy of the old pass, a letter from the *grama sevaka*, and a photocopy of the sponsor's permanent resident pass.

'I had to take all three to the police post and hand it over to the policemen at the counter. The sponsor also had to come with me.

'If you went early in the morning, say by 6 or 7 a.m., you could finish the major part of the renewal by 10 or 11 a.m.

'The police would take the papers. They would ask me to come back in the afternoon.

'I would go and collect it. The sponsor did not have to be present at that time.

'The one-month pass was for Vavuniya only. I could not leave Vavuniya.'

*

Mahendran was twenty-four years old when he arrived in Vavuniya in November 1996. Mahendran had had to leave Jaffna with his aunt and her two daughters during the exodus of October 1995. They trekked first to Chavakachcheri in the peninsula and then, on orders from the Tigers, crossed the Kilali lagoon to the northern Vanni mainland. For a while they lived in Kilinochchi.

Conditions in Tiger-controlled Sri Lanka were difficult. Refugees were everywhere, staying wherever they could find room, usually in unsanitary conditions. Food was always in short supply. The Sri Lankan government sent essential supplies to the Vanni for the refugees from Jaffna but the quantities were inadequate. Traders from Vavuniya took up bags of supplies but few could afford to buy.

Mahendran and his family crammed into the home of a relative. The only consolation was that they were away from the fighting. Then, in September 1996, the war came right up to them once again. Having conquered Jaffna peninsula, government troops decided to work their way downwards into the Tiger-controlled mainland. Kilinochchi was their target.

Unlike in the peninsula in 1995, the Tigers put up a fight but finally decided to withdraw from Kilinochchi when they realized they could not stop the troops. The entire population of Kilinochchi went with them, deeper into the Vanni.

Like many people at the time, Mahendran decided that rather than move each time fighting erupted, it might be simpler to live in government-administered Sri Lanka. With his aunt and cousins, he moved south to Vavuniya.

Through twenty years of war, many Tamils displaced from the Tamil mainland had decided to settle in Vavuniya and call it home. Vavuniya was behind government lines, so it was not in the heart of the conflict zone and was unlikely to see any fighting unless the Tigers decided to launch an offensive to grab it from the government. Vavuniya was one of the few Tamil towns in Sri Lanka where life had a semblance of normality.

Unlike the Vanni, Vavuniya had electricity. It had telephones and public transport. Unlike in the Vanni where children studied in war-damaged buildings, the schools in Vavuniya functioned in proper buildings. There were plenty of shops where traders from the Vanni bought supplies and took them back across the 'border'. Vavuniya bustled with commerce. There were job possibilities. If nothing worked, there was always Colombo, connected to Vavuniya by rail and road.

Mahendran had to apply to the Tigers for 'exit' passes to leave their territory for government-controlled Vavuniya. He was plain lucky they let him go, because he was of fighting age. He paid Rs 750 for each pass. The family took a bus to Omanthai, the final Tiger checkpoint. From there, they trekked across the stretch of no-man's land to reach Thandikulam, the military checkpoint at the boundary. When refugees from the Vanni arrived at Thandikulam, soldiers usually kept them in a holding area to question them and check for connections to the Tigers. In 1996, with the threat of suicide bomb attacks by the Tigers hanging over Colombo, Mahendran had to go through three agencies, each with its own set of interrogators and questions: the National Intelligence Bureau (NIB) of the police, military intelligence and the counter-subversive unit of the military.

Mahendran and his family survived the screening. But they discovered that they had arrived in a vast open-air prison.

I met Mahendran months after the war had given way to a ceasefire between the Tigers and a new government led by Kumaratunga's arch opponent from the UNP, Ranil Wickremesinghe, in February 2002. Eager to win the trust of the Tamils as he wooed the Tigers for peace talks, Wickremesinghe revoked the pass system immediately after signing the ceasefire.

A friend in Vavuniya introduced me to Mahendran. We met at the Vavuniya Rest House, a run-down government motel popular mainly with travelling salesmen and the town drunks who began hitting the brandy in its bar right from morning. Mahendran had taken time off from his lathe shop to meet me, and he smelt of hot metal.

We sat in the dusty veranda and as Mahendran began talking about the pass system, I expected him to tell me stories of great suffering. Instead, I realized the system had become so much a part of him that it was now a mere procedure in his memory.

We spoke in Tamil. With a deadpan look on his face, the small-built man reeled off the procedure to me step by step, as if he was teaching me to fill a credit card application. Frequently, he slipped into the present tense as he described a system that had ceased to exist.

'If you needed to travel outside Vavuniya, you had to apply for a travel pass.

'Say you wanted to go to Colombo urgently on some work. First, you have to produce a sponsorship from a permanent resident. Then, you have to give the address in Colombo where you are going to stay. The Vavuniya police would send a message to the police station in that particular area of Colombo to check the address and also the people living there.

'They will get back to the Vavuniya police to give the clearance. Then the Vavuniya police will issue the travel pass. The whole process could take about two or three weeks.

'But the travel pass was only for fourteen days. You had to come back in that time otherwise the sponsor would be in trouble. The police took the sponsor's permanent pass and national identity card and kept it with them when they gave you the travel pass. And you would be arrested in Colombo for overstaying,' Mahendran said.

Ten-to-Ten, a story about township life in 1950s' South Africa by the journalist–writer Can Themba, is a tragicomic depiction of the pass laws the white rulers of that country imposed on its black people. In Marabastad, a township in Pretoria that he wrote about, curfew hour for all black Africans was 10 p.m.

'By that hour every African man, woman and child had to be indoors, preferably in bed; if the police caught you abroad without a "special permit", you were hauled off to the battleship-grey little police station in First Avenue near the Apies River and clapped in jail.' The next morning, the magistrate would set the transgressor free after a 'scathing lecture' and a hefty fine.[1]

No such luck in Sri Lanka. In Vavuniya, from 1996 to 2002, a Tamil without a permit at any hour of the day could be jailed under Sri Lanka's Emergency laws, including for up to eighteen months without being charged under PTA.

'I never went out of Vavuniya.' Not until he obtained a permanent pass five years later. Mahendran said he had now made Vavuniya his home.

*

The Procedure Which Is Now Followed To Issue Passes In Vavuniya Division (To Enter Vavuniya, Stay In Vavuniya and Leave From Vavuniya).

These words, in bold and underlined, on a memo from the superintendent of police of Vavuniya to 'Police Officers and Public Servants', are the prelude to six pages of details on the fifteen types of passes defence ministry bureaucrats thought up to regulate the movement of more than 100,000 Tamils who had poured into Vavuniya at that time.

Police, Police Officer and Police Station appear in upper case all through the memo, just in case the reader needs reminding who is boss. With its Orwellian rules and conditions, all set out in bewildering and often ungrammatical English, the memo is a crucial document in the history of the Sri Lankan conflict.

Under Travel Pass, the memo had this to say:

For travel pass a surety is compulsory and permanent pass of the surety will be retained as surety. A photocopy of the pass duly certified will be given to the surety . . .

Computer pass will be issued for travel to the South with the photograph and details of the pass holder and a lodging pass for the period he has to stay will be prepared and sent to Colombo Information Technology Division and through that it will be referred to respective Police. In case of station outside Colombo, the lodging pass will be sent by fax by the OIC [officer-in-charge] in charge of division. It will be referred to the relevant Police Officer by him. The person who travel with the travelling pass, after reaching his destination, should report within 24 hours to the relevant Police Station and obtain that pass. The pass, which he carried, will be kept at the Police Station. After the necessary period is over he should produce the lodging pass to the relevant Police and return before due date.

When an application is submitted for a travel pass, it will be referred to the Police where he intend to go for a report regarding person mentioned in the address given in the application and only after this, travel pass will be issued . . .

Those with a three-month 'open' pass could travel out of Vavuniya but 'they have no right to settle down in outstation'. Only those with a three-month 'card' pass could apply for a three-month open pass. And only those who had renewed their one-month pass six times were eligible for the three-month pass.

Even people visiting Vavuniya from the south could not escape the pass system. On each visit to Sri Lanka in 1995 and 1996, I travelled to Vavuniya looking for what editors called the 'refugee angle' of the story.

At Erataiperiyakulam, about 10 km short of Vavuniya on the A9 Highway, military police and regular police would wave down the car, look in through the window, and ask where I was headed. All I had to do then was show my press accreditation card issued by the Sri Lankan government and they would wave me through.

By mid-1997, the system had changed; and with it, the checkpoint. It had grown to include a couple of sheds where policemen sat at counters registering vehicles and the people in them. A dozen vehicles stood in a makeshift parking area by the side of the road while the drivers went through the procedure. I got a pink slip that gave me a day to finish my work in Vavuniya. The policeman told me that if I intended to stay longer, I would have to apply for an extension—known as a 'white pass'—at a police post in Vavuniya called Brown, the name of an old British trading company in whose vacant premises the police post functioned.

The next morning saw me in line with scores of other people outside Brown to get the white pass.

It threatened to take up all morning. I thought I would make use of the time by interviewing people ahead and behind me in the line. Soon there was a crowd around me. Everyone was speaking at once. Two armed soldiers walked up and asked me who I was. I showed them the press ID. They said I was causing a disturbance and asked me to leave the area. When I said I needed to extend my pass, the soldiers curtly repeated their order. They asked me to meet the government agent, the senior civilian administrator of Vavuniya.

*

The government agent in Sri Lanka is literally what his designation says: the representative of the government in a geographical area defined as a district. The system, known as the Sri Lanka Administrative Service, is a legacy of the British. India has its equivalent in the Indian Administrative Service. As with the Indian district collector, the government agent in Sri Lanka is the main figure of power and authority in a district.

But in reality, from 1995 when refugees from Tiger-held areas began flooding Vavuniya, the commander of the massive army base outside the town was the person running the district. The government agent merely did his bidding. From his *kachcheri*, Ganesh ran fourteen refugee camps—the government called them welfare centres—under the tight security regime of the army and police.

Kandiah Ganesh, the government agent, was so soft-spoken I had to lean forward over the glass-topped table to hear him. His office was a vast room in the Vavuniya divisional secretariat, known as the kachcheri. Four long tables arranged in a rectangle took up most of the room. Behind this conference hall arrangement, looking almost birdlike, sat Ganesh at his table.

I met Ganesh every time I was in Vavuniya. He was always in a rush but made the time to speak to me, even if it was only for a few minutes. But he was conscious of his position and was always careful in what he said. He was not just the government agent, he was also Tamil, and he did not want to be seen as making comments that might be construed as political statements by either the government or the Tigers. Ganesh was most comfortable when reeling off statistics: numbers of refugees, numbers of camps, numbers of food trucks, numbers of water bowsers, any other kind of numbers. For my ready reference, he would hand out entire booklets full of numbers that he had prepared.

Ganesh knew by heart the exact amounts of food rations for each category: weekly dry rations to the value of Rs 84 for single-member families; Rs 252 for two-member families; Rs 210 for three-member families. A family of four got rations worth Rs 252 every week. For a family of five, the allocation was Rs 315.

He spoke little and chose his words with care. As with many bureaucrats caught in trying times, what he said between the lines was more important than the lines themselves. When he said he was trying to get the rations increased, I understood he was trying to tell me the rations were inadequate. Tucked away in one of the many booklets that he gave me was a comparison between the food quotas that refugees got and the actual requirements of a Sri Lankan family according to a government survey in 1995. The refugees were getting less than half of what they needed.

When the refugees first began coming in to Vavuniya, he told a Sri Lankan journalist: 'These people will not be allowed to step out of the schools allocated to them and police will restrict their movements from outside the camps, making sure that nobody escapes.'[2]

It sounded like a hidden warning to the refugees of the fate that awaited them in Vavuniya.

When I questioned him about the pass system, he said the civil administration had nothing to do with it. 'It is administered by the security forces. Police mainly, and army. It's a very strict system. They say it is necessary for the security of Colombo and the rest of the country.'

Of late, he said, in addition to his other work, it had become part of his duties to 'intervene' with security officials on behalf of people seeking passes to travel out of Vavuniya. Most wanted to visit Colombo. In the spacious compound of the kachcheri, people stood huddled in anxious bunches holding petitions addressed to him explaining why they needed to travel to Colombo and requesting his help.

'I try to help all genuine cases,' he said. But his recommendation was no guarantee that a person would get a pass.

Vavuniya abounded with stories about people who needed to travel out for all sorts of emergencies but were refused passes. Passed around from person to person by word of mouth, the stories were almost folklore. There was the story of a woman who developed complications in the last stages of pregnancy. Doctors at the Vavuniya hopsital sent her in an ambulance 60 km south to the better-equipped hospital at Anuradhapura. But her husband was not allowed to travel with her. At Anuradhapura, the woman delivered a baby that lived for only two days. The husband tried every way he knew to get a pass so he could be with his wife, including an appeal to the government agent and the UNHCR, but it was useless. Finally, the woman buried her child in Anuradhapura with the help of the hospital staff and came back to Vavuniya by herself.

Even those who considered themselves influential found their influence did not go far when it came to the pass system. A member of a Tamil political party represented in the Sri Lankan parliament discovered he could not get a travel pass in time to attend his brother-in-law's funeral in central Sri Lanka.

Another restriction on movement was a 'fuel control plan' that limited the amount of petrol and diesel that vehicle owners could buy.

'According to this plan, petrol and diesel will be issued to government departments/NGO officials/private individuals only on permit/coupons issued by the Sri Lankan army,' an internal government memo said.

Motorcycle owners could buy only 15 litres of petrol a month. Those with cars were limited to 30 litres or less than one full tank

a month. Commercial vehicles like trishaws, trucks, buses and vans
could get up to 100 litres.

*

Did the pass system prevent the Tigers from carrying out their
agenda of relentless terrorist attacks in southern Sri Lanka? Between
1996 and 2000, there were eleven suicide bombings in the Sri
Lankan capital and one in Kandy in central Sri Lanka. The attacks
grew in frequency around the time of the fiftieth anniversary of Sri
Lanka's independence on 4 February 1998, which the government
had grand plans to celebrate. From October 1997, the Tigers struck
with devastating precision, first at a five-star hotel in Colombo,
then at a power station, then at the Temple of the Tooth, Sri Lanka's
most venerated Buddhist shrine in Kandy. The fiftieth anniversary
celebrations were to be held in Kandy at a stadium near the temple.
But the bombing of the temple a week before the anniversary forced
the government to move the celebrations to Colombo.

The government managed to convince the chief guest, Prince
Charles, heir to the British throne, not to cancel his visit. But the
celebrations were low-key and under a security blanket so
widespread that people spent the day under virtual house arrest.
Vehicles and people were not allowed on the roads. The Sri Lankan
flag fluttered prettily on empty streets. Six months earlier, India
had celebrated its fiftieth anniversary, recreating the midnight
session of parliament at which Nehru had made his famous Tryst
with Destiny speech. Outside, on Rajpath, the road leading up to
the pink-sandstone Rashtrapati Bhavan, the President's House,
the people celebrated with music and dancing. In contrast, Sri
Lanka's fiftieth anniversary was one of its gloomiest, quietest days.
As if to prove a point, the Tigers struck again, this time in the
capital, hours after Charles boarded a plane to go back home, and
yet again, a month later, blowing up a school bus and killing thirty-
three children.

The pass system was not able to stop the Tigers. Instead, it
achieved exactly what the Tigers were aiming at—the alienation of

the Tamils from a leader who wanted to bypass the Tigers and reach out to the Tamil people directly. President Chandrika Kumaratunga, who had declared her intention to wage an all-out war against the Tamil Tigers and at the same time win the hearts of the Tamils, was losing on both fronts.

*

It would be six years before someone decided to challenge the pass system in the courts. In June 2001, Arumugam Vadivelu Peter of Sithamparapuram camp, had to take his three-year-old granddaughter to Colombo to get her treated for epilepsy. Doctors both at Vavuniya and Anuradhapura had told him that facilities to treat her existed only in the capital.

He needed travel passes for himself and his daughter, the mother of the child. After he found a permanent pass-holder who would stand guarantee for both of them, the police gave the two of them seven-day travel passes. They had to return to Vavuniya before the seven days ended even though the child's treatment was not complete.

Then in December 2001, Vadivelu had to travel out again. His wife's uncle was seriously ill and wanted his family to visit him in Colombo. He had to apply once again for travel passes. After going through the entire procedure for the second time in a year, Vadivelu decided enough was enough.

He filed a fundamental rights petition in the Supreme Court of Sri Lanka. This is what he said in it:

> I had to purchase an application form to apply for the travel pass for myself and two children who wanted to travel to Colombo for this purpose. We also had to supply photographs of each person.[3]
>
> I was then told to go back to the camp and await response from the Modera police, where we were intending to reside in Colombo. We had to wait for about 10 days before we were told that passes would be given for the said travel to Colombo.

I and my children had to also produce a guarantor who would guarantee our return to Vavuniya. I had to pay thousand rupees to a person who was deemed as a qualified surety by the police for this purpose.

I and my children had to present ourselves at an inquiry at the Sanasa police post of the Vavuniya police and satisfy that our travel to Colombo was for a bona fide purpose.

I and my two children were then granted 'travel passes' valid from 2 January 2002 to 15 January 2002.

The guarantor also had to surrender her 'pass' and her national identity card to the Sanasa police post of the Vavuniya police. The guarantor has been given time till 25 January 2002 to produce me and my two children in order to reclaim her national identity card and 'pass'.

At the time I and my two children left for Colombo, we were videographed at the Sanasa police station and told to leave Vavuniya within 24 hours. We were also directed to report to the Modera police with the householder of the residence we were residing in.

I and my two children duly arrived in Colombo on the 3 January 2002 and registered ourselves with the Modera police.

I and my children will have to now return to Vavuniya before 15 January 2002. If we do not return, I fear the police at Modera will take me into custody and that the said guarantor too will be called for questioning. The guarantor will also lose her identity card and the pass issued to her and consequently even her present limited freedom of movement.

In view of the above I will be returning to Vavuniya although the restrictions on my freedom of movement placed by the actions aforesaid are unlawful and illegal. The purported 'pass system' has no legal sanction whatsoever and violates several basic and fundamental rights of me and my family.

Ten months later, the Supreme Court found that the pass system had no basis in law. It ruled in favour of Vadivelu and granted him Rs 30,000 as compensation. But by then, his victory was academic. The pass system was no longer in force, dismantled by a new government that was about to begin peace talks with the Tigers.

*

When I met Vadivelu in August 2003, he was triumphant but still fuming.

'Don't get me talking about the pass system. It makes my blood boil,' he said. The wiry sixty-one-year-old looked a street fighter, with his shirt buttons open up to his waist over a faded blue sarong, a hand-rolled cigarette tucked behind his right ear. His grey hair was slicked back.

Vadivelu fled to India in 1990 and lived in a camp for Sri Lankan Tamil refugees in south India until March 1995. He said he returned to Sri Lanka because President Kumaratunga had started peace talks with the Tigers. There was a ceasefire.

'I said to myself, it looks serious this time. Maybe it's time to go back.'

The peace process collapsed a few weeks after he returned.

'Instead of peace, we discovered the pass,' he said.

He and his family could not leave the camp that was initially supposed to be just transit accommodation until they went to their own home in the Vanni. Eight years later, they were still in the same camp. He, his wife, their five children and their families live in a concrete structure with a thatched roof and a veranda. It is supposed to be one of the better refugee camps in Vavuniya. Vadivelu believed it might well turn out to be their permanent home.

Vadivelu pulled out a couple of plastic chairs from the veranda and we sat out in the shade of a tree. As our conversation progressed, Vadivelu was getting angrier, his triumph in court now a receding memory in the face of the humiliations he had endured. After a while, Vadivelu rose and began pacing around in his fury.

'How unfair was that, you tell me. You are a refugee, you have nothing, no money, no possessions, you're dependent on crumbs of food that the government throws at you. On top of that, you are the government's prisoner. The pass system was like hitting a dead man with an iron rod.'

Notes:

1. Can Themba, *The Will to Die*, Cape Town: David Philips, 1982.
2. *The Sunday Times*, 18 August 1996.
3. The police were supposed to give the forms free of charge but the forms were always in short supply. Enterprising shopkeepers kept a sample and sold photocopies for anywhere between Rs 5 and Rs 30.

4

Victory Impossible

The attack came around 1 a.m. It started with sporadic bursts of gunfire from the rear of the camp. Senaka, who had just drifted into a troubled sleep, woke at the first sound of the firing. His immediate thought was: why are we coming under attack from our own side?

The camp—headquarters of the Sri Lankan army 55 Division—was located on the army's forward defence lines, skirting territory controlled by the Tigers. Behind the camp was territory under the control of the army. Logically, a Tiger attack should have come from across the lines in the front.

Senaka, a senior officer with plenty of field experience in the war, said it took him only a fraction of a second to realize what had happened. 'The Tigers had breached the forward defence lines in order to hit us from behind. We were under attack but not from the direction we were expecting.'

Senaka rushed into the camp's Operations Room where he found the duty officer had nodded off. The soldier had not heard the gunfire at all. Senaka asked him to sound the stand-to immediately.

'There was no time to lose. They were going to open up at us full-scale any minute,' he recalled.

True enough, within seconds of the alert, the first rocket of the attack swooshed past the Operations Room, displacing the air in its path, very sure of where it was going—an open-air ammo dump in the camp. The skies lit up and Senaka thought he would go deaf with the sound of 3000 rounds of ammunition going off together. As the munitions blew up, destroying vehicles, armoured cars and tanks parked around it, the Tigers opened fire on the camp.

Even after this early setback, for the first thirty minutes, the mood in the camp was confident. The Tigers were firing away but the officers believed they could handle the attack.

'It was only after the first half-hour, when the firing did not stop, that the gravity of the situation actually hit us. But when the attack did not end after one or two hours, we knew they had come with the intention to overrun the 55 Division headquarters.'

By then, the mood had changed dramatically. Some of the officers said it would be wiser to abandon the camp and make a retreat. After tense exchanges between those who wanted to quit and those who did not, everyone decided the honourable course was to stay and defend the camp.

'But in our minds, most of us had already given up. We were preparing to die. Everybody was in a state of shock. The seniormost officers, the ones who should have been giving orders, who should have taken charge, were totally silent,' Senaka said.

Meanwhile, the Tigers kept coming at the camp in waves. No sooner had soldiers on the perimeter managed to hold off one wave, than another rose from the undergrowth on the western flank of the camp to mount a fresh assault. Senaka said he counted up to twelve waves.

When we first began talking about the attack, Senaka made a rough sketch of the camp in my notebook to illustrate what he was saying. As he recalled the stages in the attack, he would go back to the sketch adding arrows here and lines there to point out the places where the Tigers had been hitting them. Now he whipped out his pen again and drew two dark lines, one above the camp and the other below it, to show where the Tigers eventually cut off access to the camp, preventing reinforcements from reaching it.

'If you were not scared at that time, there had to be something abnormal about you.'

*

In May 1997, the government launched what was to be the biggest, longest and most expensive military operation in Sri Lanka's history. Code-named Jaya Sekurui or Sure Victory, the operation aimed to secure a portion of a highway, the A9, in Tiger-controlled northern Sri Lanka.

Think of the A9 as the spinal cord of Sri Lanka, stretching all the way from Jaffna in the north to Kandy in the middle of the country. The middle section of this backbone—75 km of it—passed through the Vanni, a wide swathe of jungle territory in the northern mainland that the Tigers ruled. The army desperately wanted that stretch of the highway. Since taking Jaffna in 1996, 40,000 troops were camped in the peninsula to guard it against the Tigers. With no road link, the troops depended for their supplies on sea and air from Colombo. But the Tigers had brought down transport planes with shoulder-fired missiles[1] and at sea, the 'Sea Tigers' attacked ships taking supplies to the peninsula.[2] The government ruled Jaffna peninsula but its officials and troops, and the people living there, were virtually cut off from the south without a road link. Nearly 500,000 people had returned to the peninsula after fleeing in the October 1995 exodus. Keeping them supplied with food and other essentials was the government's job, but without a road, that was difficult.

I was in Vavuniya, the government's last main outpost in the northern mainland, the day before the military rolled out for Operation Jaya Sekurui. Everybody called Vavuniya a 'border area', as if this was a war between two countries. Five kilometres north of the town was the 'border', a village on the A9 called Thandikulam, where troops stood guard at a military checkpoint. The government could claim another 2 km beyond that, up to a place called Nochchimodai, but no civilians were allowed past Thandikulam unless they could prove they were residents of LTTE-controlled territory. But even they could not cross over once Jaya Sekurui began. South of Thandikulam lay government-controlled Sri Lanka, unimaginatively and predictably nicknamed 'the South'.

Four kilometres north of Thandikulam, the Tigers had their first checkpoint on the A9, at Omanthai. Everything north of that in the mainland up to Kilinochchi, a town on the A9, the Tigers controlled. From Kilinochchi to Elephant Pass—an isthmus linking mainland Sri Lanka to Jaffna peninsula—was a formidable chain of army camps that stood between the Tigers and their ambitions to wrest back control of Jaffna peninsula from the government.

The mission for the generals leading Jaya Sekurui was to ram through to Kilinochchi along the A9. It would give the army a lifeline to Jaffna. More than that, it would punch a line through the vast area controlled by the Tigers.

Vavuniya, the launching pad for the operation, was as close as reporters could get to the battlefield. The Sri Lankan government strictly enforced its ban on journalists travelling to Tiger-held territory. Forget wandering around independently in the war zone or accompanying military units on operations. On previous visits, I had driven up to Thandikulam where I would be turned back by the military police. This time, I could not get past the clock tower in the middle of Vavuniya. Standing at the main bus stop in Vavuniya, I saw trucks full of grim-faced soldiers, armoured carriers and tanks trundle past around the clock tower towards Thandikulam.

Vavuniya had always had that frontier feel to it, and that afternoon it was more on edge with news of the impending operation. All day, Tamils anticipating the fighting, streamed into Vavuniya from Thandikulam, adding to the thousands of people displaced in previous operations. But everyone I spoke to predicted the operation was ill-fated. The Tigers would hit back with everything they had. This was not going to be as easy for the Sri Lankan forces as taking Jaffna from the Tigers.

I returned to Colombo that night. There would be statements by the military and faxes from the Tigers. And there would be the leaks from military headquarters. There would be more information in the capital than 5 km from the battlefront.

Back in Colombo, I learnt 20,000 soldiers had gone into the Vanni that day. The army had raised a special force, called 55 Division, for the assault. Another division of soldiers had begun to advance towards the A9 from a place called Weli Oya in the north-east. The soldiers had to reach Puliyankulam, 20 km north on the A9 from Thandikulam, in four days.

It was easy to set an objective like that but not quite as easy to accomplish it. The soldiers took ten days just to crawl up the 4 km to Omanthai. Seventy soldiers were killed and more than 300 wounded in the first week. The Tigers were not melting away.

And then, they hit back.

*

The counter-attack by the Tigers came on 12 June, a month to the day after the operation began. They aimed at the thinning tail of the soldiers on their way up the A9 and attacked it with such ferocity that it would set back the operation by several weeks.

When the Sri Lankan forces first began their assault, 55 Division established a 'tactical' headquarters at Thandikulam, in a cluster of abandoned houses by the side of the A9. This was the camp Senaka was telling me about. He described the headquarters as 'very small', covering a roughly circular area with a radius of about 200 metres. One hundred and fifty officers and troops worked out of there to provide logistics as the soldiers moved up the A9. The picture he drew in my notebook gave me an idea of how small it was.

Right from the beginning of the operation, Senaka said, he had had a sixth sense that this camp was a sitting duck for the Tigers. There were simply not enough men to defend it as the soldiers moved up the A9.

The soldiers sensed that too and feared the worst. Senaka related how he once saw policemen—part of the Sri Lankan security forces and used by the government at the battlefront mainly to guard captured territory—who were deployed at bunkers, returning to Vavuniya in buses. Shocked, Senaka flagged them down. He asked them where they were going.

The policemen told him, 'Sir, we are from Matara and Kalutara and other faraway places in the south. Our superiors told us we were being taken to guard the Mahabodhi [Sri Lanka's main Buddhist shrine in Anuradhapura, 60 km south of Vavuniya]. No one told us we were coming to the front. Sir, we don't want to die, we have families to look after.'

On 9 June, soldiers guarding bunkers at the forward lines caught a Tiger cadre on a reconnaissance mission. He had a map as big as a door with every detail of the Thandikulam camp.

'We knew there must have been others in his team. We knew that an attack was imminent,' Senaka said.

The men stationed at the camp began to work at a feverish pace to build up defences. They pulled out twenty-five soldiers from further up the A9 and put them to work piling up sandbags and palmyra logs along the camp's boundary. But their efforts were in vain.

*

Everyone in the Operations Room was spread flat on the ground as the fire kept coming.

As the sun rose, the Tigers reduced their fire. The soldiers and officers holed up in the camp were relieved as they were running out of ammunition. The base camp at Vavuniya had sent helicopters to drop supplies but the supplies had fallen outside the camp and into the hands of the Tigers. But if the men at the Thandikulam camp thought the Tigers were withdrawing, they were mistaken. Around 8 a.m., the Tigers stepped up their attack on the camp, this time with artillery.

The officers in the Operations Room decided that the only option left was to radio the main base camp at Vavuniya and instruct them to fire artillery at the camp.

'That was the only way to prevent the Tigers from taking over the camp. We knew we would get killed too, but at that point there was no choice.'

As the first rounds of artillery from Vavuniya fell into the camp, Senaka said he saw soldiers on the perimeter being tossed into the air and torn to shreds.

'But you cannot be emotional at such times,' he said.

The tiny Operations Room was soon overflowing with wounded and moaning soldiers.

'They were crying, "Please don't let us die, please don't let us die." We did not even have field dressing to give them.'

The artillery subdued the Tigers somewhat but did not drive them away. Dozens of them were inside the camp at its south-west corner and were firing away. They withdrew only after reinforcements finally made it to Thandikulam from the eastern side at about 1 p.m., twelve hours after the attack began.

Only two full days later could the army say it was once again in control of Thandikulam. Senaka said when they cleared the camp later, they found the decomposing bodies of sixty-eight Tigers. Of the 150 soldiers and officers who were originally at the camp, only twenty, most of them officers, escaped unhurt. Sixty, including twelve officers, were killed and the rest wounded.

*

Swerving and skidding, a jeep raced across, raising clouds of dust against the setting sun. From its open back, four commandos in black jumpsuits and black bandanas on their heads fired away with automatic rifles. The ground shook with the sound of thudding mortar shells. The soldiers were now taking enemy fire—one doubled over clutching his shoulder—but the jeep did not stop, driving right up to a group of men in camouflage gear. Behind them stood a grey fort with a red flag carrying the familiar insignia of the Tamil Tigers, the face of a tiger in full roar, in bright yellow. The two sides engaged in fierce hand-to-hand combat. Even the wounded soldier was giving the Tigers a tough time. Overwhelmed, those Tigers not already on the ground ran away. The soldiers sprinted up to the ramparts of the fort, tore down the Tiger flag and quickly hoisted the Sri Lankan national pendant. The crowd broke out in thunderous applause.

I was at a military show in Hingurankgoda, 150 km from Colombo in north-central Sri Lanka, near the historic city of Polonnaruwa. Thousands of people had gathered to watch. The army had taken over a huge fairground in the town and all afternoon, soldiers worked to erect a cut-out of the fort, the main prop of the show. They arranged stands on one side of the ground but such a crowd turned up that there were people spilling out of the stands and straining against the rope barriers. The military police, turned out in their distinctive uniforms, had their hands full trying to ensure people did not stray into the special enclosure from where senior military officers watched the tattoo over tea and snacks served by army waiters in white tunics.

Besides the mock battle, several other events packed the one-hour programme. Soldiers on motorcycles jumped through flaming tyres and soldiers in white shorts and singlets formed human pyramids. The army had a helicopter fly in and simulate a getaway from the battlefield. Soldiers in full battle gear grabbed a rope ladder dangling from the helicopter, and climbed up as it hovered over the ground, its blades whipping up enormous amounts of dust. As dusk fell, soldiers sent up flares used on the battlefield as locators. Their fluorescent colours looked wonderful and the crowd loved it.

In one corner of the ground, a corporal sat under a white tent, a big thick ledger open on the table in front of him. It was three months after the launch of Operation Jaya Sekurui and the army wanted more soldiers for it. The military had launched a recruitment drive a few weeks earlier. And the show was part of the campaign to inspire young men and women to sign up to fight the Tamil Tigers. Several young men stood kicking their heels outside the tent but none went inside.

I asked one if he would go in to offer himself for service to his country. His name was Sanjeewa Kumara, he was twenty-one years old and he said he had a 'small' job at an insurance company in the town. A soldier's basic salary was Rs 7000. The army would provide his food. In addition, there were medical benefits for the family. It would be much more than what he made at the insurance company, which was tempting, he said.

'But I am the only child of my mother. My father is no more. If I die in the war, there is no one to look after my mother,' he said.

Sanjeewa then pointed to his reedy frame and said, 'I am weak, always falling sick.'

He told me he was not sure if his body could withstand the rigours of the army.

'But I will tell my friend about it. Maybe he can join,' he said with a smile before wandering away into the crowd.

The stony-faced corporal was sitting upright in front of the register. I waited there for an hour or so chatting with a young officer who had been detailed by the army's media division to escort me around the fairground.

He certainly was no advertisement for the jobs the army wanted to fill. He held his arm at an awkward angle and when I asked him about it, he told me it was because of a splintered bone from a battlefield wound some months earlier. His sleeve was rolled up to his elbow but he pushed it further up so I could take a closer look. His still unhealed forearm had a bluish tinge to it. He said it needed further surgery.

Two days later, I called the military spokesman, Brigadier Sarath Munasinghe, to find out if anyone had signed up that evening. Five, came the reply.

*

Bad news from the front first reached the rest of the country through the ambulances that came screaming along Galle Road, Colombo's main artery, from the Ratmalana airbase, 15 km away. Once front-line hospitals filled up, wounded soldiers were loaded in planes and brought to Ratmalana where they were transferred to waiting ambulances. With sirens switched on to clear the traffic, military drivers raced the ambulances to the hospital at the military headquarters right next to Galle Face, Colombo's main oceanfront promenade. When that filled up, they drove them to the National Hospital, and once that began overflowing, they went to the hospitals in the capital's suburbs.

The injured flowed into hospitals as the Tigers resisted the advance of Jaya Sekurui at every step. They called their counter-attacks 'Do or Die' and gave them numbers. Thandikulam was Do or Die One. A week later, they carried out Do or Die Two at Omanthai.

'For every metre we advanced on that road, our calculation now is that one soldier got killed and three got wounded,' Senaka said.

But the army stood firm that the offensive would go on. Brigadier Munasinghe, the spokesman, ended every press release he sent out and every briefing he gave with 'Operation Jaya Sekurui continues'.

Wherever you lived in Colombo, it was difficult to escape the sound of the ambulance sirens. For most of my time in Sri Lanka, I lived 5 km inland from the sea-straddling Galle Road, but the wailing managed to reach me over that distance. At night, especially, it was a troubling sound. When I was at Harvard University for a year after leaving Sri Lanka, I lived close to a fire station and a hospital in Cambridge. Whenever I heard the sirens going, I would find myself automatically thinking of war. Sometimes, an ambulance would go past when I was on a long-distance call to friends in Colombo. They would hear it and ask: 'What's going on there?' Such was our collective association of that sound with war.

The sirens were sometimes the first indication of an 'incident' in the north-east. The number of ambulances provided an idea of how big. A friend living on Galle Road had developed his own system for calculating the number of casualties from the sirens. He estimated that every ambulance could carry up to four wounded people. He would then arrive at the number of soldiers killed using a standard ratio of wounded to dead. Despite the unreliability of his method, my friend preferred to believe his numbers rather than the government's.

Florists and funeral parlours too told their own story. Flower shops in Maradana, close to the National Hospital, stacked piles of wreaths after every attack on Operation Jaya Sekurui. When news of an attack came through, journalists first called military headquarters to find out the official count. Then they called Jayaratne, the funeral parlour that had the army account, to check the tally. Old-timers remember Jayaratne as a small business on Dean's Road in Maradana. It moved to a prime location opposite Colombo's Kanatte cemetery as the ethnic conflict turned into a full-blown war. People had another name for the refurbished Jayaratne. They called it the War Memorial.

*

Am I painting too grim a picture? I should clarify that Colombo is actually a neat little place and was quite the party town even at the height of the war. It is not New York or London or even Mumbai or Delhi. Cinemas in Colombo show five-year-old movies from India and Hollywood. There isn't much other entertainment but that never stopped people from having a good time, right through the war.

Michael Ondaatje has a passage in *Running in the Family* where he describes the annual August horse races in Colombo. After the races, everyone would go to dinner together, dance into the morning and have breakfast at the Mount Lavinia hotel. They would sleep until noon when it was time for the races again. The races were not postponed even during the war. Ceylon, Ondaatje wrote, could have been invaded during the late afternoon because most of the Light Infantry was at the races.[3]

That was about the 1930s and 1940s, but it could well have described Colombo in the late 1990s, if you substitute races with the Royal-Thomian cricket match, a school fixture that is the most important event in the social calendar of a certain breed of Colombo male. Played over three days between two blue-blooded Colombo schools, Royal College and St Thomas, the event is more an annual get-together of the mostly male Sri Lankan political and military establishment. The list of 'old boys' of the two schools combined reads like a Who's Who of Sri Lanka. One 'old boy' boasted to me that the match—called the Battle of the Blues after the colour of the two school ties—had once brought parliament to a standstill because so many members were at the stadium. The speaker decided there was no point conducting the day's business and adjourned the House.

In March 1998, when Operation Jaya Sekurui was on full throttle, a general who was supposed to be up at the front, called me in Colombo.

'I am in town, let's meet up,' he said.

What was he doing in Colombo, I asked.

'I never miss the Royal-Thomian,' he said.

For nearly a week around the match—war or peace—army officers, parliamentarians, ministers, politicians, businessmen meet at dinners, at dances and at plain old stag booze-ups. Past students of the two schools living abroad even time their visits back home to coincide with the event and everyone has a whale of a time.

Then in April every year, Colombo's wealthy pack into their latest four-wheel acquisitions and drive up to Nuwara Eliya, a picturesque colonial-era hill station in tea-growing central Sri Lanka, for the 'season'. The three-day programme of horse races and shows is a make-believe Ascot at which young women vie with each other to win the 'filly of the year' contest.

Sri Lanka is tiny but it was entirely possible to shut out the war in Colombo's five-star hotels, its casinos with their 'Foreigners Only' signs, in its night clubs, and in the gracious homes of the rich where little girls learned to play Mozart and *Dhanna Budungee*, a Sinhala patriotic song, on old Steinways. The soldiers were poor youth from rural Sri Lanka. Colombo's youngsters hung out at the shopping malls, in the American fast-food chains or they just partied by the sea at Galle Face, the *baila*—Sri Lankan dance music— blaring from their cars. The kids with money packed the Blue Elephant, a night club at the Hilton. Their moms took afternoon tea at Tittle Tattle, the hotel's coffee shop, which sponsored a popular fashion show every Wednesday. The dads gravitated after dusk towards private clubs where membership is pretty much hereditary. Indian and Western expatriates crowded the Colombo Swimming Club.

Weekdays could go past in a blur of garden parties, while at weekends, the beaches in the south beckoned. International journalists covering the region out of New Delhi loved Sri Lanka, but Sri Lanka as a story did not enjoy the sustained interest of their newspapers. They flew in once in a while when something big happened and got back on the plane to India wishing they could have stayed longer.

'It's the only city in the entire subcontinent where you can have a beer and beef in the same place, in one restaurant,' joked the South Asia correspondent of a European newspaper. The joke was about how difficult it was to find a good steak in India because of the official ban on cow slaughter, and to get a drink in Pakistan, where alcohol is banned. We were sitting in the courtyard of a restaurant in Colombo under a huge shade tree. The air smelt of rain, of the ocean just across the road, of frangipani blossoms, of Italian coffee and freshly baked bread. The restaurant was one of those chic places that packaged the best of Sri Lankan architecture and design, with avant garde art on the walls and an eclectic East-meets-West menu served by graceful sarong-clad male waiters. In there, the war outside just did not exist.

When I commented to an Indian friend about the ease with which people in Colombo could shut out the unpleasantness, she said, 'It's like poverty in India. Unless you have to deal with it directly, you stop noticing it after a while.'

*

The recruitment campaign continued for several months but there were few takers for jobs in the military. The government glossed over its battlefield casualties, but people knew. Back in 1990, when the Tigers broke off peace talks with President Ranasinghe Premadasa and launched an all-out war against the government, many thought the Tigers, weakened by the Indian army, would be easy to finish off. Indian troops flew in to the north-east to supervise the disarmament of the Tamil militants but the Tigers refused to surrender their weapons. Fighting then broke out between the Indian troops and the Tigers. The Tigers called it Eelam War.[4]

Three years later, Premadasa began peace talks with the Tigers, so he asked the Indians to leave. Three months after Indian troops withdrew, in March 1990, the Tigers broke away from the talks and launched Eelam War Two, but Sri Lankans believed victory would be quick. The Indians had not been able to defeat the Tigers but had kept them on the run and depleted their resources. Thousands of Sinhalese youth rallied to the government's call to join the Sri Lankan armed forces. There were long lines outside army recruitment centres. Morale was high and people were willing to shed blood to protect the country. But the war dragged on. On 1 May 1993, a little more than a year before Kumaratunga came to power, a suicide bomber of the Tigers killed President Premadasa as he marched in a May Day parade in Colombo.

The Tigers called the present war, which they began after pulling out of talks with President Kumaratunga, Eelam War Three. It was not going well for the government. Following the initial victories in Jaffna peninsula, the armed forces had suffered one setback after another, starting with the Tiger attack on the isolated Mullaithivu camp in north-east Sri Lanka in July 1996, in which more than a thousand soldiers perished. Now, people were seeing the fallout of Operation Jaya Sekurui.

Sometimes, after an attack by the Tigers, the army would give bodies of soldiers decomposed beyond identification a mass funeral, cremating them all together. Those families fortunate enough to receive a coffin were advised not to open it.

In 1998, Sri Lankan film-maker Prasanna Vithanage depicted the tragedy unfolding in the villages in his Sinhalese language film *Pura Handa Kaluwara*, or *Death on a Full Moon Day*. The film won praise at many international film festivals but was banned in Sri Lanka because it came when the government was in the thick of war and was still desperately trying to recruit soldiers.

In the film, a blind man in a village is told that his son has been killed at the front. The army sends him a coffin but tells him not to open it. The man refuses to accept his son's death. The final scenes show the blind man prising open the coffin to check the truth of the army's claim. He gropes in it for his son's body and instead finds a large stone and a few sticks. The government and the military accused the film-maker of being anti-national and said he was attempting to scare people into not joining the army.

But for years before Vithanage made his film, the money and benefits that the army offered lured very few recruits despite widespread poverty in the countryside. Desperate for soldiers, the army kept up valiant propaganda that thousands of youth, inspired by the victory in Jaffna, were flocking to its recruitment centres. In truth, thousands were actually leaving the army, deserting it.

*

Soldiers went on leave and never came back. Or they just disappeared from the front during an attack. Sometimes they hopped on a plane or helicopter taking the wounded from the front lines to Colombo, pretending to be wounded themselves. Sri Lanka's army had 130,000 soldiers, a small number for a country that had been in a constant state of war since 1983. The generals said they could easily win the war if they had 30,000 more soldiers. That was about the number of deserters from the army.

The first wave of desertions began much before Operation Jaya Sekurui, after the July 1996 attack on Mullaithivu. The Tigers overran the camp on the first day of the attack. Of 1400 soldiers there, only sixty-four survived. The rest were killed or went missing in action. From then on, the army faced an uphill task getting recruits and even keeping the soldiers that it had.

In November 1996, a few days after I arrived to take up my *Indian Express* post, the army commander announced an amnesty for deserters. Come back to your regiments, all will be forgiven, he said. Deserters would be treated well, they would be given back the seniority they had held and the pay they were drawing when they deserted. But by the time the four-week amnesty ended, only 4000 deserters showed up at their regiments to take up the commander's offer.

The army tried to bring them back forcibly. Military policemen pasted posters in villages carrying names of deserters and told village headmen to inform them if any came back home. They requested Buddhist monks in village temples to help them. They alerted airports and job agencies. The operation was called Desert Rat. At the end of December, they managed to round up 13,000 deserters. They gave them back their weapons and uniforms, put them through a two-week training course and sent them back to the front. But as some returned, others left.

'It is difficult to keep track of the exact number of deserters because it is like a revolving door,' Brigadier Munasinghe said at one briefing.

After the first two counter-attacks by the Tigers on Operation Jaya Sekurui, the army announced it was going to be tough again with deserters and threatened them with court martials. But with recruits hard to come by, the generals had no choice but to declare more amnesties and take back deserters.

I met a one-time deserter who went back to the army under one of the amnesty schemes eight months after running away from it. I shall call him Nissanka. He had deserted from Jaffna, deciding not to return after going home on sick leave. I asked him how he had managed to hide for such a long time without being tracked down. His reply was simple. He was never in hiding. He was living openly in his village in central Sri Lanka. For a living, he ran a grocery store. What about the people in his village, I asked. Why did they not turn him in?

'I had good support from the village people,' Nissanka said. 'They liked me very much.'

He told me there were twelve other soldiers from his village of 150 families. Two had been killed in Mullaithivu, one was missing in action. Six had returned to the village wounded, two of them with legs amputated after stepping on anti-personnel mines.

Deserters were becoming a problem not just for the army but for the police as well. The police attributed a wave of robberies and hold-ups sweeping across cities in Sri Lanka to deserters.

'I told the area assistant superintendent of police about my problem. He told me, "Nissanka, don't create any law problems for me. Enjoy quietly with your family and you will be OK,"' he said.

Why did he then decide to go back? Nissanka said he had already put in sixteen years in the army. When the army offered one of its amnesties, a senior officer under whom he had worked contacted him and asked him to take advantage of it.

'He told me I would get a lot of benefits in a few years but I would lose all that if I did not go back,' Nissanka said. The officer had assured him he would not be sent to the front, that he would find him a posting in Colombo. Nissanka shut down the grocery store and returned to the army under the amnesty scheme.

*

When the 55 Division camp was fighting to survive the Tigers, Senaka said he was so exhausted one day, he took a drink of water, sat on a chair and closed his eyes for a few seconds.

'I must have fallen asleep immediately because I had a dream that I was killed. My body was in a coffin. They had taken it to my home in Kandy. I could see my wife and children standing and crying.'

Senaka said it was his staunch belief as a Buddhist in reincarnation that prevented him from cracking under the pressure of that day.

'I have no fear of dying. Even if I die, I know I will be born again. So I was prepared to stay and fight.'

The government needed thousands of Senakas to complete Operation Jaya Sekurui. The other option was to call off the operation, which it did eighteen months later, in November 1998. The troops of 55 Division had managed to advance 43 km on the A9, from Thandikulam up to a point called Mankulam. They were 32 km short of Kilinochchi, their destination, where they should have linked up with the army camp to establish the road link.

They did not manage to get that far. But in any case, by then, Kilinochchi was no longer with the army. In September 1998, the Tigers had overrun the garrison there in an offensive they called Unceasing Waves Two,[5] forcing the government to abandon its initial objective of linking Thandikulam to Kilinochchi.

When Operation Jaya Sekurui ended, it had killed 1418 soldiers and left over 10,000 wounded. The army took consolation that more than 2000 Tigers, by its estimates, were killed defending the road,[6] which came to be known as the Highway of Death.

Exactly a year after the end of Operation Jaya Sekurui, the Tigers mounted an offensive that they named Unceasing Waves Three. In just two weeks, they took every bit of the road they had lost during the eighteen-month Operation Jaya Sekurui, and pushed the soldiers back to where they had started—Thandikulam.

Notes:

1. Between 28 April 1995 and 18 November 1995, the Sri Lankan air force lost five aircraft, at least four of them to LTTE missiles. See the *Hindu*, 19 November 1995.
2. Sea Tigers are the naval wing of the LTTE. With their light fibreglass boats rigged up with motorcycle engines, the Sea Tigers were a deadly adversary for both the Sri Lankan air force and navy. They fired at air force planes carrying troops and supplies to the peninsula using shoulder-fired missiles and anti-aircraft guns. Several times, the suicide units of the Sea Tigers packed a boat with explosives and rammed it against a navy ship with devastating effect. It was a Sea Tiger team that swam underwater to attach limpet mines to the two gunships in Trincomalee Harbour, blowing them up and ending the three-month truce in April 1995.
3. Michael Ondaatje, *Running in the Family*, Toronto: McClelland and Stewart, 1982.
4. See Chapter 2, note 7 for details on the Indo-Sri Lanka Accord and the subsequent fighting between the IPKF and the Tigers in north-eastern Sri Lanka.
5. The Mullaithivu battle was Unceasing Waves One.
6. Ministry of Defence, Government of Sri Lanka.

Maid to Measure

Twenty young women sat in a classroom, repeating after their instructor—a middle-aged woman in glasses—a sentence she had just written on the board.

'You give a very bad impression to your employer if they see you chatting/talking, or laughing with your Sri Lankan friends outside their flats or down the street.'

The class repeated the sentence after her twice. Next, the instructor translated the sentence into Sinhalese to make sure the whole class had understood it. She then asked the students to copy the sentence into their notebooks, which they did obediently and painstakingly.

I was watching an English language class in progress at a government-run school in Colombo. Located in a quiet cul-de-sac on Adam's Avenue, a posh tree-lined street in the Colombo Three neighbourhood, this girls' school had an unusual curriculum. It trained its pupils to find jobs abroad as housemaids.

World War II was good for the American economy. It spurred the growth of heavy industry and created jobs. War did no such thing for Sri Lanka. Terrorism had scared away business. Foreign and domestic investors sat on their money waiting for the fighting to stop. For the war, the government imported everything from military hardware to potatoes for soldiers' meals. The main employment the war generated was in the armed forces. That was mainly for men, but in the late 1990s, there were few takers for jobs in the military.

Sri Lankan women, on the other hand, were—unwittingly—

helping to power the war. The country's two main export industries—garments and tea—depended on women workers. Nearly 100,000[1] women worked in garment manufacturing units, making clothes that went out under big labels like Marks & Spencer and Victoria's Secret. The tea industry employed a similar number of women as pluckers in the tea gardens. While these two industries formed the backbone of the Sri Lankan economy, bringing in the dollars that enabled imports, Sri Lanka had a third, less famous but equally important export: the women themselves. Thousands of women were going abroad to work as housemaids. The remittances they sent back home helped to keep the country's foreign exchange reserves out of the red. That was one reason why the government actively encouraged women to look for menial jobs outside the country and, through schools such as the one on Adam's Avenue, provided the training for such jobs.

In the school, a spacious room at the back functioned as the training kitchen and was stocked with all the standard appliances. A young woman fiddled with a microwave oven while two others contemplated a blender. In another room, a group of women bunched around an instructor demonstrating the use of a vacuum cleaner. At the back of the house, two women were learning to run a washing machine. Upstairs, another English class was in progress. One room was dressed up as the standard living room, with a settee, two armchairs, a centre table and side tables. Next to it was the model bedroom where students learnt to fold sheets and make beds the right way. Upstairs and downstairs, the house was filled with the sounds of humming home machines and eager students chanting useful English phrases.

'Sri Lanka Bureau of Foreign Employment Training Institute', said a yellow board at the gate outside the school, in English, Tamil and Sinhalese. But for this loud announcement, the school might well have been someone's home in this classy neighbourhood. The solid metal gates, painted grey, were shut firmly and I had to ring a bell and wait for a security guard to swing them back in order to get in. Unlike other schools, there were no knots of young women laughing and chattering outside the gates of this one. No snack carts. No boys hanging around. The scene matched the English teacher's instructions to her students: 'Never gather with other Sri Lankan maids near your employer's house, especially if you are with their children.'

*

Swarnatilaka Fonseka, a twenty-one-year-old I met at the school, wanted to go to Nicosia in Cyprus. Her sister was already working there.

'She told me, "Learn some English, get some training in housework, you will find a better-paying job,"' Swarnatilaka said.

She was taking the advice seriously. The English language teacher introduced her to me as one of her best pupils. I had asked the teacher if I could speak to some of the students and she had pointed to Swarnatilaka. 'Her English is good. You can speak to her.'

Swarnatilaka was dressed in the regulation Western-style ankle-length skirt and long top that export-surplus clothes stores made available cheap to Sri Lankan women. She came to the school all the way from Negombo, a town 35 km north of Colombo. It was a four-hour commute by bus, each way. But, she reasoned with a wide smile, the course was only for twenty-one days, it was free, and if it could improve her job prospects, it was trouble worth taking.

Swarnatilaka's father was a fisherman. 'Now my family income is only Rs 3000 [less than $50]. If I go to Cyprus as a housemaid, I can earn nearly $300 and I can send the whole amount back,' she said in passable English.

When she found a job, her employer would give her food and accommodation and provide for her medical needs. That meant she could save everything she earned, she said.

There was a time when Swarnatilaka's father had made enough money to support them all. That was many years ago. A Sinhalese, he had made his home in Trincomalee in the Tamil north-east because the fishing there was good. Swarnatilaka and her sister were born there. Her mother died when Swarnatilaka was still a baby. In 1983, one day after the anti-Tamil riots in Colombo, her father found his boat gutted. He decided then to return to Negombo, his hometown, with his two daughters.

In Negombo, the family lived in a small one-room house. Her sister went off to work in Cyprus so that they could build an extra room. Now Swarnatilaka wanted to help as well. She had studied up to Class 10. She had even worked as a trainee nurse in a doctor's clinic in Negombo for a while but discovered there was 'no money' in that. Better to be a housemaid if that fetched a higher salary than the Rs 3000 that the doctor gave her, Swarnatilaka said. Plus, she could see a 'foreign country', impossible even to dream of on Sri Lankan wages.

*

At the time I met Swarnatilaka at the end of 1997, there were already more than half a million Sri Lankan women abroad, most of them working as housemaids in countries across the Middle East.[2] Sri Lankan women had first begun going abroad to the Middle East for employment in the early 1980s, during the oil boom there.[3] Beckoned by the construction boom, thousands of men from India, Pakistan, Bangladesh and Sri Lanka went to work as cheap labour on building sites in Saudi Arabia, Kuwait, Qatar and other countries in the region. When cash-rich families in the Gulf began looking for women to work as maids in their homes, Sri Lankan women grabbed the opportunity.

The economic take-off that President J.R. Jayawardene promised when he came to power in 1977 and replaced Sri Lanka's socialist policies with free market capitalism had not materialized. Jayawardene dreamt of turning Sri Lanka into a Singapore, but economic development had to take a back seat as the government struggled to contain the ethnic conflict, particularly after the 1983 anti-Tamil riots. As part of the economic reforms, Jayawardene's government had removed the previous government's restrictions on foreign travel. Thousands of Tamils fled to the West for asylum, and thousands of Sinhalese left for jobs in the Middle East.

Fourteen years and two governments later, the war against the Tamil Tigers was still on and it was being fought much more intensely than before. President Chandrika Kumaratunga's government was spending unprecedented amounts on strengthening its army to pursue its 'war for peace'.[4] The Tigers were hitting back with suicide bombers in Colombo. A state of siege prevailed over the whole country, especially after the Tigers destroyed the Central Bank, Sri Lanka's government reserves bank, in January 1996.

At the end of 1996, over 11 per cent of Sri Lanka's workforce was unemployed.[5] That year also saw a record number of 160,000 women go abroad to earn a living in order to support their families. The next year, another 150,000 women left for jobs abroad.[6]

The government was doing everything it could to help them go. Back in 1985, it had set up the Sri Lanka Bureau of Foreign Employment to administer and regulate the migration. The Bureau set up the first maid training schools in 1995. By 1997, Sri Lanka had thirty-five of these schools, in nearly every district of the country outside the north-east conflict zone. Between them, the schools had trained nearly 19,000 women in the first nine months of 1997.[7] In addition, there were countless private training institutes that had churned out more than 20,000 trained maids.

On the one hand it seemed like a cynical plot to exploit women. On the other, the women would probably go anyway because of the unemployment in Sri Lanka. They were probably better off being able to speak a few phrases in English or Arabic. And if knowing how to work a vacuum cleaner or washing machine could get them a few dollars more, it did not seem like a bad idea. After all, the women needed the money.

*

Lekha Fernando was clear about what she needed the money for. She had already done one stint of four years in Lebanon. Her mother, who had gone to Lebanon before her, had fixed her a job in the same house. After working together, mother and daughter had come back ten months ago and now, Lekha was preparing to go back again.

'Two reasons I join my mother in Lebanon: first, earn money for plastic surgery for my hare lip, second earn money for dowry. I manage plastic surgery first time,' she said in her imperfect English.

She pointed to the scar from the surgery, which she had got done at the American University hospital in Beirut. She was not completely satisfied with the surgery but her face looked much better now than before, the twenty-nine-year-old Lekha said.

'Now, second time, I go for dowry.'

Lekha's father had been employed in the state electricity supply company but his salary was not enough to feed seven children. That was the reason her mother had gone in 1988. She sent money whenever she had saved up enough and it had been a welcome addition to their father's salary. But Lekha's father had retired and the money their mother sent was proving insufficient by itself.

What stopped her from working as a housemaid in Sri Lanka, I asked. Lekha laughed. 'Here? No money for housemaid. Only getting Rs 1000, Rs 2000. In Lebanon, I earn $300 a month.'

Well, what about some other job then? Lekha's reply was matter-of-fact. You had to know good English for a well-paying job in Sri Lanka and that was a language that she had not learnt in school. Moreover, Lekha said, she had studied only up to the O level, two years less than the A level school-leaving exam, a qualification that every employer looked for in job-seekers. She had worked briefly at a snack bar in Kadawatta, some distance from her home in Moratuwa, but it was too much work for very little money.

Lekha was speaking to me as she waited in line at a counter of the Bureau holding a form in her hand. When she reached the counter, she would hand over the form with Rs 2500, the fee that the Bureau charged to register maids going abroad.

How would registration help her, I asked. Lekha replied it would entitle her to a few automatic benefits. For one, she would get a life insurance cover and her family would get medical benefits. If she had had children, the Bureau would have provided them scholarships, she said.

*

Finding an official of the Bureau willing to talk about its work proved almost as difficult as fixing an interview with the president of Sri Lanka. There had been a run of negative reports in the press. Newspapers were highlighting incidents of maids coming back to Sri Lanka after being physically assaulted by their employers, and of women duped by job agents stranded in the Middle East without a job and no means of getting back. The reports accused the government of not doing anything to help the women and even of complicity in the incidents. In its eagerness to market Sri Lankan women abroad, many of the reports said, the government did not have in place adequate measures to protect them from being abused by their employers.

Even the 'founder chairman' of the Bureau, David Soysa, who headed it for eight years till 1993, had turned a critic. He accused Sri Lanka of 'selling' Sri Lankan women abroad as 'slaves' without the slightest thought to the credentials of the people who employed them. He said the government was scared to ask Middle East countries to safeguard the rights of Sri Lankan citizens who went to work there.

Reacting to the negative reports, the government minister for labour, John Seneviratne, said Sri Lanka had no choice but to depend on remittances from foreign employment despite the harrowing experiences of housemaids, and suggested that giving publicity to such cases might affect the country's economy by 'scaring' away 'village girls'.[8]

At the main office of the Bureau in Colombo, a long line of women stood waiting to get past the security at the gates while their fathers, brothers and husbands waited outside, bunched in little clusters. Inside, the Bureau was a warren of partitioned offices with dusty files stacked everywhere. I was there to speak to a bureaucrat who reluctantly agreed to see me but asked not to be quoted.

He gave me a mouthful of statistics on Sri Lankan employment abroad and the numbers trained by the Bureau's own institutes. The total number of girls the Bureau had trained to send to the Middle East since 1995 had crossed 100,000 the previous week, he said with a touch of pride.

The government offered several carrots to women going abroad: insurance, financial assistance to the families they left behind, scholarship schemes for their children, and the promise of loans to help them set up small enterprises when their contracts abroad ran out and they wanted to come back to Sri Lanka.

To make it easier for the women, the Bureau had licensed contractors who worked as middlemen between employers and employees. For its part, the Bureau was also doing everything to encourage wealthy people around the globe to hire Sri Lankan housemaids.

'We advertise in all parts of the world, like the Middle East, and many European countries also,' the official said.

Despite the stories about maids who came back battered by their employers, the government's strategy was paying off. More and more women were going abroad. And they were sending back more and more money. In 1996, Sri Lankan housemaids in the Middle East sent $484 million, the equivalent of nearly Rs 27 billion in private remittances back to banks in Sri Lanka. Along with tea and garments, the export of women workers had become one of the top foreign exchange earners for the country.[9]

In 1997, private remittances increased to $562 million or Rs 33.2 billion, only slightly lower than the defence budget for that year.[10] Of course, the government could not dip into private earnings. But the dollar remittances swelled the government's foreign exchange reserves and helped improve the country's balance-of-payments position.

In its annual report for 1997, Sri Lanka's Central Bank made glowing references to the contribution women working abroad made to the country's economy. Housemaids got a special mention in the bank's report, which said: 'The government continued to improve and expand facilities for the welfare of these employees as well as their families since they have become a major source of foreign exchange earnings to the country.'

President Kumaratunga would later praise the contribution of Sri Lankan women workers abroad to the country's economy.[12]

*

Lekha and Swarnatilaka were no feminists, but over the years, women like them had been engineering quiet changes in the small towns and villages of Sri Lanka. Colombo University sociologist S.T. Hettige told me how the mass migration of women to the Middle East was one reason for the decrease in national fertility and birth rates.[13]

Sri Lankan women were already the most literate in South Asia.[14] They married later than women in India or Pakistan or Bangladesh. Now, because they went abroad to work, they were putting off getting married more than before. Married women were separated from their husbands for a long time. The large-scale migration had changed the way people traditionally viewed the institution of the family.

Women went away leaving their children in the care of their husbands or other relatives. The woman's earnings abroad became the principal source of income or a crucial supplement for the family, displacing traditional notions of the husband or father as the sole breadwinner of the family.

While some saw this as progress and inevitable, others— including some women themselves—viewed the changes as bad and were trying to stop women from going abroad to work.

One organization actively involved in this was the Solidarity Organization for the Foreign Employed (SOFE), affiliated to the Catholic church. Its main office was in the crowded Fort area in Colombo in a building called Paul Sixth, after an earlier pope. The president of SOFE, Anthony Manchanayake, was a former factory worker and a Marxist trade unionist. Now in his sixties, he was canvassing to keep the Sri Lankan family intact.

'The mother is the first person of the family. She is the person who does everything. The minute she goes, problems come up in the family,' Manchanayake told me.

But, he conceded, he could not prevent anyone from going abroad because there were not enough job opportunities in Sri Lanka. And there would be no jobs until the economy could take off, and that would not happen unless there was peace in Sri Lanka. Finally, it all came back to the war.

So, SOFE was doing the next best thing. It was running 'self-help' centres where women and teenaged girls could learn a skill they could use to earn a living in Sri Lanka.

'The money they might earn through tailoring may not be the same as what they can make as a housemaid in a foreign county, but at least they can be with their families and happy,' Manchanayake said.

But, as I found out after a visit to a self-help centre—a sewing school in the Colombo suburb of Kaduwela—Manchanayake was fighting a losing battle. The centre trained women so they could find work in Sri Lanka. But the women went there to learn a skill so that they would get better jobs abroad.

Nanda Rohini, the woman who ran the self-help centre, had herself returned from Kuwait in 1990 when the first Gulf War broke out. She had done well in her time abroad. In the nine years she was away, her husband—an attendant in a government hospital—had raised their three daughters and two boys. Their eldest child, a boy, was twelve years old when she left and the youngest just three. Her first salary in Kuwait was the equivalent of Rs 3500, Rs 2000 more than what her husband was earning. By the time she returned, she was earning Rs 7000, while her husband's salary had remained more or less static.

'When I left in 1981, my aim was to save enough money to build a house. I achieved that,' she said.

Then why was she stopping other women from doing the same, I asked her.

'I never say to anyone, don't go. We cannot prevent a woman from earning money for her family's sake. But I try to give awareness. They have to know that before going abroad, they must make good arrangements for their children, they must have good understanding with husband,' Nanda Rohini said.

Of the forty-one students in her sewing school, a few were 'returnees', the word commonly used in Sri Lanka to describe women who had come back after a stint in the Middle East. Mostly they were the daughters of women who had gone abroad or women who were waiting to hear from job agents for placements in the

Middle East, using the time to learn something new before leaving.

Nanda Rohini, a pleasant-faced woman in her early fifties, cited her own example. She said she could not have done anything without her husband's help.

'He is a very good man, we had a good understanding before I left,' she said, immediately touching a wooden table in front of her for luck.

But not all husbands were like hers. She had seen other Sri Lankan women in Kuwait suffer because their families were breaking down while they were away. Their husbands had become wayward or they had taken to drink and were neglecting the children.

She led me to one such child right there in the school. Yamuna Jeewanthi, a fourteen-year-old who was learning embroidery, was born deaf and mute. Her mother worked in Doha, the capital of Qatar. She went abroad to earn a living because her husband, a heavy drinker, did not have a job. She had left her daughter and son in the care of their maternal grandmother. The first time she returned home on vacation from Doha, the husband attacked her with a knife. Then, when she was back in Doha, he attacked the son, slashing the boy's upper arms. Fortunately, the boy escaped with minor injuries. The parents were now divorced.

There was another woman called Sriyani who, like Nanda Rohini, had returned home when the first Gulf War started. Nine years later, she was waiting for another opening to go back to the Middle East but equally, she was worried about the consequences, especially after the experience of her cousin Dhammika.

Dhammika, her mother's sister's daughter, had gone to Kuwait leaving her four children with their father.

'The husband spent all the money she sent home on drink. The children did not go to school. When she came back home, the husband could not show his face to her, so he committed suicide,' Sriyani said.

Nanda Rohini said she wanted to share with other women her experience of the understanding required between a husband and wife for a woman to leave the family with confidence in order to earn a living abroad.

'I thought, my family is OK, now I should help others,' she said.

Without really knowing it, Nanda Rohini was saying exactly what sophisticated radical women activists in Colombo were also saying. Instead of accusing women for abandoning their families, when in fact, they were going abroad mainly to give their families a better life, it was time men learnt to help them by doing what women traditionally did—mother the children and become the principal care-givers in the family.

*

Back at the Adam's Avenue school, unaware that they were the subject of so much debate, the twenty young women worked hard at their English. They had come to this particular training school only because it offered English language classes. Instead of aspiring to go to the Middle East, like most other women wishing to work abroad did, those who trained here had their sights set on jobs in the English-speaking world. Singapore was a favoured destination.

The class I watched included a crash course in English, spoken with a Chinese accent. The instructor wrote on the board: 'You go on the heether.' Next, she read the sentence aloud as if it were all one word. Bewildered, the class looked at her.

Standing at the back, I could not follow her either. The teacher then explained: 'If your employer says that to you, it means, go and switch on the heater.'

After translating the sentence into Sinhalese so that everybody in the class understood her, she gave a further explanation.

'Chinese people don't know how to say T, so they say heater like heether.'

The class nodded in grave understanding. But Swarnatilaka was not keen on Singapore. She had made up her mind about Cyprus.

'Singapore people good but money not good,' she continued. She had not even considered the Middle East because of the stories in the newspapers about women being raped by their 'boss' or beaten to near death by their 'madam'.

She aspired to work in a Western country because she believed she would be treated well there. To her, Cyprus was a good enough representation of the West.

She said, 'In Cyprus, all English-speaking people. Treating workers good, paying good money.'

The Sri Lankan government, in the midst of its economically crippling war, was looking forward to the money as much as she and her family were.

Notes:

1. Department of Census and Statistics (www.statistics.gov.lk).
2. Sri Lanka Bureau of Foreign Employment.
3. Gamburd, Michel, *Transnationalism and Sri Lanka's Migrant Household: Kitchen Spoon's Handle*, New Delhi: Vistar, 2002.
4. Sri Lanka's defence budget rose from SL Rs 25.3 billion (US $468 million) in 1995 to SL Rs 33.6 (US $594 million) in 1996. In 1997, it fell marginally to SL Rs 33.2 billion (US $543 million). Defence spending was 5.8 per cent of the GDP in 1996 and 5.1 per cent the next year. Source: Central Bank of Sri Lanka Annual Report, 1997.
5. Statistical Handbook, Department of Census and Statistics.
6. Sri Lanka Bureau of Foreign Employment.
7. ibid.
8. Daily News, 31 December 1997.
9. Central Bank of Sri Lanka Annual Report, 1997.
10. ibid.
11. ibid.
12. Message on International Women's Day, 8 March 2001.
13. Sri Lanka's fertility rate fell from 5.0 in 1963 to 2.3 in 1993. Source: Department of Census and Statistics (www.statistics.gov.lk).
14. Female adult literacy in Sri Lanka is 89.6 per cent, compared to 46.4 per cent in India, 31.4 per cent in Bangladesh, 26.4 per cent in Nepal and 28.5 per cent in Pakistan. Sri Lanka's overall adult literacy rate is 92.1 per cent. Source: Human Development Report 2004.

6

Like a Line Drawn on Water

Dayani sat upright in a high-backed chair, legs crossed, hands in her lap primly holding a white kerchief and tears flowing down her thin face in an unstoppable flood. Occasionally, she lifted a hand to her eyes to wipe her tears with the crumpled kerchief. We were seated in the living room of her parents' home, a little cottage in the town of Veyangoda, just off the main Colombo–Gampaha highway, 40 km east of Sri Lanka's capital. It was a room crowded with chunky furniture and other bric-a-brac—the sort of living room where members of the neighbourhood ladies' association might gather of a peaceful afternoon to embroider cushion covers or exchange recipes, in normal times.

But this was wartime Sri Lanka. Veyangoda was one of the towns that had sent a number of its young men to the battlefront and visitors to Dayani's home usually came to condole. That is why, Dayani said, she did not want anyone coming home.

'My husband is not dead,' Dayani said. 'Sure, I know it. Recently I went to a soothsayer. He said my husband is alive.'

On a table in a corner, among the assortment of stuffed toys and framed pictures, was a picture of a man in uniform. Dayani's husband, Vajira Gamlath, was a major in the Sinha regiment of the Sri Lankan army. He had been missing in action, or MIA, since July 1996 when the Tigers attacked the Mullaithivu army camp where he was posted, just six months after she and Vajira were married.

In line with normal practice in Sri Lanka, Dayani and Vajira had registered their marriage first and were to have a traditional wedding ceremony a month later. But they postponed the ceremony when Vajira got recalled to the front at short notice. On his return, Vajira was to go to India for a course at a military training school. He was then planning to get an assignment as an instructor at his regimental headquarters in Ambepussa in central Sri Lanka to be near his wife. But the war changed all that.

The twenty-eight-year-old Dayani said she had turned down a request from the Sinha regiment for a photograph of Vajira. The regiment wanted to hang it up with a commemorative plaque at its headquarters to bestow on Vajira an honour they reserved for all their officers killed in combat. Dayani said she found the regiment's request inappropriate and in bad taste.

Her voice turning angry at the memory, Dayani recalled that she had called an officer at the regiment and ticked him off for daring to presume that Vajira was dead. He was only missing in action, not dead, she had reminded the officer. It did not matter that he had been missing for nearly two years. For Dayani, he was alive until the army could prove he was dead.

'The proof of death is a body. If Vajira is dead, where is his body? I will not accept a death certificate for Vajira. I am waiting for him to return,' she said.

*

Mullaithivu is a small village on the north-eastern coast of the Vanni mainland of Sri Lanka, 60 km north of Trincomalee port. In 1996, it provided the setting for one of Sri Lanka's bloodiest battles, and of the Sri Lankan army's worst debacle in the war until then.

The battle centred on an isolated army camp in Mullaithivu. The camp was a solitary symbol of the Sri Lankan state in territory that was otherwise fully controlled by the Tigers. The camp had existed since the 1970s, expanding as Tamil militancy grew in the 1980s. As the Tigers established themselves over the years, other military presence in the area decreased but the camp in Mullaithivu, and a few other scattered camps, held out. Having them there was important for the Sri Lankan government. As long as the camps remained, the Tigers could not claim they had full control of the northern Sri Lankan mainland. The main task of the soldiers in the camps was not to carry out offensive operations but to guard what they had against the Tigers.

That sounds simple, but the Mullaithivu camp had to defend itself from the Tigers on three landlocked sides, and from the Sea Tigers on its beachhead. Tirelessly, the Tigers looked for chinks in the camp's forward defence lines. Constantly they attacked the camp. For years, the soldiers had defended the camp by pounding Tiger positions around it with heavy artillery from within the camp.

In 1996, the security forces felt that they had finally gained the upper hand in the war that had see-sawed between the two sides for so many years. They had taken Jaffna peninsula from the Tigers virtually unopposed. The Tigers were now hemmed into the Vanni. Despite the daily give and take around the Mullaithivu camp, the security forces believed the Tigers would never find a gap in the camp's defences. They were mistaken.

On 18 July 1996, a little after midnight, the Tigers launched an attack on Mullaithivu. Within a few hours, hundreds of Tiger fighters had breached the camp defences. Wave after wave of Tigers walked into the heart of the camp before the eyes of the stunned soldiers. The Tigers called the operation Unceasing Waves. They had evidently spent months planning this operation. The soldiers put up all the resistance they could and the navy tried to land reinforcements on the coast, but the Tigers were prepared for that eventuality. By the evening of 19 July, the camp was in the hands of the Tigers. The fighting continued for several days as the security forces tried to wrest the camp back. The Tigers beat back every counter-attack. On 25 July, the military finally gave up.

Only a handful of soldiers managed to survive the assault. They did so by fleeing the camp and hiding in the jungles to avoid being hunted down by the Tigers. Only when the Tigers withdrew back to their own bases after cleaning out the camp of all its guns, artillery and other arms and munitions did the survivors emerge, trekking to the nearest army posts, exhausted and delirious with hunger and thirst.

One soldier who escaped by shinning up a coconut tree and staying there until it was all over would later say the soldiers were overpowered by the sheer numbers of their attackers. From his vantage point, he said, he could see 'bodies of soldiers all over the camp'.[1]

It was the government's worst defeat at the hands of the Tigers in thirteen years. The casualties were in the hundreds. As usual, the Sri Lankan media and international press based in Colombo could report the military debacle at Mullaithivu only second-hand, from statements faxed to them by both sides. But the faxed statements reduced the gravity of the event to an absurd game of numbers where each side played up the losses of the other and played down its own. At the time of the attack, nearly 1500 soldiers were stationed in the camp. The Tigers said they had killed eight hundred soldiers and lost 120 of their own fighters. For days, the government maintained that only 177 soldiers were killed and said the security forces had killed 380 Tigers.

The government also followed up its travel restrictions on the media with a censorship on war news in Sri Lankan newspapers. The newspapers could give their readers only hints of what happened at Mullaithivu. The English-language *Sunday Times* continued to run its military news column with white spaces to let readers know where the censor had used his scissors. Under an editorial captioned 'Military Debacles', the *Island*, an English-language daily said: 'Today we comment on military debacles making no reference to any particular debacles and we hope that our readers would realise the reason for it.'[2]

But many in Sri Lanka knew the exact extent of the debacle. Leaks from the military establishment spread by word of mouth. The censorship regulations did not apply to foreign journalists, and Indian newspapers with Sri Lanka-based correspondents, international wire agencies such as Reuters and AFP, and the BBC, relayed the news. The use of the Internet was not so widespread, but those who had access to it, especially Sri Lankans living abroad, knew what had happened. They called relatives back in Sri Lanka. Soon everyone knew. It exposed the government censorship for what it was: a pathetic attempt to control the news in an age of information explosion.

From their office in London, the Tigers sent out a statement that they had 'handed over four hundred and forty-one bodies of Sri Lankan soldiers killed in the Mullaithivu battle to the International Committee of the Red Cross' on 21 July. In the same statement, the Tigers said 'hundreds of severely decomposed bodies of soldiers killed at the Mullaithivu army camp have been cremated in the camp area'.

But the government continued to stonewall all questions by journalists about the casualties. At one briefing, the military spokesman began by laying down an incredible rule that journalists must not ask for casualty numbers. At another news conference five days after the attack on Mullaithivu, the deputy minister for defence—President Kumaratunga held the main portfolio— Anuruddha Ratwatte, said a 'responsible government will not give numbers in haste'.

'We have to be sure when we give figures as the parents, brothers, sisters and relatives would be anxious to know,' he said.

With the government refusing to say anything, the family members, who Ratwatte rightly described as anxious, turned to the ICRC. The Colombo office of the organization was besieged by people wanting to find out if there was a possibility that any of the soldiers at the camp might have been taken away alive by the Tigers.

All that the Red Cross could tell them was that they had accepted fifty-five of the 441 bodies that the Tigers had given them. The rest they had declined to take charge of, because the bodies were decomposed and unidentifiable. They had handed over the fifty-five bodies to the Sri Lankan army.

Three weeks later, at the beginning of August, Ratwatte made a statement in parliament on Mullaithivu. It was the government's first official acknowledgement that it had lost the camp to the Tigers even though this was common knowledge by then. For the first time, Ratwatte set out the casualties. There were 1407 people in the camp, of which the majority were soldiers, he said. There were also a few personnel from the navy and the police as well as civilian staff. Sixty-eight soldiers, including two officers, survived by escaping from the camp. Then, to the shock of the House and the rest of the country, Ratwatte said only twelve soldiers were killed in the attack. As for the remaining, the minister declared them missing in action.

The rationale behind the government statement was this: of the fifty-five bodies the ICRC had accepted from the Tigers to hand over to the Sri Lankan army, the army could identify only twelve. Therefore, only twelve soldiers were taken as killed.

On purely technical grounds, the government was right. When bodies of combatants killed in action cannot be found or cannot be identified, they fall into the MIA category. This military convention gave the Sri Lankan government a fig leaf to play down the debacle at Mullaithivu. Unfortunately, it also gave the families false hope that their loved ones might still be alive. The government would use this fig leaf many times in the coming years. But if the government thought the families of these soldiers would recede quietly into the villages and learn to accept their loss over time, it was mistaken. As the numbers of missing soldiers grew, the family members began to demand collectively that the government make efforts to trace them and reunite them with their families.

In early 1998, I went to the first meeting of the Association of the Families of Soldiers Missing in Action (AFSMIA) to which all its members had been invited. By then, the Association, which was just a few months old, had nearly a thousand members. More than 500 showed up at the Royal College school hall in Colombo where the meeting took place. They were mostly family members of the Mullaithivu soldiers. Many were young women whose husbands had gone missing. Little children clung to their legs. Or else they were ageing couples with missing sons. They came from far-off places outside Colombo, making the long journey to Colombo in the belief that collective action could bring back their loved ones. It was a beautiful Saturday morning outside, but in the school hall, the shared anxiety and sorrow of so many people hung over the gathering like a cloud. A lot of people were dressed in white, the colour of both mourning and prayer in Sri Lanka.

By the time of this meeting, the defence ministry had revised its rules, hoping that this would put an end to the badgering by the missing soldiers' families. Earlier, the army went by the convention that a soldier had to be missing for seven years before he was considered killed. But the convention was never tested because before 1995, the Sri Lankan armed forces did not have any MIA soldiers. The new rules reduced the time period to one year. When the one year was up, the defence establishment would give the soldier's family a death certificate and a compensation package. Additionally, the government continued to pay the dead soldier's salary to his family. The family could collect his monthly pay cheque until the day on which he would have normally retired had he lived. But the government had not reckoned with the determination of many of the families not to accept the closure that it was offering them.

The people I spoke to at the AFSMIA meeting were not prepared to make the mental leap from 'missing' to 'killed' that the Sri Lankan military bureaucracy was now demanding of them. Ganga Priyanthi, a twenty-three-year-old woman who had come for the meeting from Balapitiya, a town off the south-western coast of Sri Lanka, 100 km from Colombo, told me she felt in her bones that her husband, Chandrasiri, who went missing in Mullaithivu, was going to come back any day. Her husband's regimental headquarters had recently sent her a letter saying that for all purposes, her husband would now be considered killed in action.

'But they could give no reasons. How can a person go from missing to dead just like that?' she asked.

Soma Ratnayake, a forty-five-year-old woman who was working in Saudi Arabia as a housemaid gave up her job and came back to Sri Lanka to trace her twenty-one-year-old son Priyantha Kumara, who too went missing at Mullaithivu.

'I did not get his body as proof of his death. So how can they say he is now killed?' she asked me.

Soma had come from Kurunegala in central Sri Lanka, 120 km from Colombo, for the meeting. She pointed to all the people in the hall. 'We are so many in this Association. With commitment, we can force the government to give us some information.'

*

I first met Druki Martenstyn, the energetic woman who founded AFSMIA, in September 1997. She lived not far from my home in Rosmead Place in Colombo. One afternoon, after making an appointment to meet her, I walked down to her home in a little cul-de-sac off the main road. She led me to a large living room on the first floor. It was cluttered with sailing knick-knacks, books on marine life, cups, medals and memorabilia from various regattas in Sri Lanka.

'These are all my husband's things,' she explained, shifting papers and books out of the way to make some room for me to sit.

Her husband, Cedric, was in a Russian-made Mi-17 helicopter that came under fire from the Tigers off the northern coast of Jaffna peninsula in January 1996. He was one of two soldiers who managed to jump out into the sea as the helicopter went down. He was not seen again, but Druki believed that Cedric, an excellent swimmer, was alive and in the custody of the Tigers.

'One of my husband's friends in the military told me that an LTTE cadre who was arrested some time ago told them the Tigers have up to 200 prisoners,' she said.

At that time, the Tigers acknowledged only twenty-eight prisoners. The ICRC met these prisoners regularly, and carried letters to and from their family members.

'We have to get the LTTE to acknowledge the rest. That has to be the first step in tracing them,' Druki said.

At first, she and the wife of the other missing soldier from the helicopter waged a lone struggle to trace their missing husbands. They wrote to the Tigers through the ICRC. They met senior officials in the military who had been friends and colleagues of their husbands to press their case. But they made no progress. Then, Mullaithivu happened. The two women found they were no longer alone. That was when they decided to form the AFSMIA.

At the meeting in the school hall, AFSMIA members decided to seek an appointment with President Kumaratunga. They wondered if she knew the full extent of the problem and they wanted to make her aware of it. They also wanted the government to begin a dialogue with the Tigers on the issue of prisoners. They wanted a special cell in the ministry to deal with missing soldiers.

Martenstyn told me the government must consult other countries that had a similar problem. 'After every battle we have more numbers of missing. We must learn from the American experience in Vietnam, how they went about tracing their missing soldiers.'

I asked her if the Association was not prolonging the agony for its members by keeping alive their hopes that the missing soldiers might still be living. The Sri Lankan conflict was a take-no-prisoners war, and the Tigers were not known to take soldiers captive in the battlefield save in exceptional circumstances, I argued with her. Would it not be better if the Association were instead to help these families accept that their loved ones would never come back? Was that not the more humane thing to do?

But Druki was adamant that the MIA should not be given up for dead.

'I am not saying they are all alive. But how can we say for sure they are all dead when there is not even a single body?' she asked.

Just a few months before Cedric's disappearance, in July 1995, Druki's eldest son Jason, an air force pilot, was killed when his plane came under attack from the Tigers while transporting soldiers to Jaffna.

'I have made peace with my son's death. In his case, there was a body and I accepted his death. But in my husband's case, there is no evidence that he died. All I think is, is he dead or is he alive.'

She had spent most of the twenty months since Cedric's disappearance pinning her hopes on reported sightings of him. Her husband's friends in the security forces had permitted her to meet an arrested Tiger.

'He told me the LTTE has at least 100 prisoners,' she said.

Cedric was light-skinned after his Dutch ancestors, and Druki recalled that the Tiger whom she spoke to said he remembered seeing a 'Western-looking' man in one of their prisons. On the advice of friends, she had even travelled to India to consult a famous astrologer who, she said, had confirmed to her that Cedric had survived the attack on his helicopter.

'Like me, there are hundreds of families in limbo, not really knowing what has happened. For the government, it may be easier if we all gave up hope, but how can we?' she asked.

*

Back in Veyangoda, a few minutes away from Dayani, in another house off the same highway, Leticia and Lester de Vas Goonewardene were awaiting the return of their son Harshana Pradeep.

'The army has not told us we should give up hope, so why should we? They have said some missing soldiers might be alive but that they don't know who or how many,' said Leticia.

Like Dayani's husband, twenty-five-year-old Harshana, a lieutenant, was also missing from Mullaithivu. He was the fourth of the couple's five children. Like Dayani and all the others, the couple were convinced he was alive. Their periodic visits to fortune-tellers reinforced their belief.

Leticia was sixty-two and Lester sixty-nine. Grief seemed to have aged the couple more. As we spoke, Leticia, a retired teacher and Lester, a lawyer, drew by turn on circumstantial evidence, faith and superstition to explain why they believed their son was alive.

First they said Harshana was on leave and was due to arrive home the day following the attack, so it was more than likely that he had left the camp before the attack began.

Then they said an army doctor had spoken to Harshana on 22 July over radio, three days after the attack on the camp began. That meant he had not left the camp, as they had earlier said at the beginning. But the contradiction did not matter, because to his parents it meant that he had not perished on the first and worst day of the attack. This, they believed, gave rise to a strong possibility that he was still alive. He had been wounded in action twice before and his seniors had ensured he was not assigned combat duties at Mullaithivu, so it was likely he had retreated into the jungles during the attack, they said.

Three times before in his short career in the army he had narrowly escaped death; so he must have survived this time too, they said.

And the only one explanation, they said, for their identical dreams the night before I met them—of a letter from Harshana telling them he was coming home—was that he was alive.

Like the others I had met, the couple believed the Tigers were holding their son captive and using him to train their own cadres.

'We are prepared to go anywhere—Mullaithivu, Jaffna—meet anyone, even Mr Velupillai Prabhakaran, do anything to get our son released,' Leticia said.

In the hour or so that I spent with them, both Leticia and her husband were completely composed. They looked exhausted but were neither angry nor tearful.

'This house we are giving to him,' Leticia said, pointing around the long and narrow wood-panelled living room where we sat. The furniture was old and like its owners, the house looked a little tired. Lester led me to a glass showcase in the wall with framed pictures of Harshana. He pointed with pride to a picture of Harshana at the Pakistan Defence Academy where he trained for a few months a couple of years before he went to Mullaithivu. The photograph was the usual class picture. Harshana stood out, a wide smile on his handsome face.

When the news got around that the de Vas Goonewardenes' son had gone missing at Mullaithivu, their little cottage by the highway had filled with visitors. 'But we were quite normal. We did not wear mourning clothes. Why should we have done that? We can believe he is dead only when the army gives us some proof. If not a body, at least his number tag.'

Instead, a year after the Mullaithivu attack, the government, going by the rule book, gave Harshana's parents a death certificate and the compensation given to soldiers killed in action. Leticia and Lester said they had decided not to accept either the certificate or the compensation. The army was sending them Harshana's monthly pay cheque. Under the rules of military service, they would get it till his retirement day. The money was piling up in Harshana's account, untouched by his parents.

'The government must be thinking we will be satisfied with money. But we don't need money. We are ready to donate it. What we want is our son,' Leticia said.

*

In October 1999, the Sri Lankan army celebrated its fiftieth anniversary. It brought out a book to mark the anniversary. At the back of the book was a section on soldiers who had been killed in battle since 1983.

Captioned 'Life is like a line drawn on water', a saying of the Buddha, the section was 213 pages long. It carried the names of all the 10,688 soldiers killed in action, detailing their regiment and battalion and the day, year and place they were killed. Of all those soldiers, 6180 were killed between 22 April 1995 and 30 June 1999.

A note in very small print at the bottom of the first page of this section said this: 'The names of those Missing in Action are not included in this list.'

*

Dayani had not yet received a death certificate for Vajira but she had already decided not to take it. She too got the monthly pay cheque. Dayani had quit her job as a stenographer when she married because Vajira did not want her to work, but she had no intention of dipping into her husband's salary to support herself. Like her husband had done, she did use some of it to pay for his younger brother's education. She also gave part of it to Vajira's mother. The rest was going for a little nest egg for the two for when he came back.

'When he left home, he was a healthy man. When he comes back, he may not be that healthy, and the money may be needed for his treatment,' she said.

Dayani believed leading a normal life would reduce her chances of seeing her husband alive again. She had vowed to eat only vegetarian food until he returned, and she would not go out anywhere except to visit his mother. When I asked if she might not feel better going out to the movies or to meet friends, she replied with a smile, 'When Vajira comes back, we will visit all our friends together.'

Dayani reserved her most bitter feelings not for the Tigers who had most likely killed her husband, but for the government that had sent him to battle and for those who supported the war. Dayani said supporting the war was a luxury enjoyed only by those who were not affected by it.

'It is because of this war that we are suffering. How can anyone support this war? It has destroyed me,' she said.

'The ones who support this war are those whose sons have not gone to fight. Some people say war is the only solution to the country's problem. But they don't know what it is like to lose someone in a war.'

Dayani said she had heard the US government had spent millions of dollars to trace its missing soldiers in Vietnam. But from the Sri Lankan government, she said, people like her had got only evasive replies.

'For us, it is not fighting that we want, it is talking, talking to the Tigers, to help us get the answers to our questions.'

Notes:

1. Soldier W.G. Dhammika's testimony from his hospital bed, as reported by the *Midweek Mirror*, 24 July 1996.
2. *Island*, 23 July 1996.

7

The Ghosts of Chemmani

Nearly three years had passed since Rasiah Satheeshkumar had said goodbye to his wife Shanthini and cycled off to work. That was the last time Shanthini saw him. Since then, the only scrap of information she had about him was that soldiers at a military checkpoint had detained him as he rode back home from work that evening. Shanthini—three months pregnant at the time with their third child—had gone from one army camp to another in Jaffna in search of her missing husband. But everywhere, they turned her away. No one had apparently seen or heard of the twenty-nine-year-old Satheeshkumar.

Now, it seemed he might have been traced—to a shallow grave in an abandoned saltern at Chemmani, a few kilometres outside Jaffna town. There were two sets of human remains in the grave, one on top of the other. Both bodies had turned to bones. The one on top was facing up, knees bent. There was a gaping hole on one side of the skull. A rope tied around the hands still held them together. Shreds of dark blue trousers hung from the bent legs. The skeleton below was lying on its side, a black blindfold around the eyes. The knot at the back of the skull was still intact. A tattered T-shirt and underwear were hanging on to the bones. Separating the two bodies was a wooden sleeper from a railway track, as if the people who had dumped the two bodies into the four-foot grave had decided to grant them the dignity of a separate burial.

The next day, at a police station in Jaffna, Shanthini sobbed uncontrollably as she identified the tattered trousers as those of her missing husband's. She was among nearly 300 women who filed past the bits of clothing and trinkets on display at the courthouse. Their husbands were missing too, and the Jaffna magistrate had invited them all to the identification. They came with their families and friends. From a silver pendant hanging on a black cord, one of the items found in the grave, Suppiah Ravi, the owner of the garage where Satheeshkumar had worked, identified the second skeleton as that of his other employee, Mahendran Uthaskaran.

Both men had been on their way back from work on the evening of 22 August 1996.

'Satheesh had taken ten days off from work from the next day. He and my daughter were to come and spend time with me,' Shanthini's mother said.

Some days after Satheeshkumar failed to come back home Shanthini heard from witnesses that soldiers at a roadblock in Ariyalai, 5 km from Jaffna town and right next to Chemmani, had stopped him and Mahendran Uthaskaran for an ID check and bag-and-body search. It was an everyday routine in checkpoint-saturated Jaffna. But this time, the soldiers had not waved them off after the check.

*

When the Sri Lankan army pushed the Tamil Tigers out of Jaffna peninsula after a six-month offensive that ended in April 1996, it was the first time in more than a decade that a government in Colombo could actually claim its rule extended over the peninsula. But when the Tigers retreated from the peninsula, they ensured that the soldiers would rule over an empty land. As the army moved in, the Tigers ordered the entire population of nearly 500,000 Tamils to leave their homes and retreat with them into the northern mainland (see Chapter 2).

President Chandrika Kumaratunga lost no time in trying to woo the people to return. Thousands of people were camping on the southern edges of the peninsula, in the town of Chavakachcheri, undecided about following the Tigers into the mainland but equally frightened of the all-Sinhala Sri Lankan army now in the peninsula. President Kumaratunga promised that the soldiers would not harm them. By the end of May 1996, even if people did not fully trust the soldiers, they were tired of their refugee existence. They began defying the Tigers by returning to their homes in Jaffna town, first in a trickle of tens and hundreds, then in a flood of thousands. With them, and unknown to most of them, scores of Tigers also re-entered the peninsula.

I visited Jaffna for the first time that May, flying there from Colombo in an army transporter. The government was taking journalists to the peninsula to write about the 'returnees', as officials described them. I was a day tripper—up there early morning and back in the evening. Like most first-timers, I was slack-jawed at the destruction—buildings hollowed out by heavy gunfire, roofs torn by shells, splintered and headless palmyra trees. Not all this was from the recent fighting. Much of it had happened in the 1980s. But it amazed me more that the people I spoke to described their recent return to a destroyed region as coming back to 'normal' life. Small white flags fluttered on their gates where they had stuck them to let patrolling soldiers know they were back.

On my way to Chavakachcheri from Jaffna town that day, I saw bleeding schoolchildren being piled into an ambulance near a checkpoint. Soldiers were running up and down the street, taking positions and shouting at people to get out of the way. Minutes earlier, someone had thrown a grenade at the checkpoint. The explosion had caught the schoolchildren as they made their way home. The soldiers were bracing for a possible second attack. People were running for cover, expecting the soldiers to retaliate against them in anger. That did not happen. But in the days to come, many more such checkpoints sprang up as the army tried to hunt down the Tigers in the peninsula.

Everyone—it did not matter if you were walking, riding a bicycle, or driving one of those outdated Jaffna cars—had to stop at these heavily fortified roadblocks, produce their government-issued national identity cards and another pass that identified them as a 'returnee', submit their bags for a check and answer questions about where they were coming from and where they were going. Life became strenuous, tense and uncertain even for the most uncomplaining in Jaffna as the soldiers, who had started out being courteous and smiling, turned rude and rough under the constant pressure of the hit-and-run attacks that the Tigers carried out with increasing frequency.

The real turning point came on 5 July 1996 when a government minister, Nimal Siripala de Silva, flew to Jaffna peninsula as the personal emissary of President Kumaratunga to check the progress of the relief and rehabilitation work there. For the first time in fifteen years, a government minister was visiting Jaffna. De Silva, a personable politician, toured the marketplace with senior officials of the army, stopping to talk to people about their hardships and listening to their complaints of shortages of food and other essential commodities. He was climbing back into the army Land Rover when a suicide bomber walked up to the vehicle and blew herself up. De Silva escaped with minor injuries but twenty people were killed and more than fifty were wounded, including many onlookers crowding around for a glimpse of the minister. A brigadier of the Sri Lankan army in the minister's entourage was among those killed. He was the first senior army officer to die since the beginning of the operation to regain control of Jaffna.

That suicide attack finally got the Tigers what they wanted—a furious backlash from the army. Amnesty International documented that from July to November that year, nearly 600 Tamils disappeared after being picked up by the army for 'questioning'. The disappearances lost President Kumaratunga her battle to wean the Tamil people away from the Tigers to her side even before she had properly started out on her mission.

During a visit to Jaffna the following year, in October 1997, I met Lionel Balagalle, then a major general in the army, at his heavily fortified 51 Division headquarters at Achchelu, a suburb of Jaffna town. How could 600 people have just vanished into thin air, I asked him. The general, a soft-spoken man who rose to become the commander of the army a few years later, was known to be an intelligent and serious officer, not the blustering type of soldier.

He replied, 'I believe the majority [of the disappeared] will not be traced. We have been making our own enquiries to see if they are being held in any of the camps and the answers we get are negative. We have to consider the possibility that they could be dead.'

In the presence of two other reporters and a photographer who were with me, I asked if he could tell us how they might have died.

'I am not ruling out extrajudicial killings, but I cannot be sure,' the general said. It was time for the government to settle the cases by paying out compensation to the families, he suggested.

In Argentina, where nearly 9000 people disappeared between 1974 and 1979, the government enacted a legislation called Presumption of Death Due to Disappearance.[1] The ostensible purpose of this law was to 'regularize' the rights of the missing persons, but it actually served to short-circuit investigations into the disappearances and to fix responsibility. General Balagalle appeared to be suggesting a similar resolution in Sri Lanka. But it was not going to be as simple.

*

A packed courtroom in the Colombo High Court waited for the judge to read out his verdict in the Krishanthy Kumaraswamy rape case on 3 July 1998. Krishanthy, a fifteen-year-old Tamil schoolgirl, had been gang-raped and murdered by soldiers in Jaffna two years earlier, in September 1996. The same soldiers had then killed Krishanthy's mother, her brother and their neighbour when they went looking for her. The crime shocked Sri Lanka and deeply embarrassed the government of President Kumaratunga. To the Tigers, the incident provided ammunition against the government more effective than artillery and mortars. Opposition politicians locked horns with the government over the crime, parliament debated it and international and Sri Lankan human rights organizations clamoured for action against the guilty. Eager to put it all behind her, Kumaratunga ordered a speedy trial.

A three-judge bench heard the case. Of the nine soldiers and two policemen who were indicted, two turned witnesses for the prosecution. The state laid charges against the remaining nine. But despite that and the swiftness with which the case progressed, several developments raised doubts about the government's sincerity: one of the accused died in custody; another was discharged for lack of evidence; two managed to escape from right under the nose of the police. One of them was later caught while the other remained untraceable. Finally, on judgement day, one more soldier was discharged for want of evidence.

As Judge Nimal Dissanayake pronounced the court's verdict against the remaining six, including the absconding soldier, a loud murmur went up in the courtroom. A stunned look came over the faces of the accused. The mother of one of the soldiers fainted in shock and the sister of another began to weep. The court had found all six guilty of the rape and the multiple murders, and sentenced all of them to death. In keeping with Sri Lankan courtroom convention, court attenders switched off the lights in the courtroom as the judge wrote out the individual death sentences and ceremonially broke the nib of his pen after each. Though Sri Lanka stopped implementing death sentences in the mid-1980s, judges still handed out the punishment, usually commuted to a life sentence.

The courtroom was pulling itself to order when the judge asked the first accused in the crime, Lance Corporal Somaratna Rajapakse, whether he wanted to say anything. Rajapakse, who had just been sentenced to ten years' imprisonment and a fine of Rs 50,000 for abduction, twenty years for rape and the death penalty for four murders, replied in the affirmative and began speaking in Sinhalese: 'We did not kill anyone. We only buried the bodies. I can show you the place in Chemmani where 400 bodies are buried.'

The judge showed no reaction and the six men were led away, but Rajapakse's exit lines hung heavy in the hot and airless courtroom.

*

The weekly press briefings of the government spokesman were such dull affairs that I had to drag myself to them. Mangala Samaraweera, the media minister and the designated spokesman, would arrive late as a rule. When he finally showed up, he and the two other fixtures at these events—the military spokesman and the foreign ministry spokesman—would have little to say that was worth reporting. The briefings would routinely deteriorate into a diatribe against the Opposition party, first in Sinhalese and then, for the benefit of those who did not speak the language, in English. Most of the briefings that I attended left me secretly relieved that the government did not diligently implement its official three-language policy, or we would have had to put up with a Tamil translation too. So, it was with the feeling of boredom foretold that I went to the so-called Cabinet briefing on 11 February 1999.

Brigadier Sunil Tennekoon, the military spokesman, reeled off his usual 'three Tigers killed, two soldiers wounded, search operations, arms recovered' routine.

Since 1995, once every week, the Sri Lankan government had been feeding this stuff to the media instead of permitting journalists to go north and see it all first-hand. I wrote it all down just as a matter of self-discipline and to keep from nodding off. As the brigadier continued to speak, I found myself taking down this unexpected sentence:

'All arrangements have been made for commencing the exhumation of the alleged mass grave at Chemmani on 5 March.'

The official machinery had finally begun trundling on Lance Corporal Rajapakse's seemingly desperate eight-month-old courtroom accusations, even though a number of high-echelon military careers hung by them, and despite the rumblings that the investigations might affect troop morale. Rajapakse had even been assaulted in prison by guards after he refused to sign a statement retracting his allegations. His family had said they feared for his life.

Now, the exhumation was to be conducted in the presence of the government analyst, international and Sri Lankan forensic experts and human rights activists. Brigadier Tennekoon read out from a piece of paper in front of him. Even journalists could go to Jaffna and watch. The government's sudden transparency came as a bit of a shock but there were good reasons for it.

Both presidential and parliamentary elections were still more than a year away but President Kumaratunga was seriously considering holding at least one of those ahead of time. The only problem: her popularity with the Tamils was touching empty. The war against the Tigers since 1998 had displaced thousands of Tamils, turning them homeless. Her 1995 proposals for power-sharing between the Sinhalese and the Tamils were sinking under endless discussions in a parliamentary committee that was supposed to arrive at an all-party consensus on these proposals. More than anything else, the disappearances in Jaffna peninsula had totally alienated the Tamil people from her. For Kumaratunga, excavating Chemmani was crucial.

*

'I would be shattered if the remains of my son were found buried at Chemmani; but then, I would be shattered even if they were not,' Paramanathan Selvarajah said to me outside the small house on Stanley Road that served as the Jaffna courthouse.

He was a stocky, grey-haired man who worked in a hardware store for a living. His eyes filled with tears for his missing son as we talked.

Inside the courthouse, the magistrate was about to issue orders permitting the government to begin excavations at Chemmani in the search for the bodies of the peninsula's disappeared persons.

'I can be happy only if my son is returned to me alive,' Selvarajah said.

His words mirrored the hope of all the families that awaited a missing father, son or husband, and their fears that the disappeared might be found in Chemmani.

The only way to travel to Jaffna quickly those days was by Sri Lankan Air Force transporters. Operation Jaya Sekurui had failed to open a land route from Vavuniya through the Vanni to the peninsula. Civilian flights to Jaffna stopped in September 1998 after the Tigers had brought down a plane of the only commerical airline that flew the Colombo–Jaffna route, killing all passengers and crew on board.

After that, international organizations like the Red Cross and the United Nations advised civilians to travel to Jaffna only by sea because the Antonov planes with their air force markings were legitimate military targets. But the process was tedious, involving first a journey by road from Colombo to Trincomalee and then an uncertain wait in Trincomalee to get a berth on the earliest ship out.

Journalists just took the easy way out and did not venture up to the peninsula too often. As a result, the story of the 'disappeared' appeared only sporadically in newspapers, and that too, through second-hand sources. Now, the military, the main accused in the disappearances, was assisting in media coverage of the excavation of an alleged mass grave, by laying on the transport. Despite the obvious risk of travelling with the military, an Antonov-load of journalists flew into Jaffna to witness the proceedings and to give it the coverage the government evidently wanted.

A military bus took us from the Jaffna airbase to the courthouse. As we got off the bus, scores of women waiting at the courthouse mobbed us. They were the mothers and wives of the disappeared men and they were now appealing to us to help trace their missing family members. Many of them were sobbing. They were also angry, and as we got off the bus, they turned their anger upon us, ordering us to take down every detail of their individual stories. Several pages of the spiral notebook that I used that day are covered with a hasty scrawl as I fought to keep up with all their names, the names of their missing family members and the circumstances in which they disappeared.

The women were members of the Jaffna Guardian Association for Families of the Disappeared (JGAFD). Selvarajah set up the association when he found he was not the only one grieving for his missing son. At least twenty-two other young men had been detained on the same day at the same checkpoint where his son was seen last, and Selvarajah had decided to marshal forces with the others. The association had documented the names of all those who had gone missing, but it had encountered an army stubborn in its refusal to extend any assistance in tracing them.

The word 'disappeared' first came into human rights usage from the Spanish *desaparacido* that the Guatemalan press used to describe the thousands of people who went missing in that country in 1966. Human rights activists have described the mental trauma suffered by families of the disappeared as 'sustained shock' arising from a sense of loss and the 'suspension of bereavement'.[2]

After three years, the sixty-four-year-old Selvarajah had not permitted the pain of his loss to cloud the memory of the day his son went missing. Every detail was etched in his mind as if it had all happened just yesterday. His son, Prabhakaran, had vanished on 31 July 1996. Selvarajah had carefully preserved in his memory the details he believed would be crucial for identification when Prabhakaran was found—the clothes and jewellery he was wearing on that day: grey trousers, a light-blue shirt, a wristwatch on his left hand, a gold chain around his neck and two rings.

To all outward appearances, Selvarajah staunchly held to his belief that his son Prabhakaran was still alive, detained in an army camp. But as he listed the details that would help him to identify Prabhakaran, I could not help thinking that the distraught Selvarajah was perhaps acknowledging that his son, twenty-four years old when he disappeared, was now dead.

Prabhakaran had been a salesman in a cloth shop. On the day he disappeared, Prabhakaran had got off his scooter at the Chemmani checkpoint on his way back home so that the soldiers on duty could inspect his identity card. He probably expected to be waved through as usual. But the soldiers held him back. In Jaffna, it is not unusual for people to look out for others, especially at checkpoints. When something unusual happens between soldiers and civilians, news of it travels fast.

When Selvarajah heard from a friend that Prabhakaran had been detained at an army camp near the lonely Chemmani checkpoint, he hastened to it. He was filled with relief when he saw his son's scooter parked at the entrance to the camp. But the relief was short-lived. The soldiers said they had not detained anyone answering to the name or description of Prabhakaran. When he pointed to the scooter, the soldiers simply refused to accept it as evidence that Prabhakaran was inside and asked Selvarajah to leave.

As Selvarajah told his story outside the courthouse, inside, Rajapakse—the death-row soldier who had made the mass grave allegation nearly a year ago—prepared to make a statement before the magistrate that would give Selvarajah an idea of what might have happened to his son.

Rajapakse was in Jaffna to point out the exact spots where the forensics team would find the bodies he said were buried there. The government had flown him in the day before under heavy guard. In Jaffna prison where he had spent the night, jail guards mounted a special protective watch over him. Such were the fears for his life.

As two policemen led him in before the magistrate, it was obvious Rajapakse was in a state of extreme agitation. The year in prison had further thinned his slender frame. Except for the well-groomed pencil-line moustache, his face was, like the rest of him, nondescript. But once again, this nondescript man managed to create a courtroom sensation.

Rajapakse had evidently been waiting for this day. Now, there was no stopping him as he angrily spat out names of senior officers who, he alleged, were involved in the torture and killings of detained Tamils, the locations where the torture was carried out, the methods the officers had used and the cover-up afterwards. He spoke for an hour, giving details of how detained Tiger suspects were paraded by two officers before two masked informants. When the informants nodded, the suspect was separated from the others. The separated suspects went to another camp. Some were lodged in a school building that the army had taken over.

'One day they arrested a government official, Selvaratnam, who worked at the education department, and brought him to the camp. The next day his wife came and asked me if I had seen Selvaratnam. Although I did not know where Selvaratnam was held at the time, when I later went to the building which was used to torture people, Selvaratnam was among twenty-five others who were tortured there. Selvaratnam's legs were tied. He pleaded with me, saying he didn't have any Tiger connections. I asked Captain Hewa to release him. He agreed. But that same night he was killed. The next morning I saw ten dead bodies there,' Rajapakse said to the magistrate.

The magistrate, a Tamil, had been flown in from another part of the country after the Jaffna magistrate excused himself on grounds of illness. His face was an impassive mask as he listened to Rajapakse.

'The next day another man, one Udayakumar, was arrested and brought to the camp. Later his family came and pleaded with me for his release. I went to Captain Jayawardena and asked him to release Udayakumar. That afternoon he was transferred to another camp. When I went there, the officers in charge of that camp got a radio message to release Udayakumar. By that time he was hanging from his feet inside the camp and his body was cut with razor blades. They could not release him in that condition. He was killed later by a bullet. I know the weapons they used to torture people, and I think even now I can show them to you in that building.'

It seemed Rajapakse could go on and on.

'One day I was asked to bring a spade by Captain Lalith Hewa. When I took it to him he was with a woman who had no clothes on. This woman and her husband were brought to the camp earlier that day. Lalith Hewa had raped the woman and later attacked her and her husband with the spade I brought to him. Both of them died. Lalith Hewa tried to bury them there himself but he couldn't do it. Then the bodies were brought to Chemmani. I can show you where the bodies are buried.'

The former lance corporal, stripped of his rank and staring at life in prison, said he had decided to blow the whistle because he had been falsely convicted in the Krishanthy case. Those in the army who had actually committed the crime had escaped by pinning the blame on him, he said.

'I did not do it. I was asked to bury her body. But at that time I didn't know that it was Krishanthy's body that I buried. I know of two workers who worked as mechanics in a garage who were taken to the main camp and killed. I can show you the place where they were buried.'

*

Before us was a vast and desolate marshland. A thin strip of road, optimistically called the Jaffna–Kandy A9 highway but blocked 6 km south of Jaffna town—from where it was a 90-km-long battlefield up to Vavuniya, cut the marsh in two. The bleak landscape stretched into the horizon on either side. This was Chemmani.

On one side of the road, a man-made sandbank ran across the marsh. Bunkers constructed out of coconut tree trunks were embedded in the sandbank at regular intervals. Each bunker was connected to the next with tangled-up rolls of concertina wire. Constructed by the Tigers several years ago when they were in control of the peninsula, the bunkers were now used by the security forces to guard their forward defence line. The A9, on which we stood, was heavily fortified with checkpoints every few metres.

As far as the eye could see on the other side—to the left as I stood facing south on that road with a gaggle of reporters, TV crews, human rights activists, lawyers, Sri Lankan and international forensic science experts, policemen, soldiers and government officials—were old, waterlogged salt pans, long in disuse.

It was about noon. Rajapakse had finished his testimony to the magistrate sometime earlier and was now all set to point out the sites where he claimed bodies of torture victims were buried. The sun was beating down with the special ferocity it reserves for Jaffna but unmindful of it, and a little away from us, stood a bunch of people patiently waiting for the digging to begin. They were the same men and women—family members of the disappeared—who had been at the courthouse. They had followed us all this way to watch the next stage of the government's investigation.

A road overgrown with weeds ran through the saltern. Rajapakse indicated to the authorities that the graves were a little distance down that road. We waited till a group of soldiers, wearing fibreglass face masks and wellingtons with high platform heels—dangerously inadequate protection—went down the road with a minesweeper and rakes to 'clear' it for embedded mines. They did not find any, and we could only hope their search had been thorough because a few minutes later, we were all following Rajapakse as he walked confidently down that road to a small junction, half a kilometre off the A9, and pointed to two sites.

The investigators marked off the area with wooden pegs and a string of coir. After what seemed like ages as the excavators went through various technical procedures like surveying and mapping the area, the digging finally began. The group of family members of the disappeared had also moved with us but along a parallel road that they evidently knew or believed to be mine-free. Not permitted by the authorities to come too close to the digging site, they sat in a row along the edge of one of the salt pans watching the digging from a distance. The journalists too were asked to keep their distance from the excavation site, but we did not strictly comply with that request.

It was a painfully slow process. We were a bunch of impatient journalists but the chief forensic scientist, Dr Niriellage Chandrasiri, was like the conductor of an orchestra, proceeding step by step with studied deliberation. As the shadows lengthened over the marsh, many of the reporters, myself included, had concluded there might be nothing after all to Rajapakse's claims. We strode up and down the cleared road purposelessly, in two minds whether to stay or leave.

When the workers had dug about two feet into the ground, Chandrasiri suddenly stopped them with a dramatic gesture. He had spotted a change in the soil colour and he wanted to examine it. A few seconds later, he was saying there was a possibility the site contained human remains. That brought all the straying journalists back to the dig. The first sign of a buried body came at about four feet. It was a bone, sticking out from under the soil covered with a scrap of cloth.

The journalists were now eager for more but the light was fading and Chandrasiri called a halt to the excavation. His assistants covered the site with plastic sheets.

The next morning saw us all back at the site, greedily waiting for the digging to begin. The relatives of the disappeared were also back, gathered exactly at the same spot as the day before to watch the proceedings from a distance. The forensics people carefully brushed away the soil. It took hours but bit by bit, a skeleton came into view. The workers carefully removed it from the grave and laid it out on a plastic sheet. There was a wooden plank under it, a sleeper from a railway track. And under the sleeper was the second skeleton. Both were almost intact.

As word of the discovery reached the knot of family members, several women broke down, weeping uncontrollably. They knew the find was a blow for at least two people in their group, the final confirmation that their loved ones were not alive, but they did not know which two yet. Shanthini was among them, and like all the others, she cried fearing the worst for herself, and in sympathy for the women whose husbands the two skeletons might turn out to be.

*

From the report on the investigation from Professor Niriellage Chandrasiri to M. Illanchezian, additional magistrate, magistrate court, Jaffna:[3]

There were 15 bodies disinterred including the two bodies exhumed in the pilot phase on June 16, 17 and 18, 1999. One was a female and the rest were males. Body numbers 3 to 15 are to be identified later . . . Two bodies were identified provisionally in the pilot phase, with clothes as body number one (B1) to be that of Rasiah Sathis Kumar and body number two (B2) to be that of Mahendran Uthaskaran.

Rasiah Sathis Kumar (B1) was a male, age between 25–30 years with a height of 5 feet 8 inches . . . died of severe brain injury resulting from skull fracture resulting from assaulting the head with a club-like weapon. This is a case of homicide.

Mahendran Uthaskaran (B2) was a male aged 20–25 years with a height of 5 feet 3 inches. Mahendran Uthaskaran had died from injury to brain and lungs resulting from fractures of skull and ribs resulting from assaulting with clubs on the face and chest. This is a case of homicide.

*

The thirteen other skeletal remains found over the next three months were also dug out from near the site of the first excavation but were not subjected to identification procedures as the first two.

The last of the excavations was carried out in September 1999. No more excavations were possible after that. Jaffna became a no-go zone due to the eruption of a full-scale war between the army and the Tigers. From December 1999 to June 2000, Chemmani turned into a battlefield as the Tigers mounted a renewed battle for the control of Jaffna peninsula.

Niriellage's recommendation that in the absence of sophisticated equipment in Sri Lanka, DNA samples from the excavated remains should be sent abroad for identification was not taken up immediately. Asked about the delay, the defence minister, Anuruddha Ratwatte, cited budget constraints.

In 2000, the government finally sent the samples for testing to Hyderabad, India. The tests turned up negative. That is, none of the samples from the remains matched the DNA samples from the family members of the missing, not even those from the skeletons that had been tentatively identified as those of Satheeshkumar and Uthaskaran. The Attorney-General's office said it was not satisfied with the results and would carry out a more detailed test but cited a shortage of funds.

Were the samples not taken correctly or were they not preserved properly? Or were the tests not carried out rigorously? If the tests were correct and the bodies were not those of any of the disappeared, whose were they? And the big question: who was responsible for killing these thirteen people and dumping them in Chemmani? The family members of the disappeared got no answers.

Rajapakse's claim of a mass grave was corroborated by the others sentenced in the Krishanthy Kumaraswamy case. They alleged they had buried between 120 and 140 bodies in the area. In all, they named twenty security personnel, including former policemen.[4] Four officers of the Sri Lankan army were arrested in early 2000 for their suspected involvement in the torture and disappearance of detained Tamils in Jaffna. They were released on bail soon after.

Notes:

1. Passed on 12 September 1979, it allowed the Argentinian state and relatives to declare dead anyone regarded as missing between 6 November 1974 and 12 September 1979, a period when nearly 9000 people went missing in that country. *See* 'Nunca Mas', the report by Argentina's National Commission on Disappeared People (CONADEP), September 1984, London: Faber & Faber, 1986.
2. Amnesty International, '"Disappearances": A Workbook', 1981.
3. Made available to the writer.
4. US State Department Country Report on Human Rights Practices, 2002.

8

The Tiger-Trapper

I met Razeek just two days before he was murdered.

'Okay, come tomorrow at 11 a.m.,' said a raspy voice at the other end when I called his office.

I was taken aback, almost disappointed, at the ease with which I was able to set up a meeting with him. He answered the phone himself, picking it up on the first ring. The address was as much of a let-down. No secret hideout, no long journey over Batticaloa's grim topography. Just a house on Lake Road, the town's most respectable neighbourhood skirting the lagoon, a short distance from the Lake View Inn where I was staying.

I drove down to his place the next day with Marwaan Macan-Markar of the *Sunday Leader* and Suzy Price of the BBC. The three of us had come to this corner of eastern Sri Lanka to get away from the boredom of reporting routine press conferences and military briefings in Colombo and to find something new to write about.

Razeek was a possible story. But his ready accessibility came as a real surprise to us. Even more so his appearance. When we were ushered into his presence, there were five or six men in the room and it might have been impossible to pick him out from that group had one of them not got up, hand extended in welcome.

'I am Razeek,' he introduced himself, his face breaking into a shy smile. With his neatly trimmed beard, a receding hairline and a paunch that a loose knock-down Tommy Hilfiger T-shirt could not camouflage, he might have been a shopkeeper in the Batticaloa market.

He dismissed the others in the room with a discreet nod and, except for one big-built man who was evidently his bodyguard, they all left. Razeek seemed talkative, eager to tell his story. We spoke to him for over an hour and when we rose to leave, he came out of the room and walked us to the gate where he stood chatting with us for a few more minutes.

We scrambled back into our van with relief after that long goodbye. 'Should he be doing that, standing like that at his gate and talking to his visitors? Anyone could get him easily,' Marwaan said.

I had had the identical thought as we lingered with Razeek at his gate. We joked about what would have been the easiest way for anyone to kill him then—a gun or a well-aimed grenade.

As it turned out, the Tigers gave him the ultimate honour—one they reserved only for their most important adversaries—by sending him a suicide bomber, two days after our meeting. We were back in Colombo by then.

Razeek was waiting at a garage that morning while one of his motorcycles was being repaired when a boy on a bicycle came speeding up to where he stood talking to the owner of the garage with another member of his group. His bodyguard stood close by. Four of his men waited in the double cab in which he had come to the garage. But it happened so quickly that neither Razeek nor any of the others had time to react. The boy leapt off the bicycle, and grabbing Razeek in a tight embrace from behind, detonated the explosives-packed suicide jacket that he was wearing.

*

Batticaloa is on the east coast of Sri Lanka, in the 'troubled northeast' in the shorthand of journalists. Unlike Jaffna, it was accessible by road. Until 1995, there was an overnight train between Colombo and Batticaloa and an air service too. But the government discontinued the first fearing the Tigers would bomb the tracks and the second because the airfield, run by the Sri Lankan air force, was uncomfortably close to the Tiger-controlled areas of Batticaloa. Planes taking off from or landing there were within reach of the Tigers' long-range guns.

The journey by road meant cutting diagonally across the breadth of the island, 240 km from the west coast, where Colombo was located, to the east coast. The checkpoints began in the last quarter or so of that expedition, at Welikanda, commonly known as 'Welikanda border' because the Tamil area began there. It was also the beginning of the officially designated conflict zone. At Welikanda, the military closed the road to Batticaloa at dusk every day and reopened it at 9 in the mornings. The border regime grew tighter after some of the big bomb attacks in Colombo were traced to Batticaloa. Vehicles, especially trucks going in and out of Batticaloa, had to submit themselves to the military for a cumbersome check. The soldiers got trucks to disgorge their entire freight, and went through both the unloaded goods and the empty vehicle for bombs and explosives. The process was painfully slow and the lines of vehicles grew faster than the soldiers could check them. Many drivers just resigned themselves to waiting more than a day for their turn.

It was easier for us but not entirely so. The ban on journalists travelling to Tiger-controlled areas should not have applied to Batticaloa, because, like Vavuniya in the north, it was under the control of the government. But unlike Vavuniya, the situation in Batti, as we called it, was a lot more fluid. There was no proper line demarcating territory between the government and Tigers. The Tigers controlled swathes of land around the main town, but this territory was not contiguous. Farmers, fishermen, government employees, students—everyone—had to pass through territory controlled by the one and then the other in turn to reach anywhere.

Unless the army banned all civilian activity, it could not prevent the Tigers from moving in and out of its territory. Technically, Batticaloa town came under the government. The civil administration of the entire Batticaloa district was based in the town. It was answerable to the Sri Lankan army brigade headquarters. That was by day. By night, the town took orders from the Tigers.

With a little effort, journalists could get in touch with the Tigers in Batti, and for this reason the government was reluctant to allow journalists to travel there. The government could not totally bar the media from travelling to the east as it could to LTTE-controlled areas in the north, but it certainly made going there cumbersome. We could not just jump into a car and drive to Batti. We had to write to the topmost bureaucrat in the defence ministry for permission, give him the car number and the identity particulars of the passengers and drivers in the vehicle. We had to follow up the letter with phone calls to ensure that we got a reply from the ministry with permission to travel. A last-minute change that did not tally with the details mentioned in the permit could mean the turn-back sign from the military police at Welikanda.

The rule applied to all foreigners, whether or not from the press. Even diplomats were not exempt. On this particular journey, the Australian deputy high commissioner to Sri Lanka, Kathy Klugman, was travelling with us, but in her own car. She did not have the defence ministry permit but believed her diplomatic status might get her across the checkpoint. It did not work and she had to scramble to get a permit from the local brigadier, the seniormost military authority in the area.

Beyond Welikanda, the road was a straight thin ribbon, just about serviceable. The army, the most frequent user of that road, made sure of at least that. But what made the ride a real nightmare each time was the series of mini-army camps located at gaps of 3 or 4 km on the road. The camps were there to ensure the road remained in military hands. Two hundred metres or so before every camp, we had to get off the road into a rough-hewn track around the camp and rejoin the highway at some distance beyond the camp's sandbagged fortifications.

Except for military transporters and the trucks in which traders transported goods to sell in Batticaloa, we did not see much traffic on that road. Small groups of soldiers patrolled the road between the camps. Scrubby vegetation covered the land on either side of the road, as far as the eye could see.

An hour's drive later, a giant welcome arch announced Batticaloa town. 'Land of the singing fish', Batti liked to call itself, after a myth that on *poya*—full moon—nights the fish in the lagoon sang. People claimed to have heard it but said the fish had stopped singing when the troubles began.

Compared to the road we had left behind, the town was a frenzy of activity—bands of schoolchildren and office workers on bicycles, bustling markets, fishing boats out in the lagoon, fishermen selling their catch on the shore, and lines of people waiting at the checkpoints. Sometimes, wandering into the quieter narrow side streets with their little yellow houses and red-tiled roofs, it was even possible to imagine a provincial idyll. But in reality, Batti was tense.

From their base in Kokkadicholai, a village 35 km from the town, the Tigers ran a parallel administration in the entire district that was feared as much as, if not more than, the army. They ran courts that dispensed quick justice and handed down punishments in cases ranging from adultery to property disputes to murder. They ran a police force whose members slipped past checkpoints to enter the town to make 'arrests'. Their 'tax unit' dropped in at the homes of people to demand money. No one could say they did not have money to give because the Tigers carried with them copies of their salary slips and bank balances.

Every now and then, the Tigers made their presence felt even more strongly. Bombs and grenade attacks were common in Batti. Soldiers going on leave were a favourite target of the Tigers. The soldiers saw safety in numbers and usually travelled out of Batti in a convoy of buses but that made them easier to pick out for the Tigers. On at least two occasions, LTTE gunmen on motorcycles picked off targets—political rivals—in broad daylight.

*

Razeek was a counter-insurgent. He helped the army hunt down the Tigers in the Batticaloa area. The day we met him, he had just returned from an 'operation'—an unsuccessful one. That morning, he had information that three members of a Tiger pistol gang had slipped into town, but his quarry had got away by the time he reached the spot. He pointed to a slight bulge on one side of his waist to show us the Browning 9 mm tucked into his trousers, under his baggy T-shirt.

But he was not unduly worried about the morning's failure. He brushed it aside to share with us a statistic of which he was evidently quite proud. His force of a 150 men—the Razeek Group—had killed thirty Tigers from the time he had set it up in 1996.

What about casualties on his side, we asked.

'Twenty-one,' he replied, pointing to the framed pictures of young men that lined one wall of the room.

But Razeek shrugged off his losses. 'This is a war we are fighting and we have to be prepared for anything,' he said.

Razeek occupied a sprawling house at the end of Lake Drive, a road that ran alongside the lagoon. It was an area where the town's wealthy had once lived. The houses were generously built, with long verandas where their owners might have sat out on rattan chairs in the evenings, enjoying a commanding view of the sunset over the water.

But Batti's wealthy had long departed for safer havens in Colombo or abroad. Now the homes looked run-down, needing at least a coat of paint. The large frontages, where once there were well-tended lawns, were overgrown with weeds. Some of the houses had been turned into offices.

The original owner of Razeek's house, Sam Thambimuttu, was long dead. He and his wife Kala were well known in Batticaloa. Thambimuttu had been a high-profile Tamil businessman turned politician. The Tigers did not like him because he was not on their side. They shot him and Kala outside the Canadian embassy in Colombo where they had gone to get visas. That was in 1990. Now Razeek had taken over their house. Dozens of young men of the Razeek Group lived in the house. People in the neighbourhood knew it not by its number but as Razeek Camp. And camp it was, fully fortified with rolls of concertina wire, sandbags, bunkers, and a sentry box at the gate, which was patrolled by several armed guards.

What about his own life, was he not worried he was a target, we asked Razeek.

His reply was more philosophical than confident. 'Oh, not at all. I am not scared of the Tigers or anybody. This has become a way of life for me and that is how I live it.'

*

Muthulingam Ganesh Kumar was a fifteen-year-old boy in 1978 when he joined the General Union of Eelam Students (GUES), which was the forerunner of the militant group called the Eelam Revolutionary Organisation of Students. Tamil students were just then beginning to get involved in the struggle for their political rights. For them, militancy held more appeal than the give-and-take brand of moderate politics practised by the TULF, a venerable political party that had represented the Tamils since the 1950s.

Ganesh Kumar's mother, a schoolteacher, and his father, a clerk in a government department, did not approve of their teenaged son's political activism, but there was nothing they could do to stop him.

Five years later, in July 1983, anti-Tamil riots swept through Colombo, giving Tamil militancy a spur. By then, EROS had split with some of its members leaving to form a new organization called the Eelam People's Revolutionary Liberation Front. These were just two of several militant groups that sprang up around that time. After the riots, Tamil youth flocked to the militant groups to volunteer in the fight for liberation from the Sinhalese.

Ganesh Kumar joined the EPRLF. Karaithivu, the coastal village where Ganesh Kumar was born and raised, was a stronghold of the EPRLF. The usual practice for recruits in any of the groups was to take a nom de guerre. Ganesh Kumar took the name Razeek.

When Indian intelligence agencies began giving Sri Lankan Tamil militants covert training in weapons for their liberation struggle, they chose 119 cadres from the EPRLF. Razeek was one of them. Within days of landing on the Tamil Nadu coast by boat from Sri Lanka, Razeek found himself on the slopes of the Garhwal

Himalayas in north India with instructors from the Indian army barking commands at him and his comrades.

'At the time, I did not even know exactly where we were,' he told us the day we met him. 'But it was good training.'

The way he recalled it, he got two-and-a-half months of training in the basics of warfare, then a month of advanced training in guns and weapons, and after that, three months of commando training.

Razeek returned to Sri Lanka soon after, the same way he had left it, secretly by boat. He took part in several ambushes and attacks on the Sri Lankan army. Three years later, he was on the run, not from the army, but from the Tigers. The Tigers were on a rampage, out to eliminate all the other militant groups.

In April 1986, they decimated the most powerful of them all, the TELO. In October that year, they turned their fire on the EPRLF. For his own protection, Razeek turned himself in to the Sri Lankan army.

A year later, when India sent a peacekeeping force to Sri Lanka to disarm all militants, the Indian army propped up the EPRLF against the Tigers. Razeek was in business again.

The EPRLF had accepted the accord under which the Sri Lankan government made several political concessions to the Tamils, incorporating these concessions into the country's constitution as its thirteenth amendment. Cadres of the EPRLF and many other militant groups surrendered their weapons to the Indian army and became part of Sri Lanka's larger democratic process.

The Tigers, who like the other militant groups had been arm-twisted by India into accepting the Accord, later changed their mind. They refused to disarm fully and made known their opposition to the Accord and its provisions. Their hostility against the Indian forces finally blew up into a full-scale war that lasted three years. Those were the best years of Razeek's life. He became a Tiger-spotter for the Indian army.

'I killed 237 Tigers during the three years that the Indians were here,' he said.

That was when Razeek began to view counter-insurgency as a way to define his politics, earn a living and protect himself from the Tigers, all at once. He had a small band of men with whom he worked. Those days, they were known as the Mandaiyan Group. *Mandai* is the Tamil word for head. Tamil militants commonly used the euphemistic and crude Tamil phrase 'hit the head' for 'kill'. But in 1990, Razeek was once again on the run. The Sri Lankan government had asked the Indian army to leave, and by March 1990, the Indian forces had completed their pull-out, leaving the EPRLF to fend for itself against the heavily armed Tigers.

What followed was a series of massacres of members and supporters of the EPRLF. Razeek was then a commander of the Tamil National Army (TNA), a force that the EPRLF had hastily put together—by forcibly recruiting youngsters—for its own defence once the Indian army pulled out. But this bunch of ill-trained conscripted schoolboys stood no chance, and hundreds of its members were simply rounded up by the Tigers and shot.

Razeek fled to India, this time as a refugee, and lived there from 1991 to 1995. When peace talks between the government and the Tigers broke down in April 1995 and President Chandrika Kumaratunga decided a war against the Tigers was the only option, Razeek saw the counter-insurgency job market opening up again. He decided it was time to come back home and offer his services to the Sri Lankan army.

*

'We were like the Tigers once. We know how they think, what their strategies are likely to be, what their reactions and movements might be at any given time and in any given situation.'

Razeek was explaining the advantages he and his men had over the regular army when it came to fighting the Tigers. Plus, unlike the soldiers, they spoke Tamil.

'That is our biggest advantage. We know the language, we know the area inside out. We can tell who is a Tiger and who is not.'

Razeek boasted he was the sort of man who was not afraid to meet the Tigers head-on. The army never sent its soldiers into areas controlled by the Tigers for any covert operations because they would be immediately found out. Razeek said he did that job for them.

'We go hunting for the Tiger in its own lair,' he bragged.

But did the Tigers not know him and his men well by now, I asked Razeek. Surely, they had their spotters too, especially in Kokkadicholai, a village under LTTE control where Razeek said he went often to gather intelligence.

'Disguises,' he replied. 'I use them all the time.'

What sort, I asked him. The ones he told me about did not sound impressive at all: a pair of sunglasses, sometimes a skullcap over his head to make him look like a Muslim trader from Batticaloa. But he seemed to think they worked.

I asked him if he believed eliminating the Tigers would end the conflict he had witnessed from his childhood. He was emphatic.

'It's the only way.'

Of course, the Sri Lankan government needed to settle the grievances of the Tamil people through a political solution, he said.

'But the Tigers, they will never come for a settlement. They will oppose all political solutions. We have to finish them militarily,' he declared.

All his men had undergone a two-month training programme at Minneriya, a Sri Lankan army garrison 150 km from Batticaloa. The army had offered them ranks. Razeek, who had undergone an officer's training course with the Sri Lankan army, was offered the rank of second lieutenant. But he had refused it because he felt he was equal to at least a major or colonel.

'You can describe me as the commander of the army special support group,' he told us.

*

Since 1995, the war had caused suffering to the Tamil people on a scale they had not experienced before. The Sri Lankan army had come down heavily on Tamil civilians, imposing restrictions on travel and other individual freedoms. People were arbitrarily detained under emergency regulations. Tens of thousands of people had been displaced by the fighting in the north. Tamils hated the all-Sinhala Sri Lankan army.

But even more, they hated Tamils like Razeek who associated with it. There were other Tamils helping the army. All the so-called former Tamil militant groups that had entered the democratic process in 1987 still had weapon-carrying cadres. The Sri Lankan army gave them the weapons. This was in part for their protection against the Tigers. The government also gave them money. In return, the groups helped the armed forces conduct counter-insurgency operations. In Vavuniya, cadres of two former militant groups, TELO and PLOTE, were assisting soldiers of the anti-subversive unit. Cadres of one of the groups even policed forward defence lines with regular soldiers. But unlike Razeek, these groups did not openly admit to these activities. Even so, people knew and loathed them for it. The Tigers fuelled the hatred with their own propaganda about the 'traitors'.

Around the time we met Razeek, the Sri Lankan army had announced that it would enlist Tamil soldiers to give the force a multi-ethnic look. It took out advertisements in the Tamil newspapers in Jaffna and opened two recruitment centres in the peninsula. But there were no takers.

Tamils might have welcomed the move for an ethnic balance in the army had the government followed such a policy from the beginning. Now, in the middle of a war that was affecting them directly, they only thought it disingenuous.

Fearing a political fallout from his activities, the EPRLF threw Razeek out of the party. Completely discredited by the Tigers for supporting the Indian government and troops between 1987 and 1990, the party was trying hard to regain support among the Tamils. It hoped to contest the next elections and win at least one seat to the Sri Lankan parliament. The last thing the EPRLF wanted was someone like Razeek in its ranks.

'We have no connections with Razeek,' the leader of the party, Suresh Premachandran, told me in Colombo. 'We had to ask him to leave the party because he was becoming a major embarrassment for us.'

It was also an embarrassment to the party that Razeek operated out of Sam Thambimuttu's house because that perpetuated the link between him and the EPRLF. Thambimuttu had been a member of the EPRLF, and in 1989 had been a member of parliament representing the party.

But Razeek was unfazed by the EPRLF's discomfiture.

'Politically, we are still on the same side. We are all opposed to the Tigers. The only difference between me and them is that I carry weapons and they don't.'

He remained friendly with the party's local members. They visited him regularly. At least to us he displayed no bitterness over his ejection from the EPRLF.

Razeek said the army had given him rocket grenade launchers and an assortment of machine guns and automatic weapons. He believed the weapons made all the difference to his survival. Razeek looked at his job not just as his political platform but also as his life insurance. He rationalized his association with the army as essential for his self-protection because it gave him licence to carry weapons.

'I could not have done that as an ordinary civilian. As long as the LTTE continues to have weapons, we must have them too, otherwise we become easy targets for them.'

It was employment too. It helped him and the others in his force keep their heads up financially. Razeek did not tell us how much he was paid by the army, but he said each of his cadres received a monthly salary of Rs 9000, same as a solider. He said the Razeek Group had opened up job opportunities for the youth of Batticaloa.

'A lot of youngsters want to join my group. We recently sent a fresh batch of thirty for training,' Razeek told us.

*

Besides the obvious dangers, a job as a counter-insurgent had its perks. In Vavuniya, those in the counter-insurgency business used their clout with the security forces to set up their own regimes in the northern 'border' town. Different sets of counter-insurgents carved up Vavuniya between themselves. One group had sole rights to charge unofficial tax on every truckload of goods entering the town, another had a monopoly running the parking lot for the trucks. Sometimes they clashed with each other. In Batticaloa, Razeek had no competition. His was the only group in counter-insurgency work, and his perk was a carte blanche from the army to do pretty much as he pleased as he went about tracking the Tigers. Batti abounded with dark stories about Razeek.

We ran into the president of the Batticaloa Traders' Association (BTA), a thin, nervous-looking man by the name of Rajan Sathiyamoorthy, at the Lake View Inn. Taking quick puffs from his cigarette, he made indirect references to the Razeek Group's activities in the town. 'Local groups' had become a major problem, he told us. They were harassing the traders.

'They summon us to their office and tell us, these are our needs, you must help us,' he said.

Father Harry Miller was more direct. 'They arrest civilians and then take their time handing these people back to their families. The families will go to Razeek pleading for the release, and he might agree to do so for a monetary consideration,' he told us.

Father Miller was an American Jesuit who had lived in Batticaloa for forty years and was the chairman of its Citizens' Committee. He had originally come to teach at St. Michael's School in the town and had stayed on. No one ever referred to him by his full name.

He spoke fluent Tamil. Everything that happened in Batticaloa, Father Miller knew. Information just seemed to walk up the three flights of stairs to his disorderly rooftop office at the school and present itself to him in a way that any journalist would envy. And unlike other people in Batticaloa who spoke in whispers, looking over their shoulders all the time, the diminutive priest was afraid of neither the army nor the Tigers. He spoke his mind.

There were piles of papers on his desk when we went to see

him. He was preparing for yet another meeting of the Citizens'
Committee but said he could give us a few minutes. Father Miller
said he had complained to the town commander of the Sri Lankan
army, a brigadier, about Razeek's activities.

'The brigadier says the Razeek Group are army and they have
all the justification to do what they are doing,' Father Miller said.
'He told me they are our [the army's] eyes and ears.'

The Tigers were doing the same thing, summoning people from
the town to their side of Batticaloa and extorting money, Father
Miller said. In fact, the Tigers ran a much more systematic extortion
racket. But there was a difference.

'It's given resignedly to the Tigers. It's the only way to live free
from their persecution or from being branded a traitor. Some people
will say that the LTTE is putting their lives on the line for the
Tamil people and they owe them this money,' Father Miller said.

But in Razeek's case, there was fear, hate and contempt because
he derived his power to harass the people solely from the army.

According to whispers in the town, Razeek had used his
influence with the army for personal profit. Besides the allegations
of extortion from traders in the town, there were allegations that
he had his fingers in the lucrative sand-mining business. Sand is
used in construction. The coastal areas from where it was mined
were in the high-security zone. The military controlled access to
those areas and Razeek controlled access to the army.

There were other more gory stories about Razeek. Once, or so
the story went, he had tied a Tiger to his motorbike and dragged
the man behind him on the streets of Batticaloa. There were
allegations of torture against him. Two years before we met him,
his men had detained a nineteen-year-old LTTE cadre by the name
of Periyathamby Subramanian. The security forces later produced
Subramanian before the Batticaloa High Court to face charges under
PTA.

But in a fundamental rights plea to the Sri Lankan Supreme
Court, the teenager said he had been beaten with wooden rods at
the Razeek Camp. They had given him a 'dry submarino'—pushed
his nose into a plastic bag that contained petrol mixed with chilli

powder. They jabbed his body with pins and his penis had burn marks where they had stubbed cigarette butts on it. From the Razeek Camp, he was transferred to the Patpodi army camp, where his tormentors poured hot wax over his body. The district medical officer who examined Subramanian said the injuries on his body were consistent with the allegations of torture.[1] The case made headlines. Human rights groups around the world knew of it.

Razeek regularly made it into their annual reports under the subheading 'Torture and Disappearances'.

*

'We don't harm civilians in any way,' Razeek said. He was hurt at the suggestion that he was a profiteer, extortionist, torturer and killer.

'These are things that our enemies do in our name just to tarnish our reputation. We are sons of the same soil, I was born here. I would never do anything that would give the people a bad opinion about me,' he said.

Razeek said he carried weapons only to fight the Tigers, never to use them against the Tamil people.

'When the army says it wants to defeat the Tigers in order to help the Tamil people, it sounds fraudulent, because they are all Sinhalese. When we say it, they are more convinced,' he said.

He was wrong. Razeek was killed in May during the season of Vesak, a festival to commemorate the triple benediction of Buddha's birth, death and enlightenment, all of which Buddhists believe happened on the same day.

Batticaloa is a Tamil town but it also has a Sinhalese Buddhist population. Lanterns are a big part of the traditional Vesak celebrations. All over town, there were rows of stalls displaying lanterns of all kinds, shapes and sizes. Large crowds of people moved from stall to stall gawking at the lanterns. His assassination did not disrupt the celebrations. Evidently, not many were mourning Razeek.

Had Razeek known, he would have brushed it off with one of

the ready explanations he had for all the unsavoury aspects of his life. He would have said people did not attend his funeral because they were too scared of retribution by the Tigers.

Note:

1.   Amnesty International, Report on Torture in Custody, Sri Lanka, 1 June 1999 (Online Documentation Archive).

9

The Smell of Death

One Saturday afternoon in May 2000, the commander of the Sri Lankan army, General Sri Lal Weerasooriya, summoned one of his officers, Brigadier Sanath Karunaratne, to his office at the military headquarters in Colombo. As the brigadier recalled, the usually dapper General Weerasooriya, looked pale, tired and shaken.

'He told me, "Sanath, you are flying to Prague tonight. You have to get down the MBRLs immediately. Unless we have those . . . I don't have to tell you about the situation in Jaffna,"' Karunaratne said.

The situation in Jaffna in May 2000 was that the Tamil Tigers were on the verge of recapturing the peninsula they had lost in 1996. In April, they had demolished the chain of army camps that made up the garrison at the Elephant Pass isthmus. Then they had made inroads into the peninsula, taking much of its southern neck back from the army. They named the offensive Unceasing Waves Three.

From their new, advanced positions, the Tigers fired artillery at the Palaly airbase at the northern end of the peninsula where the military base camp housed 30,000 soldiers. They damaged the runway of the peninsula's only airfield, hampering the movement of planes ferrying supplies to the troops and transporting soldiers wounded in the battle back to Colombo. At one stage during the two months of fighting, the Tigers were pounding at the door of Jaffna town, the administrative capital of the peninsula.

The multi-barrel rocket launcher (MBRL) is a long-range gun

mounted on a truck. It is capable of hitting a target with up to forty explosive-loaded rockets simultaneously. The MBRL the commander referred to was made in the old Czechoslovakia, leftover military hardware from the Warsaw Pact. After the Cold War ended, the Czechs began dumping the MBRLs.

In the late 1990s, the Czech Republic offered two MBRLs free to Sri Lanka. With it, the Czechs offered rockets at the cut price of US $324 each. Sri Lanka placed an initial order for 10,000 rockets.

But the Czechs had not yet delivered the MBRLs. Karunaratne was then in the training division at army headquarters. He was involved in an initial programme training for the gun, and the commander was roping him back in to hard-talk the Czechs into an emergency delivery.

'My mission was to get the launchers into Sri Lanka as soon as possible,' he said.

Karunaratne and another officer left for Prague that night. In Prague, Karunaratne threatened to cancel a second order of 40,000 rockets that came with four more free launchers if the first order was not delivered instantly. The Czechs, he said, scrambled to deliver.

'The Ilyushin-76 transporters to carry the rocket launchers had to arrive from Azerbaijan, the rockets by train from one place in Czechoslovakia and the launchers from another. It was a hell of a thing coordinating all three, but we somehow managed to do it,' Karunaratne said.

Karunaratne was working to Sri Lanka time and there, the Tigers were advancing into the peninsula. Karunaratne and his colleague had no time to inspect the launchers as they arrived at the military airbase in Ostrava, some 300 km east of Prague on the Polish border from where the Ilyushins were to fly out. They examined only the ammunition and waved it on for loading.

The original plan was to land the Ilyushins directly in Palaly airbase in Jaffna to save time. But Karunaratne was forced to ditch this plan because the runway, damaged by the Tigers, could not be repaired on time. In any case, it might have been risky to land a plane there with the Tigers at artillery-firing distance. The pilots were instructed to fly into Katunayake International Airport, Sri Lanka's only civilian airport, a part of which the Sri Lankan air force used as an airbase. It was, in fact, the air force's largest airbase. The pilots would stop at Sharjah to refuel. But for some reason that Karunaratne did not know, the pilot of the first plane decided to refuel in Baku in Azerbaijan. He discovered he could not take off after the refuelling because of the weight of his load.

'We got the news as we were loading the second aircraft. I said to the people back in Colombo, "Don't worry, I'll make sure this one reaches you by tomorrow,"' Karunaratne said.

But the second Ilyushin was jinxed too. As it flew into the airspace of the United Arab Emirates (UAE), the country's air force forced the pilot to land in Sharjah where he would have landed for refuelling by himself. But, Karunaratne said, there had been a communication gap. The UAE air force grounded the plane and its cargo. Getting it disentangled from the red tape would take its own time. Karunaratne was not even going there. He decided to leave that one to Sri Lanka's diplomats while he concentrated on his own mission.

'Colombo was despondent. I was getting calls all the time. They were saying to me, "If you don't send the launchers, Jaffna is falling [to the LTTE]."'

When he heard about the second plane, Karunaratne was supervising the loading of a third launcher in a third Ilyushin, to make up for the first one that could not take off from Baku.

'Finally, this one reached Sri Lanka safely. No problems. Our chaps had everything in place ready to transport it to Jaffna by sea.'

In the days that followed, Sri Lanka bought more MBRLs from Pakistan and China, its biggest arms suppliers. The army held on to Jaffna but did not manage to take back land they had lost to the Tigers. The fighting subsided into an uneasy calm along the newly established forward lines, till the first week of September.

*

A massive slab of broken concrete swung from a few twisted iron rods. It used to be a shopping complex. Like all the other buildings on the street, it was a pile of rubble. Chunks of concrete lay strewn around. Little heaps of bricks, charred wood, shattered glass and broken roof tiles covered the ground. Electricity wires, severed from their poles, snaked through the debris. A grey dust covered everything.

A few signs had escaped the devastation. They were the only visible guides now. One sign sticking out of a collapsed structure said it was a hospital. Another over a heap of bricks said it had been a high school.

'This is your town. Keep it tidy,' a blue-and-white sign said.

It was 20 September 2000, and I was in Chavakachcheri—or what remained of it. For four days, from 16 to 19 September, the Sri Lankan army had rained thousands of rockets on the town with its newly acquired MBRLs. The Tigers had taken Chavakachcheri in April at the height of the Unceasing Waves Three offensive. Now, after the heavy pounding, the town was back with the army.

It was my first visit to the Jaffna peninsula in months. When the Tigers launched the offensive to take back the peninsula from the army, the government declared the region out of bounds for reporters. Not even conducted tours. Four months later, with the recapture of Chavakachcheri and another area called Colombothurai, the government swiftly flew in journalists to show off its first real triumph in months.

More than 100,000 people had been displaced since the fighting started in April. People living in the path of the fighting fled to safer areas in the peninsula. But the Tigers kept advancing, the battle lines kept rolling forward and the people were forced to flee again and again.

No journalist, bar the handful who lived in Jaffna and worked for the single local newspaper there, witnessed any of this. And even the Jaffna journalists could not communicate the story to the outside world as the fighting cut all phone and other communication links. Shackled to their desks, journalists in Colombo were dependent on government handouts and statements the Tigers sent out from their office in London. As for the gaps, we filled those with the help of leaks from the Sri Lankan army and the scraps of information international humanitarian agencies sometimes threw our way.

Even those bits and pieces were censored heavily. Early in the fighting, when newspapers put out accounts—second-hand but detailed—of the army's capitulation to the Tigers at Elephant Pass, the government reacted by clamping down on war news. Before sending it to their newspapers or agencies, reporters had to submit a copy to Ariya Rubasinghe, the director of the department of information, who was now also the chief censor.

He sent it back after blacking out words, sentences and entire paragraphs with a thick marker pen. The censorship had begun to loosen a little by June when the army managed to hold back the Tigers' advance into the peninsula. But the fragile stalemate was not good enough for the government to permit journalists to travel to the north again until it could trumpet a victory.

Chavakachcheri—even if it had been destroyed to its foundations—was that victory. Escorting us on the trip was Brigadier Sanath Karunaratne, the same officer who had flown to Prague in May to ship the MBRLs to Sri Lanka. Now he was the military spokesman and flew with us on an air force transport to the Palaly airbase where we clambered into a bus that took us to Chavakachcheri.

In Chavakachcheri, our yellow bus stopped in the middle of what had been the market area, unable to go further because of the wreckage strewn all around. There were about twenty of us, and the destruction stunned us into an awed silence.

Chavakachcheri was a ghost town even before it was destroyed. The 60,000 people who lived there had fled in April, days before the battle in which the Tigers took control. No civilians were killed in the September battle for Chavakachcheri. Its residents had locked up their homes and shops when they fled six months earlier, hoping to return when the fighting ended. But there was nothing to return to.

Before leaving for the conducted tour, we stopped to meet Major General Anton Wijendra, commander of the security forces in the peninsula. His barricaded office was in the Palaly camp, minutes from the airfield.

'The people will now be able to move back into the homes they abandoned in the early part of this year,' the general said.

He said there had been 'quite a lot' of fighting. It was a long-distance battle, fought mainly with long-range guns. The Sri Lankan infantry rolled in later for mopping-up operations.

'The MBRLs are very effective,' Wijendra said. 'The Tigers are frightened of them.'

He said the Tigers also used the same weapons but added that the army's firepower had been greater. Wijendra said 500 Tigers died, many of them at Chavakachcheri. The army lost forty-two soldiers.

From the main road, there were side streets branching into residential neighbourhoods and as I walked towards one, one of the officers escorting us shouted out a warning: 'It is unsafe to walk around because of unexploded ordnance lying in the rubble.' That froze me, but from where I stood, I could see more ruins and shards of clay tiles from roofs scattered on the street. Mocking the doors the owners had carefully locked before fleeing, the bombs had punched their way into homes through roofs and walls.

Lingering in Chavakachcheri seemed pointless. The military schedule had given us ten minutes to gawk at the destruction. I was quite relieved when the robustly built Karunaratne began pushing everybody back into the bus after the allotted time with the cheerful threat that if it got too dark, we would have to stay in Chavakachcheri because the road out was not fully secure. The party had to reach the Palaly airfield and wing out of the peninsula before sunset.

On the way out, we passed soldiers standing guard near a destroyed building. They stood watching as our bus passed by.

'Ladies and gentlemen, give these boys a big hand, they have done a wonderful job,' one of the officers in the bus said.

Many of the journalists in the bus broke out in applause. The soldiers smiled and waved back. I turned around to a small group of Tamil journalists sitting together on the long seat in the back of the bus. They were not clapping.

'One thing is clear now,' one of them later said, 'with these MBRLs, if the fighting continues for a few more days, all of Jaffna peninsula is going to look like this.'

*

There was a foul smell in the air the next morning. I was at a guest house in Chundikuli, a suburb of Jaffna town. The smell came and went with the breeze. A clogged drain somewhere, I thought.

The rest of my group had returned to Colombo the previous evening soon after the quick tour of Chavakachcheri. I decided to stay in Jaffna for a few more days, a plan to which the army reluctantly consented. On the way back from Chavakachcheri, the brigadier stopped the bus at a military camp and found an army truck for me and Sriyantha Walpola, the photographer of the *Hindu*. A soldier drove us to Chundikuli. We had to get there before 7.30 p.m., when the daily dusk-to-dawn curfew began. With its olive-green colour and military markings, it was not the safest transport. But there was no other way to get around in Jaffna. The fighting had driven all public transport off the roads.

Chundikuli must have been a well-to-do neighbourhood before the conflict. Signs of wealth were still visible in the large houses with gardens in the front. Many of the houses were either empty or occupied by tenants. Tamils with means had fled the peninsula years ago.

Our guest house was one such bungalow. It was now with a government department in charge of the reconstruction and rehabilitation of Jaffna. President Kumaratunga set up the department in 1996 after the army took control of the peninsula. This was where its officials stayed when they visited the peninsula. They got first preference and others could stay only if bureaucrats were not in residence. For journalists, it was a choice between the guest house and Bastian, a restaurant a couple of houses down the road that had rooms upstairs. There were no hotels in Jaffna. After it took control of the peninsula in 1996, the Sri Lankan army turned Subhash, the hotel that journalists had always used until then, into the Jaffna town commander's office. Located close to the guest house were two famous Jaffna schools, the Chundikuli Girls' School and the St. John's Boys' School. The boys' school was a two-minute walk from the guest house. The yellow walls of its church carried the marks of all the shrapnel that had hit it over the years. In this round of fighting though, the church had been spared because Chundikuli was not in the line of fire.

I asked Chandrashekhar Kugharajan, the guest house manager, about the bad smell. He did not know either, but guessed, as I had done, that it might be a blocked drain in the neighbourhood.

In April, as Unceasing Waves Three began, Kugharajan moved from his home to the comparative safety of the guest house with his wife Usha, three daughters and son. Jaffna was not getting any visitors, official or ordinary, those days—we were the first in a long while—and the family had the full run of the place.

The home Kugharajan had abandoned was in Colombothurai. It was the other town that the army had wrested back from the Tigers in that week. Since the beginning of Unceasing Waves Three, Colombothurai had been the scene of several intense battles and like Kugharajan, its residents had all fled before the fighting began.

Colombothurai was on the road to Chavakachcheri and its recapture was a strategic advantage for the army. We had stopped there briefly before going on to Chavakachcheri on our bus tour. That evening, as I sat talking with Kugharajan in the guest house, I hesitated to tell him that the neat rows of houses in Colombothurai had all been flattened. His house was most likely among them. At one collapsed house, evidently used by the Tigers as a camp, there were signs of a hurried departure. A pair of fatigues and other men's clothes were hanging on a line tied to two trees. Several pairs of flip-flops lay scattered in the debris.

But Kugharajan knew already. The army had allowed residents to go and look at their homes.

'I went to check our house,' he said. 'There's nothing left.'

'This time we lost everything, even the mattresses,' Usha said.

'We have been through this every few years—1987, 1995, now 2000. We barely finish repairing the house when it is destroyed again.'

The first time was when the Indian army and the Tigers were fighting. The second time in 1995 was when the Sri Lankan army moved in to take control of Jaffna from the Tigers. Kugharajan and his family—forced to leave their home by the Tigers—went to Point Pedro in the peninsula's north-east. Returning a year later, they found that a shell had punched a hole through their roof.

'We waited three years before repairing it because we were not sure when the Tigers would try to take back Jaffna from the army. If that happened we would have to abandon the house again.'

Finally in December 1999, gambling on the Sri Lankan army's staying power, Kugharajan and his wife decided to repair the roof and redo the kitchen.

'Now this. All that effort for nothing,' Kugharajan said. He did not seem bitter, just resigned.

'This time we have decided not to go back to Colombothurai,' Usha said. 'We will look for a house somewhere else.'

The couple's priority now was to ensure their children did well at school.

'Tamils only have education left to them, we must make the best of it,' Kugharajan said.

After every round of fighting in Jaffna, the schools were always the first to reopen. People in Jaffna described education as their 'only industry'. It helped them get better jobs if they went abroad, as hundreds of thousands of Tamils had already done. Through war and displacement, children went to school looking bright and clean in their uniforms. It was the same this time.

Kugharajan's eldest daughter Meera was studying for the school-leaving A level exams. He summoned her downstairs to say hello to me. She asked about going to college in India. Meera was born when the conflict was already raging. She had never known life without war or the threat of it. But if the sixteen-year-old was affected by the disruption and the displacement, I could not tell. She had an open smile as she bombarded me with curious questions about India.

*

Seizing Jaffna town—the administrative capital of the peninsula—had been the main goal of the Tigers when they launched Unceasing Waves Three. They came close to achieving it but the army managed to stave them off at the last minute. Thousands of people who had evacuated from the town in anticipation of the fighting in May had only recently begun streaming back.

'It is surprising sometimes to see that even in the middle of battle normal life goes on,' General Wijendra said on the day we arrived.

In a sense, he was right. Crowds of people milled around the bus stop. Soldiers and civilians jostled in the market. The stalls were all fully stocked with vegetables that Jaffna farmers grew.

On the streets there was the usual flock of bicycles and trishaws. Jaffna did not have many cars except for old British Austins left over from before the conflict. The new models of Japanese and European cars that flooded Colombo did not make it to Jaffna because of the war. The Austins—the Oxford and Cambridge models—were now mostly taxis.

That was the only way their present owners could maintain them. There was an embargo on fuel shipments to Tiger-controlled Jaffna from 1990 to 1996, and the cars were adapted to run on kerosene, the only kind of fuel the government would allow into the peninsula because people used it for cooking. Petrol, the government feared, would be commandeered by the Tigers to fuel their own vehicles.

Since winning back control in 1996, the government had begun sending up petrol, but it was expensive, so the cars still ran on kerosene. Taxi drivers stored petrol in little bottles, which they used only to get the car started, disappearing under the bonnet to sparingly drop some on the carburettor before turning the key in the ignition. As usual, the cars were lined up along Hospital Road, their drivers hunting for rides from the people who streamed out of Jaffna Hospital and the nearby bus stop.

Outwardly, Jaffna did not look very different from the way it looked during any other time since I had started visiting it in 1995. But it felt different. The threat of war hung over the town. People did not believe Unceasing Waves Three was over. The town itself was teeming with displaced people from other parts of the peninsula. They were living with friends or relatives or in shelters, with no idea when they would be able to return home.

At the University of Jaffna, classes were being held as usual, but the vice chancellor, Professor Balasundarampillai, said that since May, more students than usual had been leaving Jaffna, either for Colombo or to go abroad.

'The war has accelerated the outmigration. It is natural that students will seek better pastures,' he said.

In the middle of this, elections to Sri Lanka's parliament were just two weeks away in early October. Tamil political parties had tried to get them postponed but the government was determined to hold the elections as scheduled in the peninsula in order to show it was fully in control. Fourteen political parties and six independent groups put up candidates, but elections were really the last thing on people's minds.

Tharmaraja Mahalingam, manager of Poopalasingham's, a small bookshop and news stand near the bus stop, told me he had returned only a few weeks earlier after fleeing with his wife and two children in May.

They had first gone just a short distance to a suburb of Jaffna town to stay with relatives. But once fighting came closer, they evacuated again, this time further up to Innuvil, once again staying with relatives. The bookstore remained closed. In late July, he and his wife decided to return to reopen their business. But they left their children behind at Innuvil so their schooling would not be disrupted again.

'What sort of life is this?' Mahalingam asked. 'We are in one place, our children are somewhere else, our things are in a third. When will we be able to live normally, in peace?'

He laughed when I asked him about the elections. 'What elections? People are homeless, there is fighting going on. I haven't even thought about elections,' he said.

Mahalingam said he had had high expectations after the last elections that there would be peace. 'But what we got was war and more war. So we don't pin our hopes on elections any more,' he said.

In the last few days, the noise from the fighting had driven him nearly crazy, he said. Chavakachcheri is about 7 km from Jaffna town. Colombothurai is closer.

'You should have heard those new rocket things they were firing. It's louder than anything we have heard before. And they fired hundreds of them at the same time,' he said, covering his ears with his hands as if he could still hear them. 'First a loud scream, then massive thumping sounds. I thought I was used to everything, but this was entirely new.'

*

Once, after the fighting had stopped, an officer of the Sri Lankan army was good enough to show me the MBRLs. There were seven of them, parked in a huge open field, all in various states of disrepair. I saw the Czech ones for which Brigadier Karunaratne had flown to Prague. There were also Chinese and Pakistani MBRLs.

The officer explained how the MBRL worked as we stood before the Czech forty-barrel rocket launcher, mounted on a Tatra 813 truck.

The launcher, or the gun, was an oblong structure of forty long tubes stacked together in four rows, mounted in the back of the truck. It weighed 15 tonnes, the officer said. Each of the rockets that would go into those tubes was about 10 feet in length and weighed 105 kg. It took three men to load a rocket into the launcher.

'The Czech launcher can carry two salvos,' he said.

That meant it carried forty rounds in the barrels and an additional forty in the 'feeder'. When the first set had been fired, the gun turned 180 degrees, to point at the truck's cab. Inside the cab, the soldier at the controls lowered the gun to the level of the feeder located at the end of the truck. The feeder then loaded the second set of rockets into the barrels.

Three soldiers work the MBRL: the driver of the truck, a sergeant and a corporal. They feed in the target position into the gun sights fixed outside the driver's window. The corporal, who is the bombardier, pulls a cord to trigger the rockets. The three move away from the truck as the rockets zoom out to their target.

'What is the noise like?' I asked the officer.

He struggled for the right words. 'How can I describe it?' he asked himself aloud.

'When the rockets leave the launcher, it is as if someone is scraping a thin sheet of metal,' he said. 'It's a continuous screaming sound, but we get used to it after a while.'

The rockets are propelled by fuel inside their casings. 'They leave a 20-metre long flame,' the officer said. 'We can see it at night.'

When the rockets hit their target, the leftover fuel in them explodes with the ammunition inside the rocket.

The armour-plated Tatra came with a snow plough. In Jaffna, a few degrees north of the Equator, there was no snow. The army used the plow to ram through Tiger bunkers.

*

The smell from the guest house seemed to have followed me into Jaffna town, getting progressively worse over the morning. By afternoon, it had turned into a ripe, overpowering, unbearable stench.

I was on my way to meet Thambirajah Subathiran, a former militant known by his nom de guerre Robert and the leader of the EPRLF. He was a candidate in the approaching elections. The streets were full of people going about their business as usual, but they were now walking with handkerchiefs held to their noses. The smell had to be something far worse than sewage.

Even Robert's office on the third floor of a building across from Jaffna Hospital had not escaped the odour. If anything, it was stronger there.

The smell was the first thing I asked him about.

'That's really troubling you, isn't it?' he asked. 'It's from the bodies.'

What bodies, I asked him.

'Tigers',' he replied. 'They are lying at the hospital. Thirty-eight of them from the Chavakachcheri fighting.'

The army had found the bodies when they went into Chavakachcheri. They had handed them over to the ICRC, which in turn was to give them to the Tigers—a routine Geneva Convention procedure that is supposed to make war a civilized affair.

Three days earlier, the Red Cross representatives had travelled to Kaithady, an area under the control of the Tigers, to hand over the bodies. The Tigers had taken charge of just ten bodies when the grim proceedings were interrupted by sounds of shells being fired nearby.

The Red Cross representatives, ever fastidious about the organization's safety rules for its employees in war zones, immediately decided to pull out without handing over the remaining bodies. They brought them back to Jaffna Hospital and left them in the mortuary.

'Don't worry. The smell will go soon. I made some enquiries just a little while ago and the army has decided to remove the bodies from the hospital today. They will put them down as unidentified bodies and give them a mass cremation,' Robert said.

We discussed the elections. Robert, who had spent most of his thirty-eight years actively fighting for the Tamil cause and was an opponent of the Tigers, believed the elections were necessary despite the chaos of war. He said this was the only way to keep moderate Tamil politics alive. He and his party were still living down the shame of 1990. After the Indo-Sri Lanka Accord of 1987, the EPRLF ran a short-lived provincial government in the north-east under the protection of the Indian army. As the Indians left, the EPRLF began forcibly recruiting hundreds of teenagers to raise a force called the Tamil National Army to fight the Tigers. The Tamils had not yet forgiven the EPRLF for that and the party had done poorly in the 1994 elections, not winning a single seat anywhere in the north-east.

'I am not ashamed to admit we committed mistakes in the past. But we have renounced arms and militancy. We are now a democratic party that wants a just solution for the Tamils from the Sri Lankan government, and we do not subscribe to the Tigers' separatism,' Robert said.

Despite the threat to his life from the Tigers, Robert had made Jaffna his home since 1998. Much of the time, he went around asking forgiveness for 1990, he said.

Robert said despite what people might think of his party, they were terrified of the Tigers recapturing the town.

'No one wants the Tigers back. The people may complain about life under the army, but at least they have the freedom to complain. Under the Tigers, people were scared to open their mouths for fear they would hang from the nearest lamp post,' he said.

Chavakachcheri also had a lot to do with it, he said. If the Tigers succeeded in taking Jaffna town, the army would launch a battle to wrest it back.

'People fear that it could end up like Chavakachcheri,' he said.

When I came down from Robert's office into the street, there was an army truck parked at the hospital. As Robert had said, the army was probably about to load the bodies into the truck to take them away. Sriyantha wanted to take pictures and I accompanied him to the morgue.

We followed the stench to the morgue. The bodies were lying just outside the morgue on stretchers, some covered and some not. Yellowish liquid dripped from them into little pools under the stretchers.

*

How must it feel to live continuously amidst the sight, sounds and smell of war? At least 500,000 people—the population of Jaffna since the 1990s—had been exposed to two decades of almost constant fighting. Stress, depression and trauma had to be endemic here. Yet, only one psychiatrist lived and worked in Jaffna. The problem was not Jaffna's alone. Sri Lanka, embroiled in full-scale conflict since 1983, and holding the dubious distinction for the highest number of suicides in the world in the mid-1990s, had only thirty qualified psychiatrists and eight trained clinical psychologists. Some of them were private practitioners. Not all government hospitals had a psychiatric department or the services of a psychiatrist. Even the army had woken up to the mental health needs of soldiers and their families only in 2000. Jaffna was lucky to have the one psychiatrist, and a dedicated one at that.

Unlike so many other Tamil doctors who had left the peninsula years ago for better opportunities in the West, Daya Somasundaram stayed on. A professor of psychiatry, he teaches in the faculty of medicine at Jaffna University. He is also the consultant psychiatrist at Jaffna Hospital. He trains fieldworkers in counselling and therapy. A tired-looking man in his late forties, Somasundaram—like the people around him—bicycles to his various assignments in Jaffna.

In his book *Scarred Minds*, about the ways in which the trauma of war in Jaffna has manifested itself, Somasundaram says people in northern Sri Lanka had gradually adapted to the war after years of being constantly exposed to it. The book talks of a shooting incident in 1983, at the beginning of the conflict that kept people indoors for two months. But after a few years of the war, people went about their daily chores amidst far more devastating developments.

'While helicopters were strafing on one side, cycles and buses would be plying along on the very next street.'[1]

But such adaptation is only on the surface and poses an increasing strain on the capacity of individuals to cope, Somasundaram writes.

I first met him in April 1999 at his office in Jaffna University. Even before the unearthing of fifteen skeletons at the alleged mass grave in Chemmani (see Chapter 7), two skeletons had come up in Jaffna stadium that month. I commented on the absence of public interest in the discovery. He said the stress of war and repeated displacement was showing itself in people mainly as disinterest in events unless they were directly affected by them. The community was shattered, he said.

'It is difficult to describe this kind of shattering. People have been through waves and waves of trauma. It has resulted in a lack of motivation, an absence of activity,' he said. 'Instead there is a tiredness, helplessness.'

In September 2000, that tiredness and helplessness were evident even to my untrained eye.

*

After my visit to the hospital, I was walking towards the bus stop when a middle-aged man suddenly stopped me and asked if I was a reporter. When I nodded, he asked if I had been in the group of journalists that visited Chavakachcheri the day before. The news of the trip had been reported prominently in *Uthayan*, the main Jaffna newspaper along with a photograph of the destroyed market.

The man asked me if the reports of the destruction were accurate.

'Is it true there is nothing left in Chavakachcheri?' he asked.

'Yes,' I replied.

'Everything gone?' he asked again.

'Almost everything,' I said.

What about the market, had I been there, he wanted to know.

The market had taken the worst of it, I said, and asked him why he wanted to know.

'I have a shop there,' he replied as he walked away.

Note:

1. Daya Somasundaram, *Scarred Minds—The Psychological Impact of War on Sri Lankan Tamils*, Delhi: Sage, 1998.

10

The Boy Monk of Polonnaruwa

Eight-year-old Saman Suresh Kumara was too young to attach the prefix 'venerable' to his name. For that, he would have to wait at least another twenty years. But he bore all the other trappings of the Buddhist monk: orange robe, a fully shaven head, bare feet, a wooden begging bowl in his hand, an umbrella tucked under his arm, and the new priestly name of Kandegama Rajithawansa Lankara bestowed on him after his ordination as a *bhikku*, or monk, just minutes earlier.

I was at the Dimbulagala temple in Polonnaruwa in north-central Sri Lanka in June 2001, where Saman Suresh Kumara was one of 118 boys ordained that day into the Buddhist clergy. It was mid-morning, time for the ceremonial lunch, the boys' first meal in their new life as monks. Several senior monks were bustling around getting them to stand in line so they would walk into the dining hall in an orderly fashion.

Hundreds of family members stood around. Some of the children had escaped the line and were weaving their way through the crowd of adults, searching for a familiar face. One new monk who looked not more than five years old was wailing because he could not spot his parents and steadfastly refused to be consoled by the strangers around him. Were it not for the all-pervasive orange colour and the clean-shaven heads, it could have been school sports day.

The ordination took place in a one-level building on the temple grounds. The temple itself was up on a hill. When I got there that morning, a priest was working at full speed shaving the heads of boys who stood in a long line in front of him. Parents and other relatives stood by to help the boys get into a white robe after the haircut. Shaved and dressed, the boys stumbled into a huge hall. There, they sat cross-legged in three rows, facing senior monks from the temple who sat before them in two rows. In their hands, the boys each carried a big bundle of orange cloth.

Directly behind the boys, the hall was filled to overflowing with their families, relatives and friends, all seated on the floor. Several times, a priest admonished the audience not to press forward.

The priest chanted in Pali, the language of the Theravada Buddhist texts, asking the boys to repeat after him. Obediently, their outstretched hands still holding the orange bundles, the boys repeated those life-changing words:

> For the purpose of getting beyond this sea of suffering and for the purpose of reaching the ultimate desired goal of nirvana, please give me these robes and ordain me as a monk.

The ceremony I was witnessing was not an ordinary event. Mass ordinations are rare in Sri Lanka. But in the summer of 2001, there were three. Monks were being ordained with sudden urgency. The reason: The prime minister of Sri Lanka, Ratnasiri Wickremenayake, had declared there was a 'conspiracy' against Buddhism and lamented there were not enough priests to defeat this conspiracy.

Wickremenayake was also the minister in charge of Buddhasasana, or Buddhist affairs. He ordered his officials to set about recruiting a thousand new priests immediately. The ordination at Dimbulagala was part of this campaign. Two other similar ceremonies had already been held at other temples in the country.

*

The *Mahavamsa* is a sixth-century chronicle of events in Sri Lanka from ancient times to about the fourth century. Many Sinhalese Buddhists see it as the correct and true version of the early history of the island. In it, Buddha visits Sri Lanka three times.

This is how it describes his first visit:

> ... the Conqueror, in the ninth month of his buddhahood, at the full moon of the Phussa, himself set forth for the isle of Lanka, to win Lanka for the faith. For Lanka was known to the Conqueror as the place where his doctrine should [thereafter] shine in glory ...[1]

From this and the other two visits of the Buddha that the *Mahavamsa* describes, influential Sinhalese Buddhist scholars have interpreted Sri Lanka as the chosen land of the Buddha and of Buddhism, and of the Sinhalese as the chosen people for the protection of the faith. The king, as the leader of the Sinhalese people, was the principal 'defender of the faith' and in this way, Buddhism became the religion of the state.

Walpola Rahula, a scholar–monk of the last century, wrote in his 1956 book, *History of Buddhism* that 'it became the state religion from the day of its introduction into the island'.

Rahula refers to the *Mahavamsa*'s use of the word *dhammena* to describe governance. Translating this as 'righteously', he says, '... [this] suggests they governed the country as Buddhists, or, at least according to Buddhist customs. How else could one rule *dhammena*?'[2]

In modern-day Sri Lanka, Buddhism is the religion of over 76 per cent[3] of the people, all of whom are Sinhalese. Twenty-five years after its independence from Britain, when Sri Lanka finally became a republic, the new constitution ensured that of all religions practised in the country, Buddhism got the 'foremost' position, a provision that the 1978 constitution retains. Governments made sure they did nothing to antagonize the Sinhalese Buddhist population even if their policies completely alienated Tamils. Governments in trouble worked harder to please the Sinhalese Buddhists.

*

When the boys returned to the hall they were dressed in the orange robes, more voluminous and unwieldy than the white garment. The senior monks sat them down again, this time to tutor them in the 'four noble truths' of Buddhism and in the ten 'precepts', or rules of conduct.

'*Buddham Sharanam Gachchami, Dhammam Sharanam Gachchami, Sangham Sharanam Gachchami,*' the boys said after the priests.

The lines literally mean taking refuge in the Buddha, his teachings, and in the priestly order. Women in the audience dabbed their eyes with the ends of their saris. A low chant rose up from the sea of people looking on as they blessed the novitiates with the words: '*Sadhu, sadhu.*'

At the end of the ninety-minute ceremony, the novitiates were each given new names. A priest stood up to announce the boy's original name and then his new priestly name.

The ordination over, the hall emptied. The senior monks led the novitiates to an open ground where they sat on chairs arranged in neat rows under a temporary shed. Up at the temple, senior monks and bureaucrats of the ministry of Buddhasasana, who attended the ceremony in strength, began their own meeting. Each made a speech about Buddhism, which was relayed downhill on a public address system for the benefit of everyone. Exhausted by the morning's proceedings, the orange-robed children fidgeted through the long sermons, perspiring in their new attire under the blazing mid-morning sun. Their families milled around them, adjusting a robe on a drooping shoulder, running to fetch water for a parched throat, ready to perform any little task for the new monks.

That is where I met Saman Suresh Kumara. He was tired and hungry and in no mood to respond to a stranger's questions. The sermons from the temple on the hill were white noise. Saman Suresh Kumara kept his gaze steadfastly pinned downward as he sat in his chair, swinging tiny legs that hung a few inches short of the ground.

But his mother Dayawanthie seemed more forthcoming. She looked old and tired. There were deep wrinkles on her face and around her eyes as if she was out in the sun all the time. Like the other mothers, she was dressed in a white sari—white is associated with prayer for Sinhalese Buddhists—but her hair was pulled back in a severe bun. 'I will miss him very much. I feel sad he is going away, but I am happy at the same time that my son will serve the dhamma. I can consider it my contribution to my faith,' Dayawanthie said.

*

The official status of Buddhism makes the sangha, the Buddhist priestly order of 40,000 monks, an important force in Sri Lanka. Drawing on the *Mahavamsa*, monks see themselves as custodians of the religion and believe that the legitimacy of a government hangs on their say-so.

'The influence of the sangha over the masses was so great that rulers were careful to win the hearts of the bhikkus for the sake of peaceful and successful government,' Walpola Rahula wrote in his treatise on Buddhism.

Governments in Sri Lanka keep that belief going in their own interests, mindful that the Opposition parties woo the sangha equally.

A few months into my posting in Sri Lanka, I was blown away by a news report that President Chandrika Kumaratunga gave the two heads of the Siam and Asgiriya monastic houses a new luxury Mercedes-Benz car each. And the two chief monks refused to accept the gifts unless the government paid the insurance on the vehicles too. But friends told me 'these things happen all the time'.

In July 1995, as President Kumaratunga was preparing for a war against the Tigers after her efforts at making peace had failed, her mother Sirimavo Bandaranaike, the prime minister, described the sangha in glowing terms at a public function to honour a senior monk. She said:

'We have a long history, a history more than 2500 years old. It was preserved due to actions of the *mahasangha* and our Sinhala kings. The kings of yesteryear worked for the benefit of the people and the *buddhasasana*. The *bhikkus* while spreading Buddhism throughout the world helped shape society here. The same guidance is being rendered by the *mahasangha* of today.'[4]

Several influential monks believe the Tamil problem is of the Tigers' making and that once the Tigers are defeated, the problem will disappear. Naturally, the sangha was pleased with Kumaratunga's determination to defeat the Tigers militarily. Monks organized prayers for the success of the armed forces and praised the president when the army took control of Jaffna peninsula.

They were suspicious of moves by Kumaratunga to offer Tamils political concessions through constitutional reforms, which they saw as a precursor to the break-up of the island and a death blow to Buddhism. Kumaratunga was emphatic about the political changes she would bring in to address Tamil grievances.

'Another Prabhakaran and another LTTE will be born if a political solution is not found after the military wins their ongoing offensive against the LTTE . . . There are historical reasons that resulted in the birth of the LTTE . . . Billions of rupees spent on development will be wasted if a political solution is not found to the ethnic problems, as history tells of the continued recurrence of this tragedy,' she once said in an interview.[5] It was the theme of every speech she made and every interview she gave. But as long as Kumaratunga's military strategy dominated over her political plan for Tamils, the pro-war monks were happy.

Five years later, in August 2000, President Kumaratunga fell foul of the clergy. She tried to push through parliament the package of constitutional reforms she had first proposed in 1995. The new constitution was aimed at changing Sri Lanka from a unitary to a federal state in all but name so that Tamils could govern themselves without breaking up the country. The reforms were not just about devolution, they also aimed to do away with Sri Lanka's all-powerful executive presidency—another of Kumaratunga's 1994 promises— and change to a Westminster-style parliamentary democracy, in which the government would be headed by a prime minister accountable to parliament.

From 1996 onwards, a parliamentary committee had held discussions to arrive at an all-party consensus on the reforms. But consensus proved elusive. Early in 2000, after winning a second term as president in December 1999, Kumaratunga decided to fast-track the process. The voting during the presidential election revealed a massive erosion of Tamil support for her since 1994.[6] The parliamentary elections were next in line. They had to be held by October 2000 and Kumaratunga had nothing to show besides the war for the six years since her party was first elected. A new constitution along the lines she had promised in 1995, she believed, would improve her report card.

Kumaratunga had invited the government of Norway to facilitate talks between her government and the Tigers in late 1999. She believed finalizing the draft of a new constitution would strengthen her position at negotiations with the Tigers. Unknown to her, the Tigers too wanted to strengthen their position at the table. They planned to do this by recapturing Jaffna peninsula.

In February 2000, at about the same time that the Tigers were starting to put their military plan into action, Kumaratunga invited the main Opposition party, the UNP, for discussions on the constitutional reforms package. She needed the support of the Opposition to clear the new constitution through parliament. The leader of the UNP, Ranil Wickremesinghe, who had two months earlier lost the presidential election to Kumaratunga, agreed to participate in the discussions. His party too was preparing for the parliamentary elections later that year; Wickremesinghe did not want to appear non-cooperative or confrontationist.

In April, the Tigers launched Unceasing Waves Three. It made Kumaratunga more determined to finalize a new constitution. If need be, she would even implement it without the Tigers. Just as the Sri Lankan military, after fighting desperately, managed to force a stalemate in Jaffna, the government and the UNP managed to arrive at an agreement on the reforms, even though the resulting document was a watered-down version of the original 1995 proposals. Still, it was the first time in the history of independent

Sri Lanka that the two parties had reached agreement on a plan to resolve the Tamil question.[7] But as the results of the discussions leaked to the rest of Sri Lanka, the Tamils, who wanted the Tigers to be involved in any political solution to the conflict, protested it was too little, while the Sinhalese screamed 'too much'.[8]

The UNP's support to the government on an issue sensitive with Sinhala voters in an election year was always doubtful. The party did not want to antagonize Tamils either. It found a way out of its dilemma by declaring that it could not back the passage of the new constitution through parliament unless both the sangha and the Tigers also approved of it.[9]

The Tigers had rejected the constitution-drafting exercise as early as 1995. Now the sangha made it clear they did not like the new constitution either. Thousands of monks staged protests against the reforms, which they described as a threat to the future of Buddhism in Sri Lanka.[10] The new constitution would have removed the word 'unitary' to describe Sri Lanka as a union of regions in line with the devolution of powers it was proposing for the north-east of the country, the main Tamil area.

For Sinhalese Buddhist nationalists, control over all of Sri Lanka is vital for the safeguarding of Buddhism. The monks saw a federal set-up, or its equivalent, as the first step towards splitting the country and the death of Buddhism in Sri Lanka.

A well-known monk, Madeehe Panghaseeha, said, 'If the proposed constitution is passed, it will be the end of the Sinhala-Buddhist civilisation. Therefore, patriots have to come forward to save the nation and the motherland.'[11]

The *Island* newspaper, known for its Sinhalese Buddhist leanings, reported that Hadigalle Wimalasara, a Buddhist priest and an executive committee member of the National Sangha Council (NSC), an organization of monks, had volunteered 'to sacrifice his life to save the unitary character of Sri Lanka'.

'Rather than living in a divided country, I prefer to sacrifice my life to save it,' Wimalasara said. He added:

'This country has a proud history. Our forefathers died for the cause of safeguarding it, and now the government tries to divide it and to give a portion to Tamil terrorists. If we do not come forward to fight against this conspiracy of depriving the country from the Sinhala nation, those who sacrificed their lives at wars will curse us. I will sacrifice my life for the integrity of the country. One country! One national song! One flag! Let's defeat the separatist constitutional reforms!'[12]

The newspaper said these were the monk's 'last words' before he moved to a platform erected under a banyan tree in crowded Pettah in Colombo's Fort area to begin a hunger strike to force the government to withdraw the proposed constitution.

The government tried to get across the views of a few priests who were still friendly to it. The state-owned *Daily News* prominently ran the pictures of three monks who said the draft constitution posed no threat to Buddhism or Sri Lanka.

'We have read the draft [constitution] in full, carefully, and found nothing harmful to Buddhism or the country's unity, sovereignty or territorial integrity in it. We have found that it is a constitution that will do good rather than harm to the country,' the *Daily News* reported an important priest from Polonnaruwa, Kumbukkaduwala Sri Dheerananda, as saying.[13]

Kumaratunga too made a plea to the sangha support to the new constitution. Presenting the draft constitution to parliament, she said, 'I have been practising Buddhism since my childhood. I was voted to power last year by a majority of the Sinhalese Buddhists. I appeal to the Buddhist clergy to extend their support.'[14]

It was no use. 'President Kumaratunga will pass this constitution over our dead bodies,' said Madulawave Sobitha, a muscularly built priest, at one protest meeting organized by the NSC.[15] The priest was the president of the NSC.

On 8 August 2000, on the second day of the debate in parliament on the new constitution, monks staged a sit-in on the road to the parliament complex to prevent members from reaching. The members had to get there by other routes.

The government was depending upon defectors from the Opposition to make up the numbers required for pushing the new constitution through parliament, and even hoped to engineer some of these defections. But not only did the ruling party fail to win over Opposition party members in sufficient numbers, even senior government members turned jittery at the reaction the draft constitution had provoked from the monks and were unsure of supporting it. I was at the sit-in when an important minister came out of the parliament building in the middle of the debate to reassure the monks that 'nothing would happen'.

True enough, the government, worried that the proposed new constitution would not have enough support from its own ranks, preferred not to put it to vote rather than suffer defeat.[16]

Not being able to bring in a new constitution was a big setback for President Kumaratunga. For five years, she had waged a war against the Tigers while also telling the Tamil people that she understood their misery and the pain the war caused them, promising a political solution that would truly reflect Sri Lanka's multi-ethnic character. Now she had nothing to show them. Stripped of Tamil support, her coalition, the PA, won just a narrow victory in the parliamentary elections of 5 October 2000.

After the elections, the president decided to plunge into talks with the Tigers, an option she had begun exploring way back in 1999 with the assistance of the government of Norway. Kumaratunga had then believed she would present to the Tigers a new constitution as a fait accompli. For their part, before talking, the Tigers wanted to take back territory they had lost to the government since 1995, including the Jaffna peninsula.

Both had tried and failed. Kumaratunga's plan to push through a new constitution bombed. A massive military offensive by the Tigers to wrest the Jaffna peninsula from the government between April and June 2000 had ended in a stalemate. The Tigers signalled that they too were ready for talks.

The peace process began spectacularly, with a meeting between a Norwegian diplomat, Eric Solheim, and the leader of the Tigers, Velupillai Prabhakaran.[17] But less than a year later, in May 2001, both the peace process and Kumaratunga's government were tottering. A coalition partner, the Sri Lanka Muslim Congress

(SLMC), was about to pull out, pushing the government to the verge of collapse.

The Tigers, angry with Kumaratunga because she was unwilling to concede any of their preconditions for face-to-face negotiations, made it plain that they did not want to continue the process with a shaky government. Added to that, the economy ground to a standstill as the rains failed, lakes dried up and the whole of Sri Lanka, dependent almost entirely on hydroelectricity, was slapped with daily powercuts.

Another election was in the wind—that much was certain in the hot, rainless summer of 2001. Eventually, it was held in December, but Prime Minister Wickremenayake, a loyalist of President Kumaratunga and a stalwart of her SLFP, decided to get a head start in the race by winding up the majority Sinhalese Buddhists, telling them their religion was under threat. First he ordered his officials to start the campaign to recruit more monks. The ministry of Buddhist affairs took out advertisements in the newspapers calling for 1000 volunteers to join the sangha. But the response was lukewarm. Then, he asked people to contribute to the protection of Sinhalese Buddhism by having more babies, blaming Sri Lanka's successful family planning programme for the poor response to both his campaign to recruit more priests and to the army recruitment drives. That was the reason, he said, the government was not able to finish the war against the Tigers.[18]

*

In an email interview to me, the University of Virginia-based Sri Lankan anthropologist H.L. Seneviratne, who wrote *The Work of Kings*, a masterly analysis of the role of the sangha in Sri Lanka, described the mass ordination of monks as the 'twin' to the recruitment of soldiers for the war.

In Sinhalese Buddhist lore, whenever the faith came under threat, the clergy and army always rose to protect it, hand in hand. The *Mahavamsa* tells the story of King Dutugemunu who marched his armies north and slew Elara, a damila king (*demala* in modern

Sinhalese is the word for Tamil).

Before he left on his military venture, he told the sangha, 'I will go to the land on the further side of the river to bring glory to the doctrine. Give us, that we may treat them with honour, *bhikkus* who shall go with us, since the sight of the *bhikkus* is blessing and protection for us.'[19]

The sangha gave him 500 monks. They marched with Dutugemunu's army. Kumaratunga's war was directed at the Tigers, but it had inescapable undertones of the Sinhalese Buddhist supremacy that Dutugemunu fought to protect. It was waged by an entirely Sinhalese military. Each of its operations had a Sinhalese code name that called to mind the battlefield victories of ancient Sinhalese kings over their Tamil counterparts. When the war began in 1995, the *Daily News* gave prominent coverage to three monks who enlisted for the army.

Prime Minister Wickremenayake's call for more priests was an appeal for more warrior–monks who would join the battle to protect Sinhalese Buddhism from their temples if not in the battlefield. Officials took the campaign to recruit priests seriously, setting targets for each area, almost as if recruiting soldiers.

In the area I visited, priests from every village temple fanned out under instructions from the chief priest of the main Dimbulagala temple to find at least hundred boys willing to join the sangha.

Dayawanthie, the mother of eight-year-old Saman Suresh Kumara, said the priest of the Kandegama temple paid her a visit. He asked if she would give her son to the order. She said he was too young, but the priest then put the question directly to Saman and the boy said yes.

Elle Gunavamsa, a musically inclined monk, shot to fame in the mid-1990s with his songs praising Sinhala militancy. The Sri Lankan armed forces even used his songs to inspire soldiers.

These were the words of one of his songs:

The Sangha is ever ready
At the front

If the race is threatened
So long as the Sangha robe lasts
So long as the Sangha robe lasts, so long as the Sangha robe lasts,
Our country and race, our country and race
Will shine, O son.[20]

Monks like Gunavamsa saw no contradiction in their double role as messengers of peace and propagandists of war. For Gunavamsa, the war was being fought to safeguard Buddhism, not just to defeat the Tigers.

In the *Mahavamsa*, King Dutugemunu laments the number of people killed in his battle with King Elara:

'How shall there be any comfort for me, O venerable sirs, since by me was caused the slaughter of a great host numbering millions?'

To which the eight monks who had gone to console him say:

'From this deed arises no hindrance in thy way to heaven. Only one and half human beings have been slain here by thee, O lord of men. The one had come unto the [three] refuges, the other had taken on himself the five precepts. Unbelievers and men of evil were the rest, not more to be esteemed than beasts. But as for thee, thou wilt bring glory to the doctrine of the Buddha in manifold ways; therefore cast away care from thy heart, O ruler of men!'[21]

A previous chief priest of the Dimbulagala temple, Matara Kithalagama Sri Seethalankara Thero, had fashioned himself in the image of the warrior–monk of legend that Elle Gunavamsa sang about. Seethalankara considered it his duty to protect Sri Lanka from breaking up so that Buddhism may live. He saw himself in the front line of the battle with the Tigers. The Tigers killed him.

Dimbulagala was a 'border' area, that is, it bordered the north-east conflict zone. Most of the people living in the villages surrounding the temple were Sinhalese Buddhists. They constantly feared being attacked by the Tigers. Seethalankara's killing had heightened the sense of siege. The temple, set atop a rocky cliff, high above the villages, was almost a border watchtower. A flag with the Buddhist colours—white, yellow and blue—flapped loudly in the constant breeze. Driving up to the temple that morning, I had seen the flag from 5 km away. The harsh beauty of the surroundings enhanced the outpost quality of the temple.

*

Standing there, I realized there was another striking similarity between this mass ordination and an army recruitment drive. Dimbulagala is a poor area of Polonnaruwa district. The 2001 census records a population of 63,189 in Dimbulagala. They are mainly small farmers or agricultural labourers. There were no rich people in that crowd of families waiting at the temple. Besides service to the dhamma, another compelling reason was pushing parents to send their children into the sangha.

Dayawanthie said she was a labourer and did whatever work she could find around her home, about 15 km from the Dimbulagala temple. On days she worked, she earned Rs 120 (a little more than one US dollar). Her husband was in hospital, but she did not know what was wrong with him, only that he coughed and wheezed a lot. He could not work, and they also had a ten-year-old daughter to raise.

'The monks can look after Saman Kumara much better than I,' she said, looking away.

As a student monk, Saman Kumara would be taught, in addition to the Buddhist scriptures, everything he would have learnt at a normal school. His orange cloth would give him privileged access to educational facilities in the country, something his peers back at the village school could only dream about.

One of those who had come to witness the ordination was H.W. Ariyaratne, a young English teacher from the school in Kandegama that Saman Kumara attended before his ordination. He told us thirty-eight students from his school were ordained that day.

'Their families are too poor to bring them up. They would not have been able to continue their education,' he said. 'Their parents can't even provide for their basic everyday needs, so they have sent them to the monastery where they will be assured at least of food and education.'

For their first meal as members of the sangha, the boys sat at long tables and placed their black wooden bowls on the table. Senior monks and volunteers from the village spooned generous helpings of rice, meat curries and vegetables into the bowl and the boys attacked the food with gusto. Dessert was a roughly chopped-up fruit salad, and Ariyaratne whispered to me as we stood in one corner of the dining room that some of these children might not have tasted an apple or an orange or a grape before this.

I asked Ariyaratne how many of those ordained that day would stay on in the clergy, considering that most probably had no idea of what sort of life decision they or their parents had just made for them.

His response was not a direct reply.

'We have advised the pupils from our school who have been ordained today that even if they wish to drop out, they should do so only after getting an education, so that they can make something of their lives if they do come out of the clergy,' he said.

Government officials at the ordination ceremony looked pleased at the way the event had gone off. They had packed the front rows of the audience during the ceremony. The seniormost bureaucrat in the ministry of Buddhasasana was also present, wearing all white for the occasion. I asked him the same question. How many of these children could be expected to grow up and remain in the sangha?

He was getting into his car to go back to Colombo.

'We see no problems. These children will grow up and guide the destiny of this country. The more bhikkus we have, the more the benefits to our society,' he said.

*

The boys emerged from the dining room looking less restive than they had been before lunch. They instinctively sought out their families. The families stood in little groups, each talking to their own little monk. Their brothers and sisters looked at them with a mixture of awe and curiosity. One pulled playfully at the robe, another ran his hand over his brother's shaven head.

Then it was time to say goodbye. Once again, senior monks of the Dimbulagala monastery asked their new charges to form a line. As the boys began heading towards their living quarters, their families walked with them, helping them hold on to their few belongings.

Realization was now beginning to creep in that this was also the time to say goodbye to their families. Saman Kumara was crying, as was his mother who straggled along beside him. He hardly looked the part of a warrior for Sinhalese Buddhism, the role that the government wanted him to play.

When a boy is ordained into the sangha, especially at a very young age, the family usually bids adieu to him with a suitcase filled with toys and other goodies to make his passage into the spiritual world a little less severe.

Dayawanthie held a new suitcase with a blue-and-black check pattern to give Saman Kumara. It was not an expensive box, but it had cost her a day's wages. I wanted to know what she was giving her son as a going-away gift. At first, Dayawanthie was reluctant to open it but finally gave in at the persuasion of Sriyantha, the *Hindu*'s photgrapher.

'There is nothing much in it, I had no money to buy him anything. Take a look if you want.'

The box had one small tube of toothpaste and a toothbrush.

Notes:

1. The *Mahavamsa*, translated by Wilhelm Geiger, Colombo: Ceylon Government Information Department, 1956.
2. Walpola Rahula, *History of Buddhism*, Dehiwela, Sri Lanka: The Buddhist Cultural Centre, 1956.

3. *Statistical Handbook of Sri Lanka—2002*, Department of Census and Statistics, Ministry of Interior, Government of Sri Lanka.

4. *Daily News*, 17 July 1995.

5. *Daily News*, 21 July 1995.

6. Kumaratunga survived an assassination attempt by the Tigers three days before the elections. She won a large number of sympathy votes from among the Sinhalese majority.

7. Two earlier attempts by the ruling party to resolve the Tamil question, the Bandaranaike–Chelvanayakam Pact of 1957, and the Indo-Sri Lanka Accord of 1987, failed after the Opposition party rallied Sinhala public opinion against them. See also, the *Hindu*, 8 July 2000.

8. *The Hindu*, 17 July 2000.

9. *The Hindu*, 28 July 2000. The UNP also cited disagreement with the government on the powers of the president in the transition period between the old and the new constitutions. The draft new constitution abolished the Executive Presidency but made transitory provisions for Kumaratunga to continue in office until the expiration of her second term in 2005.

10. *The Hindu*, 2 August 2000.

11. *Island*, 2 August 2000.

12. *Island*, 8 August 2000.

13. *Daily News*, 25 July 2000.

14. Kumaratunga, presenting the New Constitution Bill of Sri Lanka to parliament, 4 August 2000.

15. *Island*, 2 August 2000.

16. *The Hindu*, 9 August 2000.

17. *The Hindu*, 2 November 2000.

18. *Divaina*, 19 June 2001.

19. The *Mahavamsa*, translated by Wilhelm Geiger, Colombo: Ceylon Government Information Department, 1956.

20. From H.L. Seneviratne, *The Work of Kings—The New Buddhism in Sri Lanka*, Chicago: University of Chicago Press, 1999.

21. The *Mahavamsa*, translated by Wilhelm Geiger, Colombo: Ceylon Government Information Department, 1956.

11

'Give Us Your Children'

Finding Dharmalingam Sritharan was easy. The hard part was getting the fifteen-year-old to talk. He lived by Kattankudy, a short ride from Batticaloa town, across the bridge over the lagoon. It was early afternoon, the sun was bouncing off the uneven tar on the road and there was hardly any traffic on the bridge, not like in the mornings or evenings when it was covered with people pedalling to and from work. Nor did we—I was with Sriyantha, the *Hindu*'s photographer and Sri, our driver on long-distance trips—have to contend with the usual back-up of buses, vans, motorcycles, cyclists or pedestrians waiting to be let through at the checkpoint at the foot of the bridge. Looking relaxed, the soldiers smiled at us and waved us through.

A week had gone by since the ceasefire between the government and the Tigers—signed on 22 February 2002—and the relief showed on the soldiers' faces. When we neared Sritharan's house, we first thought we might park on the main road and walk over. But a parked van on the main road with a driver waiting inside would surely attract attention. So we navigated the narrow sand track and drove right up to his house, a two-roomed hut with a thatch of palmyra leaves in a large compound with other similar houses. Palmyra fronds woven into a fence around the compound gave it privacy.

We had no way of letting the family know in advance that we were coming. They did not have a phone. Even so, Sritharan's mother, Rupavathi, was welcoming. She first thought we were aid workers. Often, people in north-east Sri Lanka take it for granted that everyone who is obviously not local works for one of the several international agencies based in the conflict area.

'Are you from the ICRC?' she asked, as she opened the gate of the compound to let us in.

When I told her I was a reporter and that Sriyantha's job was to take photographs, she pulled back visibly.

'What do you want from us?' she asked.

'I would like to speak to your son, about his escape,' I said.

'What for?'

'I want to write about it in my newspaper.'

'Oh, no, no. How will that help? It might only go against us.'

My assurance that I would not mention her or her son's name in my report, and that Sriyantha would not take any photographs, did not convince her fully.

What was in it for her or her family, Rupavathi asked.

Nothing directly but it might help prevent other such incidents, was my reply. After a little thought, she allowed us to come into the compound and began barking orders to an assortment of family members who had gathered to watch.

'Where is your brother, call him,' she said to a little girl.

'Where's the mat, bring it out,' she said to someone else.

As she rolled out a hastily produced reed mat on the sand in the compound, a stockily built boy appeared. Acne peppered his forehead, and hair had just begun to make an appearance above his lip.

'This is Sritharan,' Rupavathi said.

After that simple introduction by his mother, Sritharan sat on the edge of the mat and doodled on the sand with his right forefinger. His replies to questions were short, as if it was an effort to speak more than a few words at a time. Three weeks earlier, Sritharan had escaped from a Tiger camp.

Sritharan was an O Level student at the Sivananda High School in nearby Kallady. Like many of his classmates keen to do well in the exam at the end of the year, Sritharan was attending extra coaching classes. On the morning of 3 February, he was returning home from the 'tutory' when two men, one wheeling a bicycle, came up to him. They first forced Sritharan to get off his bicycle.

'They asked me to come with them to the other side,' he said.

The 'other side' is a commonly used phrase in the north-east to describe LTTE-controlled territory.

'I told them I would not go with them, but they threatened to beat me up if I didn't. I was afraid. I went with them.'

Since he seemed not to have put up much resistance, I asked him if he had actually wanted to go with them.

'They threatened me,' he said again.

The men took him on the ferry across the Manmunai river, about 3 km from Kallady, to Kokkadicholai, 'the other side' of Batticaloa, where the Tigers have their main office for the area.

'There were other boys there. When it became dark, they took us in a tractor-trailer to Karadiyanaru,' said Sritharan.

Karadiyanaru is deep inside Batticaloa district in Tiger-controlled land. The Tigers had a military camp in Karadiyanaru. Part of their fighting force was based there. That is also where they trained new recruits.

They put Sritharan with a few others in a house with a compound and a palmyra fence around it. Senior male cadres in the compound took charge of them.

The next morning, Sritharan said, a senior cadre asked him to sweep the place and cut the grass in the compound. Sritharan spent the next two days keeping the compound clean. On the third day, he decided to take his chance.

'I took the cook's bicycle and escaped on it,' he said. 'There was no one else in the compound at the time. The others had all gone away somewhere, I don't know where. It was just me and the cook.'

He cycled nearly 5 km, once stopping to ask directions from a group of villagers, to reach the main Batticaloa highway at Chenkaladdy, where the first vehicle he saw was a huge white jeep with antennae rising up from it, a red cross on its hood and side.

'It was the ICRC. They rescued me,' he said.

When the fifteen-year-old Sritharan did not return home after his coaching class, his elder brother, Jayakanthan, quite certain the Tigers were behind his disappearance, went to the 'other side' looking for him.

'I had a feeling he might have been taken, so I went to Kokkadicholai to see if I could find him there,' he said.

He saw Sritharan's bicycle at the LTTE office there. Someone in the office told him some boys had been transported in a tractor-trailer the day before for Karadiyanaru.

'I thank god that he gave my boy the brains to snatch that bicycle and escape from the camp,' Rupavathi said, her hands folded in prayer, her eyes glazing over with tears.

'When he did not come back home that day from his classes, all I could do was run up and down these roads, screaming for him,' she said. 'I died a thousand deaths in those three days.'

Since being reunited with his family, Sritharan had not been out anywhere. Rupavathi was afraid to send him back to school. What about the extra classes, I asked him.

'I'm scared to go out,' was all he said.

With the ceasefire, Rupavathi wondered if the Tigers would ease off on the children. She did not have many details about the ceasefire but she had heard the Tigers could move around without being checked by the army. She was mentally preparing for the eventuality that they would come back for Sritharan.

For now, Sritharan's only protection was an emergency phone number that the ICRC had given his mother. Rupavathi would have to walk several minutes to the main road to find a payphone because she had no telephone at home. But she had another strategy.

'Let them come, they have to shoot me before they take him away again.'

*

For the first time in six years, the guns were finally silent in Sri Lanka. No more fighting, no more young men dying at the front, no more suicide bombings. Colombo was in a celebratory mood after the ceasefire.

In fact, the capital had begun celebrating two months before, in December 2001, when the government of President

Kumaratunga was defeated in the parliamentary elections. Kumaratunga was still president and the head of the government but she would have to share governance with the Opposition UNP, which, with its allies, had won the majority of seats in parliament. Its leader, Ranil Wickremesinghe, became the prime minister. We journalists described it as an 'uneasy cohabitation'.

The Tigers were more favourably disposed to the new ruling party than they had been to Kumaratunga's government. In the elections, the UNP had pledged not to pursue the war. Instead, they had promised to do everything to restart the peace process with the Tigers.

Kumaratunga's efforts to begin talks with the Tigers, which gathered momentum after the parliamentary election of 2000, ran out of steam within a few months over the Tigers' preconditions for peace talks. They wanted a ceasefire. Kumaratunga said the Tigers would only use a ceasefire to rearm and regroup to strike back more brutally, as they had done in 1995. The Tigers also wanted the government to lift the ban that had been imposed on them in 1998. Kumaratunga was firm she would not do this either, at least until the two sides began talking.

While the fighting between the Tigers and government forces continued intermittently, the PA, a carefully constructed coalition of disparate political parties, was beginning to unravel and threaten the very existence of the government. The Tigers hastened the process with a crippling terrorist attack on Sri Lanka's international airport on 24 July 2001. The attack produced exactly the result that the Tigers wanted: it consolidated the anti-PA mood in the country; it even convinced many Kumaratunga supporters that she did not have the right approach to the peace process, and that she had not done enough to enable talks with the Tigers. Dissenters from the PA left to join the UNP, reducing it to a minority in parliament. Kumaratunga explored a few options to keep her government propped up, but finally called another parliamentary election in December that year. The UNP won.

As soon as Wickremesinghe took charge, the Tigers offered a Christmas truce. The new government decided to reciprocate with a truce of its own. All at once the atmosphere in Sri Lanka changed. The military dismantled checkpoints on several roads in the capital. People went on joyrides down roads that had been closed for years. They packed the shopping malls.

Galle Face, the deserted oceanfront promenade that only the very daring or the very young frequented after dark, came alive. Roads leading to it were choked with cars trying to get there. I once had to park 2 km away and walked to reach Galle Face. Soldiers still stood in the watchtowers of the military headquarters that looked out to Galle Face but they smiled and waved at the crowds below.

Where the waves crashed against the concrete breaker, someone put up a sign with a single word—PEACE. At night, the board twinkled with lights. I had never seen a Christmas season quite like that in Colombo before. Everybody looked happy and recharged.

Two months later, in February 2002, the government and the Tigers signed a formal ceasefire agreement. Five days after the signing, I set off for Batticaloa.

Batti was in the conflict zone. If Colombo was euphoric, Batti had to be ecstatic. But it seemed untouched by the celebrations. People were fearful. Not of the army any more. Now they were only afraid of the Tigers. The ceasefire agreement allowed the Tigers to move freely even in government-controlled Batti. They could open an office right there in Batti town. For many people in Batti, that was a scary prospect.

On my first afternoon, wandering into the Lake View Inn, a run-down hotel in the town, I asked the hotel clerk, whom I knew from previous trips, what he thought of the ceasefire. He gave me a circumspect smile from under his dyed moustache, but a man slumped in the sagging sofa in the dusty veranda that passed for a lobby muttered something without taking his eyes off the television.

'Now when the boys summon us to the other side, we can't even give them the excuse that we got stopped at an army checkpoint because there are no more checkpoints.'

For people in Batticaloa, the ceasefire had removed one oppressor but empowered the other. The soldiers had backed off but the

Tigers were still around and freer to do as they pleased. Traders in the town feared more frequent visits from Tiger tax squads, politicians who had refused to toe the LTTE line feared for their lives, but most of all, parents feared for their young children.

*

One of the great open secrets of the conflict in Sri Lanka was that the Tigers forcibly recruited children for combat. Their recruiters went from school to school in the north-east, telling students it was their duty to come forward for the liberation of Tamil Eelam. But Tamil people, especially vocal supporters of the Tigers living in Colombo whose own children went to posh schools, rarely liked to discuss this aspect of the Tamil liberation struggle.

University Teachers for Human Rights (UTHR), Jaffna, was the only human rights organization in Sri Lanka that consistently endeavoured to force the issue of child conscription by the Tigers out into the open. The original group, made up of four University of Jaffna academics—two mathematics teachers and two from the medical faculty of Jaffna University—used to be based in the peninsula.

They monitored and documented violations of the human rights of Tamil people in the north-east, whether by the armed forces or by the Tigers. They did this with a zeal bordering on the missionary. In 1990, the Tigers killed one of their members, Rajini Thiranagama. The others scattered for their safety and now led low-profile lives, changing addresses and phone numbers frequently. But they continued to bring out reports based on a well-established network of sources in the north-east. Their reports on child soldiers carried names, ages and addresses of children taken away by the Tigers.

In July 2000, the UTHR reported a renewed child recruitment campaign by the Tigers on the heels of their military successes at Elephant Pass and the Jaffna peninsula.

The report said:

> On May 5, after the Elephant Pass attack . . . three days a week, all school children from [class] 9 upwards [that is in the 14–15 age group] were required to take military training.[1]

It described teams of recruiters going to schools and holding 'current affairs' classes. The current affairs topic was the LTTE victory at Elephant Pass in which they projected the beach landing of 1400 LTTE cadres north of Elephant Pass as one of the world's most remarkable military feats.

At a meeting between teachers and the Tigers, the report said, one teacher asked how long the military training for students would continue.

'Once all the students join our organization, there will be no need for further training,' came the reply.

After the propaganda sessions in the school, recruiters waited outside, and picking on individual students, engaged them in discussions about why they should join the 'movement'. The report said many students were 'tricked' into going with the recruiters in this manner.

Girls, the report said, were 'a large majority' of those who joined in that round of recruitment.

> Twenty girls were recruited recently from a school and were taken to a girls' camp. They were ordered to surrender their school uniforms and were given exercise slacks. The school uniforms were burnt in their presence. After a day, five of the girls aged 14 to 15 told the camp authorities that they wanted to go home. These girls were then isolated, taken to a room, stripped, mercilessly assaulted and pushed on to the ground . . . [and] trampled upon. This punitive violence was administered by senior girls.
>
> The girls were then locked up. Three of them escaped when they had the chance. The remaining two were too frightened to escape. The escapees made it home after walking more than 24 hours in the jungle. The father of one of the girls feared that the LTTE would come looking for his daughter . . . [he] was determined . . . he would fight them and face death at their hands.

The report talked of how parents and teachers were too terrrorized by the Tigers to protest against the recruitment in any organized fashion.

> Earlier [mid-1990s] in Jaffna the parents would rush to the school and surround it and the teachers and the principal would often help safeguard the children . . . Parents today do not rush to the school in an organised manner when the recruiters arrive. At one time the teachers and principal used to insist on being present when the recruiters addressed the children. Today as soon as the recruiters arrive the teachers walk out of the class and there is no adult present to witness the pressures being employed.

The Tigers used direct and indirect terror to make the adults compliant, the report said. They had a long, well-known history of killing or arresting dissenters. So when they made it known to teachers who resisted the recruitment drive that they were being watched, the teachers knew how to look the other way when the recruiters came.

A week after the UTHR report came out, United Nations International Children's Emergency Fund (UNICEF) held a news conference in Colombo for the release of its annual publication *Progress of Nations*. Journalists present at the news conference asked the head of UNICEF Sri Lanka, Colin Glennie, to comment on the report.

International bureaucrats usually serve bland, diplomatic fare, but Glennie was surprisingly candid. Perhaps the Scotsman in him had surfaced, or perhaps UNICEF had decided to finally go public that it had a problem with the Tigers. Glennie said some parents had reported to UNICEF that their children had been recruited.

'We don't have numbers but we know it's a serious problem,' Glennie said.[2]

UNICEF, he said, raised the issue whenever it met representatives of the Tigers. Glennie said the Tigers had broken a commitment they made to the UN Special Representative on Children in Armed Conflict, Olara Otunnu, when he visited them in 1998 and held talks with senior Tiger leaders in northern Sri

Lanka. The Tigers told Otunnu they would not recruit children below seventeen years and not send anyone under eighteen years into combat.

'Until they announce to their own people they have measures to prevent children below seventeen from being recruited, we cannot take their promises seriously,' Glennie said.

For me, the memory of the day I made my first foray into LTTE land is still vivid. It was on my first trip to Batticaloa in July 1995. I would have been stopped by soldiers at the last army checkpoint. But thanks to a helpful officer, I 'crossed over', as the journey is called, to Vakkarai, a village 45 km north of Batticaloa town.

When I reached the LTTE office there, a smooth-faced boy, no older than twelve or thirteen, stood guard holding an assault rifle in his hand. He stonewalled all my attempts to make conversation as I waited for someone to fetch a senior cadre even though he kept his gaze fixed on me.

When I came back to the town that evening, the Lake View's run-down veranda was crowded with the town drunks—the hotel bar was popular—hunched around the television set watching the night news.

The Tigers had attempted to overrun a garrison north-west of Batticaloa. The army had repulsed the attack. The news said that up to 300 Tigers were killed in the fighting. A government camera crew had been rushed up to the garrison to document the victory and the TV station was showing the pictures: rows upon rows of uncovered corpses, some mangled, some whole, the camera zooming in and out of what remained of their pubescent bodies.

'Kids, all of them,' one of the drunks said.

After losing Jaffna peninsula to the army in 1996, the Tigers had turned to Batticaloa for fresh recruits. The Tigers needed to replace the hundreds of cadres they were losing in the war. The government was not winning the war but its military operations, one after the other in quick succession, were definitely taking a toll on the Tigers' fighting strength. Recruitment squads went around Batticaloa sucking up its young to replace those who had fallen in the battlefield.

The UTHR documented another intensive recruitment drive by the Tigers in August and September 2001 even though there was no fighting then.

Unsigned notices came up on school boards, the report said, with the following message:

> The Leader is of the opinion that this war should not be prolonged. It must be brought to an end soon so that the coming generations of our people can live in dignity. We must defeat the Sinhalese armed forces that have committed aggression against our soil. We now have the weaponry, but it is fighters that we lack. We feel each family should contribute one member towards the fulfillment of our aim.[3]

Teams of recruiters went around in tractor-trailers demanding children from parents. The report said:

> When parents refused, they were beaten with palmyra fronds. Usually the children came running out when they heard parents scream. The recruiters then asked a child to come along. The child, on declining, was beaten and forced into the trailer.

In Valaichenai, an area of Batticaloa, the Tigers distributed a pamphlet that said: 'Young men and maidens of Valaichenai, rise and come to us, one from each home, to liberate the soil of Batticaloa from the enemy.'

The recruitment was taking place mostly in areas under the direct control of the Tigers. Attendance in schools in these areas dropped. People living in these areas began sending their children to live with relatives in army-controlled Batticaloa, thinking they would be safer there. Entire families moved too.

The UTHR said 900 families had gone into army-controlled areas. The Tigers responded by ordering all those who had sent out their children to bring them back or face confiscation of their properties.

Alarmed by what was happening, reported the UTHR in October 2001, the Bishop of Batticaloa, Kingsley Swamipillai, paid a visit to the Tiger area leadership on 25 September. With him went other community leaders of Batticaloa.[4]

They met Karikalan, the Tigers' eastern area leader. The bishop told him of the people's concerns about forcible recruitment of children. Karikalan denied the Tigers were taking anybody into the organization forcibly and said it was all voluntary.

Finally, the bishop said to Karikalan: '. . . see that the people are not harmed in the process of liberating them.'

But the appeal carried no weight and the recruitment continued right into the ceasefire.

*

Before the ceasefire, journalists who wanted to cross into Tiger areas in Batti were completely at the mercy of the whims of policemen or soldiers to allow them through the last checkpoint. On a couple of earlier trips to Batti, we got through without much questioning. But more often, I had been turned back at one or the other of the checkpoints beyond which lay Tiger land. Once, we were not allowed even the minor luxury of a U-turn. The two surly soldiers ordered Sri, the driver, to reverse out, their guns pointed at us. It took all his driving skills to negotiate the tight inverted S around the barrels without hitting anything.

But with the truce, everything was different. At the checkpoint at Vavunathivu, a soldier politely asked to see our press identity cards, took down our van's registration number and let us through.

We were on our way to Kokkadicholai, to meet Karikalan, the area Tiger boss. It took more than an hour of driving on a bumpy dirt track to reach the LTTE office. The office stretched down one entire side of a narrow lane. A high fence of dry palm leaves woven together into a thick curtain cut the office off from the outside.

At the gate, a thick-set youth, his dense hair cut high and flat like a table top, stood guard. He wore the usual Tiger civvies: black trousers, baggy at the top with tapered legs and a loose grey and blue checked shirt left untucked. On his feet, he wore rubber flip-flops. He looked unsure when we said we wanted to meet Karikalan.

'He's in a meeting, it could take long,' he said.

'That doesn't matter. We can wait,' I said, trying to edge my way past him.

He blocked me with his hand across the gate and asked me to stand outside while he checked with someone inside. He was back within minutes and this time, he led us to a waiting area just inside the gate where several people sat in plastic chairs. The chairs were arranged in rows facing each other under a palmyra thatch held up by wooden poles fixed in the sand. Most of the chairs were taken up. I found an empty seat next to a woman who was leaning over, talking in low whispers to some people sitting to her right. When they paused and she sat back in her chair, I asked her what had brought her there.

'What can I say . . .' she began, shaking her head. 'It's my boy, my fourth, he's just seventeen. I have already lost three sons in this war. Now they've taken my last child as well.'

She had come to ask for his return, or at least, to be allowed to meet him.

'Did they take him away by force?' I asked.

'I don't know. The boy went out one day and never came back.'

'How do you know he's with the Tigers? He could have gone anywhere.'

'No, I know he's with them,' she insisted.

But she was optimistic. Hers was a 'martyr's family', given that title by the Tigers. They gave the title to families of all their cadres killed in action.

'They know my family, the sacrifices we have made, so they might play fair by me.'

As she spoke, a functionary of the Tigers emerged from the single-storeyed buildings to one side of the waiting area and approached our group. Evidently, his task was to minimize the number of people waiting in the line, and he worked his way up our row of chairs asking each person what his business was, telling some people to leave and others to stay.

When he came to me, I told him I had been asked to wait for a meeting with Karikalan. He nodded in acknowledgement and passed on to the woman next to me.

'Thambi,' she said, using the Tamil word for younger brother, 'it's about my son . . .'

Immediately, he motioned her to follow him outside the palmyra shelter. They stood talking in the sun for a few minutes. When she returned, her face looked crumpled.

'He says they are not holding anyone here, all the boys have been sent to camp for training . . .' she said, trailing off as the same man came back towards us.

This time, it was to tell me I would be more comfortable waiting inside in the office. When I replied that I was comfortable where I was, he insisted.

He showed Sriyantha and me into a large meeting hall with more plastic chairs but no people. We waited in isolation for two hours till Karikalan was finally ready to meet us.

*

Karikalan's office was tiny, a table taking up most of the space in the room. In a grey shirt and trousers, he looked more like a middle-aged office worker than a guerilla fighter. He had been a teacher before he joined the Tigers. His wife was a government doctor, serving in another part of Tiger-controlled Batticaloa district. A picture of the leader of the Tigers, Velupillai Prabhakaran, hung behind him. There were pictures also of cadres whose death in battle had turned them into legends in Tiger folklore. A map of Tamil Eelam hung on one side.

Karikalan first ordered an underling to fetch sodas for us and then proceeded to brush away all my questions about forcible recruitment and child soldiers.

'Absolutely untrue.'

'False allegations.'

'Atrocities committed by our enemies in our name to give the Liberation Tigers a bad reputation.'

'We recruit only volunteers and no one below eighteen.'

'Panic in Batti at the prospect of the LTTE opening an office in town?'

He laughed. Probably because people living in the 'army-occupied areas' of the Tamil homeland were not familiar with the Tigers.

'Artificial fear,' he called it.

'When we move into town and set up our offices there, our contacts with the people will grow, we will come closer to them, they will come to know us better and then they will realize that all these allegations against us are untrue.'

*

Back in Batticaloa town, Chitravelan Nishanthan was spending his days at his uncle's house. Nishanthan's father had disappeared in a military crackdown in 1991 and he and his younger brother had been living with his grandmother in Morakattanchenai—one of those villages that no one was ever sure who controlled, the army or the Tigers—after his mother remarried.

A few days before, Nishanthan and his grandmother had had a brush with the Tigers. They had moved here, to his mother's brother's house, after that. A boy and a girl were swinging from the tall iron gates of the house when I arrived there with a friend of the family, whom I met through a source in Colombo.

They got off the gate and greeted him politely. A woman came out of the house. The friend did not introduce me directly. He only told her who I was and my purpose for coming there. She disappeared indoors and some minutes later, a boy emerged on the veranda.

'This is Nishanthan,' the little girl near the gate said.

With his squeaky voice and slender build, Nishanthan looked a lot younger than his seventeen years. Three weeks before, he had narrowly escaped being abducted by the Tigers.

Nishanthan said it all began when he went to the bicycle shop near his grandmother's house to get a puncture fixed one morning. At the shop, he ran into five tough-looking men, who told him an able-bodied person like him should be fighting the Sri Lankan army instead of wasting his time.

The men ordered him to get on his bicycle and follow them but he refused to go, telling them he had to look after his grandmother and younger brother and sister. The men hit him with a branch they broke off from a tree but they let him go.

The same afternoon, three of the men who had accosted Nishanthan at the shop showed up at his home. They seized Nishanthan. When his grandmother tried to pull him back, they pushed her to the ground.

'Tie them up and let's drag the boy and the old hag with him, that should teach her a lesson,' Nishanthan recalled the men saying.

They would have taken both of them but for Nishanthan's younger brother. The house was close to a checkpoint and the boy ran there screaming for help. Two soldiers from the checkpoint came back with him to the house to investigate.

'When the men saw the soldiers coming, they ran off,' Nishanthan said.

They left a bicycle behind, which the soldiers took away.

The next day, both boys and their grandmother moved from Morakattanchenai to Batti town. The boys' little sister was already living there. In the last few days, they had heard from their neighbours in Morakattanchenai that the men who had attempted to abduct Nishanthan had returned to the house.

Finding it locked, they told the neighbours to tell the family they must never come back to Morakattanchenai.

*

There is a passage in *When Memory Dies*, an epic novel about three generations in post-independence Sri Lanka by the Sri Lankan Tamil writer A. Sivanandan, in which two of the protagonists, Vijay and Yogi, have a heated exchange about Tamil Eelam. Vijay, born of a Sinhalese mother and a Tamil father, is visiting Jaffna where he runs into his friend Yogi, who is with the liberation movement.

Vijay asks Yogi:

'What are you fighting for? Yes, yes for Eelam, I know. But what sort of Eelam?'

'A socialist Eelam, of course.'

'But where's the socialism now?'

'How do you mean?'

'In the way you run things, your civil administration, law and order, that sort of thing.'

'What about them?'

'I know it's none of my business, but isn't it all very high-handed and top-down? You don't seem to take the people along with you. Or do you think you can take power on behalf of the people and then hand it over to them?'

Yogi did not say anything and encouraged by his silence, Vijay went on. 'It never happens like that, you know, Yogi. That way socialism never comes. Those who take power don't give it.'

'But then, we'll never take power,' Yogi's voice rose in irritation.

'There's that chance, of course, but this way you are bound to end up replacing one tyranny with another. Where's your socialism then?'

'It'll bloody well have to wait,' shouted Yogi, pushing back his chair angrily, 'till after the liberation.'[5]

*

In a house on Batticaloa's Lake View Road, I met a woman, Rathnamani Murugesapillai, whose only daughter lived in Switzerland. Her husband had died two years before. Till December 2001, she was the principal of a school near Chenkaladdy, 20 km north of Batticaloa town.

She used to live in Vantharamoolai, close to Chenkaladdy. She was fifty-four but she retired early and came to live in Batticaloa because the Tigers were harassing her for money.

'They wanted me to give them Rs 300,000,' she said.

They sent her three letters summoning her to their office. She finally went and they detained her for more than an hour and let her go only after she signed a letter saying she would pay up after a month.

She came away to Batticaloa before the deadline. Her mother and sister, Lilavathie, continued to live in the house in Vantharamoolai. Lilavathie had two daughters. One was studying in Russia.

'They began harassing my sister. They said why should your children learn English and study abroad when other children are fighting and dying for the liberation of Tamils. Give us your other daughter, they demanded from her,' Rathnamani said.

Lilavathie refused. In February, a few days before the ceasefire was signed, a group of Tigers went to the house and threatened to toss a grenade into the house if Lilavathie did not leave immediately.

'My sister and my mother packed up and came away immediately. We all live here now.'

The Tigers had confiscated the house in Vantharamoolai and some paddy fields that belonged to Rathnamani.

The slightly built woman was worried that with the ceasefire, the Tigers would be able to freely harass her family right there in Batticaloa.

'The ceasefire agreement says they can come into town after thirty days. Where will we run then?'

Notes:

1. *UTHR (J) Bulletin 23*, 'The Sun God's Children and the Big Lie', 11 July 2000.
2. *The Hindu*, 14 July 2000.
3. *UTHR (J) Bulletin 26*, 'The Vanishing Young and Silent Agony of Sunset Shore', 20 September 2001.
4. *UTHR (J) Bulletin 27*, 'The LTTE, Child Soldiers and Serial Disasters: A Challenge Without an Answer', 26 October 2001.
5. A. Sivanandan, *When Memory Dies*, London: Arcadia, 1997.

12

The Tiger in His Cage

The Roaring Tiger insignia rolled out of the fax machine. Below it was a letter in officious English, with aspirations to grammatical precision.

> We do not consider the present conditions as conducive for our leader to meet the media. However, we wish to assure you that this situation will change very soon and you will be able to meet him in a press conference.
>
> This will be intimated to you in time, so that you may avail this opportunity. We regret very much that we are unable to comply with your request at the present moment.
>
> Assuring you of our fullest cooperation at all times.
>
> S. Thangan,
> Political Administrative Office,
> LTTE.

The early morning fax was in reply to a letter I had sent to the leader of the Tamil Tigers, Velupillai Prabhakaran, asking for an interview. The Tigers, after contributing significantly to the early exit of the PA government and to the election victory of the UNP, had called a truce after a new government, led by Ranil Wickremesinghe, was elected in December 2001. The government responded with its own ceasefire.

One of the steps that the new government took was to lift restrictions on journalists', permitting them to travel to Tiger territory for the first time since 1995. Asking for an interview with Prabhakaran seemed the first move to make, and I did that. Tiger-controlled Sri Lanka had no phones but the Tigers worked with satellite phones. After much perseverance, I managed to send my letter to an erratic fax machine connected to the satellite phone, the only contact number I had. I was not really surprised to receive a negative reply. Prabhakaran had stopped giving interviews years ago. He had not met a journalist for seven years. A reporter for the BBC Tamil Service was the last journalist to meet him, in April 1995. Since then, the only words directly attributable to him were the speeches he made, every 27 November, the day the Tigers honour their dead cadres.

Known as the Martyrs' Day address, for years the speech had provided the only clues to Prabhakaran's thinking. It came on the Voice of Tigers, a secret radio station operated by the LTTE and heard only in northern Sri Lanka. But within minutes, it would be on the Internet, on Tamil websites. Politicians, political scientists, conflict resolutionists, diplomats, journalists, Sinhalese and Tamils would spend days dissecting the speech, trying to gain insights from Prabhakaran's choice of this word over that, the construction of sentences and sometimes even punctuation marks. The most dedicated would compare the Tamil version—Prabhakaran speaks only in Tamil—with the English translation that the Tigers put out. Even though it was all a bit like the five blind men and the elephant—everyone coming up with his own interpretation—such labour often provided several interesting leads. But still, it was not the same as talking to Prabhakaran mano-a-mano, which is what every journalist in Sri Lanka wanted.

Part of Prabhakaran's inaccessibility was due to the previous government's travel restrictions on journalists from April 1995 to January 2002. I had managed to get around the ban and cross the lines several times in eastern Sri Lanka but doing the same in the north, where the lines were better defined, was a riskier business. Several times, contacts offered to smuggle me across but finally, it was my call, and each time, I remained unconvinced that the story at the other end outweighed the personal risks of a clandestine journey across military lines and minefields. Call me an undedicated journalist if you like.

One visiting journalist, an American woman working for a British newspaper, did manage to sneak past military lines in Vavuniya into the Vanni in 2001. She spent two weeks there and as she was coming back, she was caught in a crossfire between the military and the Tigers close to the lines. She lived, but lost an eye. I was not a war reporter and had neither the stomach nor the ambition for such risk.

In any case, it was unlikely that Prabhakaran would have met me even if I had undertaken that risky journey. He did not meet the American journalist. Even before the restrictions on journalists travelling to Tiger territory, Prabhakaran was choosy about his interviewers. Now, paranoid about his life, he lived, or so the story went, surrounded by 300 bodyguards in an underground bunker most of the time. He was rarely seen in public, even in any of the areas controlled by the Tigers.

But the fax that morning mentioned Prabhakaran's intention to meet journalists 'soon'. That 'soon' arrived less than a month later. It would turn out to be a memorable event. Not so much for what Prabhakaran said at the press conference as for what the press conference said about him.

*

On a visit to the Tiger-controlled Vanni in January 2002, the day after the government lifted the travel ban on journalists, Scott McDonald of Reuters and I had jokingly asked our Tamil Tiger guide, Daya Master—the name master from his job as a teacher before joining the Tigers—if he could set up a meeting for us with Prabhakaran.

'So, Master, when can we meet Mr P?' Scott asked.

We were bumping along in a van on a moonscaped dirt track that passed for a road, somewhere between Mallavi and Madhu in the Vanni. Small patches of asphalt here and there were the only evidence that a road had existed many years ago. But years of war had left their mark and the 80-km journey took a back-breaking eight hours.

After years of being kept out of this side of the conflict, more than fifty reporters, photographers and television crews had swamped Tiger country hungering to meet someone—anyone—in the Tiger hierarchy. We had persuaded the minor Tiger functionaries who met us on their side as we crossed military lines in Vavuniya, to take us to S.P. Thamilchelvam, who carried the grand-sounding title of 'Leader of the Tigers Political Wing'.[1]

A decade-old restriction on taking in essential supplies had also been lifted and we shared the road, such as it was, with hundreds of ordinary Tamil civilians bringing in goods that they had had no access to for years. Mostly, they were bringing in bicycle tyres. With petrol supplies to northern Sri Lanka discontinued when the war began, the humble pushbike had become the most common mode of transport. But because the Tigers used it too, bicycle tyres had been on the government's list of banned items. Now the embargo was gone but no one knew how long this change of heart would last, and people were bringing in as many spare wheels as they could carry.

Bicycles could probably navigate those giant-sized potholes better than our van. When we finally reached Mallavi, it was late at night and dark everywhere. The Vanni had no electricity—the government had cut off supply since 1990—and this was the way it was every night. The people had learnt to live by daylight.

But for the Tigers, electricity was not a problem. Lights, powered by a generator, were blazing away at the bungalow to which our Tiger escorts took us. It was the middle of the war zone but the little converted bungalow did not lack anything. The rooms had beds with mosquito nets, the attached bathrooms had fresh towels, new cakes of soap, shaving cream and razors, and in the hall stood an old piano under a life-size poster of Prabhakaran. That night, most improbably, gloved waiters dressed in black-and-white served us a Chinese dinner, which we ate off tables covered with white tablecloths.

We met Thamilchelvam the next morning. A small, pleasant-faced man in glasses, Thamilchelvam walked with the help of a stick because of a leg injury sustained in a battle, and he smiled a lot. It was the Tigers' first contact with the media in a long time but Thamilchelvam was unfazed by the sight of so many journalists. He behaved as if he had done nothing but meet journalists every day of the intervening years. But exciting as it all was, it was still not as good as a meeting with 'Mr P'.

Daya Master, a wiry man in his forties, did not share our amusement at the abbreviation. He was escorting us back to the checkpoint after our meeting with Thamilchelvam. He was chatty, talking to me in Tamil and to Scott in English. But his reply to Scott's question was short.

'Meeting the leader is very, very difficult. Maybe in the future. The situation is not yet good.'

I asked Master if his leader ever came out in public.

'Sometimes, but it's very rare,' he said.

What about 27 November every year, when he makes that speech, I asked him. Wasn't that a public address?

'That one he makes in front of Black Tigers,' he said. Black Tigers are the LTTE's suicide-bomber wing.

Master lapsed into silence after that and kept his eyes on the road. But before he got off from our van at the checkpoint, he gave us a satellite telephone and fax number for the LTTE office in Mallavi.

'If you like, you can try and give a message for him at this number,' he said.

*

Late one night in March 2002, two months after the meeting with Thamilchelvam and days after my fax exchange with the Tigers, I saw an announcement on a Tamil Internet site that Prabhakaran would meet journalists at a conference on 10 April. A couple of days later, true to his word, Thangan, who had faxed the interview turndown, sent another polite note with the promised 'intimation' of the news conference. But the Internet notice had been enough to set off a buzz among journalists. The government had signed a formal ceasefire with the Tigers in February and the peace process looked set to take off. While the United States had already begun its 'war on terror', Sri Lanka was about to begin talks with a terrorist group. The Tigers were still banned in Sri Lanka but that seemed irrelevant—the terms of the ceasefire agreement had bestowed on them legitimacy and parity of status with the Sri Lankan government. The press conference was the first opportunity to meet the man behind this victory. Even if they had not received any polite faxes from the Tigers, hundreds of journalists immediately began to ready for the press conference. As the day approached, I was fielding phone calls daily from reporters in New Delhi, where several international newspapers are represented. Many wanted packaged advice on everything from the peace process to accommodation in the Vanni. One American journalist wanted to know which was the best hotel in the Vanni, an underdeveloped wilderness even before the war, where no one had ever thought a hotel would become necessary.

'The Hilton,' I was tempted to reply.

Preparing for the event was like preparing to scale Everest and my home office had begun to resemble base camp. Apart from computer, camera, taperecorder, notebooks, pens, I would carry food and water to last four days, bedding, torches, batteries, candles, mosquito coils and a first-aid kit. The Vanni had no electricity, so Scott even carried a generator to power his high-speed photo-transfer equipment. Only satellite phones worked in the Vanni. I did not have one but a journalist friend from New Delhi offered to share his with me. Foreshadowing an elaborate security procedure, the Tigers had told journalists to get to Kilinochchi by the afternoon of 9 April, a day ahead of the conference. That meant leaving Colombo on 8 April for the 320-km drive north on the A9 highway.

*

The war between the Sri Lankan armed forces and the Tigers in the Vanni for control of the A9 through 1997 and 1998, the stories of the attacks and counter-attacks on it and the number of men

who had died for it in those eighteen months, had given the
highway an almost folkloric quality (see Chapter 4). When the
battle ended—the government called off the offensive after it
realized it could not overcome the resistance that the Tigers put
up—both sides sealed off their respective ends of the highway. It
stayed that way until January 2002, when the government and
the Tigers agreed to reopen it and permit civilians to travel on it
once again.

Riding down the same road for the appointment with Mr P
felt strange, especially because of the moniker 'Highway of Blood'
that had got attached to it. Both sides still retained their parts of
the highway, with formal checkpoints demarcating respective lines
of control. I was with two colleagues from India, T.S. Subramanian
from *Frontline*, a sister publication of the *Hindu*, and M.R. Narayan
Swamy of the Indo-Asian News Service, both veteran Sri Lanka
observers. We drove on the Tigers' stretch of the A9, past places on
the highway that, four years before, the army had struggled for
months to reach, only to be beaten back by the Tigers in under
two weeks. My travelling companions had driven down that road
many times in the 1980s and were shocked by how much it had
changed through the war. Not much of the road remained. And
on both sides of the road, the war had ravaged houses and ripped
apart trees or reduced them to stumps. A UN demining team that
had recently started work in the area had taped off huge swathes of
open scrubland with mine warnings. The A9 got progressively worse
as we went deeper into Tiger territory. For much of the way to
Kilinochchi, we saw no people.

But Kilinochchi turned out to be a busy town. The new climate
of détente had inspired a group of athletes to do a symbolic 'peace
run' from Vavuniya to Kilinochchi and large numbers of people
had turned out to greet them. A bus service between Kilinochchi
and Jaffna had just begun. To add to it, three hundred journalists
were attending the press conference and our convoy of vehicles
caused a traffic jam. Tiger policemen, outfitted in blue uniforms
distinct from the khaki of the Sri Lankan police force, directed
traffic.

Kilinochchi was the scene of two ferocious battles, the first in 1996, when Sri Lankan forces fought the Tigers to take control of the town, and the second two years later, when the Tigers recaptured the town. The Tigers were running the town from a few buildings that had somehow survived the fighting. Outside the office of the Voice of Tigers radio station, empty artillery shells formed a neat boundary around a little flowerbed.

With no hotels or other accommodation in Kilinochchi, we were dependent on the Tigers for accommodation and they had made military-style plans to billet us for the night. I was in a large compound with three separate houses. Seventy journalists spent the night in that compound. The houses might have belonged to some people years ago, but now, the LTTE used them as offices and dormitories for its cadres. No fancy guest house this time with gloved service. That, we realized later, the Tigers had reserved for Western journalists.

Where we were, the men slept on straw mats on the floor. Unused to sleeping on the floor, some retreated into their vans. The women—just five of us—shared two bedrooms with attached bathrooms, a luxury in that setting. They fed us simple meals as we waited for word about the time and venue of our meeting with Prabhakaran the next day. There were television sets in each of the houses in the compound, and the Tigers had decided we should be entertained with non-stop screenings of videos showing their battlefield successes.

A woman cadre bearing a cup of milky sweet tea shook me awake at 6.30 a.m. the next morning.

'Get ready, we will leave in half an hour,' she said.

I scrambled to get going, and soon we were all back on the road, our vehicles in a long motorcade, following two Tigers on a motorcycle. After a ten-minute drive, we pulled up at another Tiger office—three long, low barrack-like buildings around a huge ground. Chairs had been set out in neat rows in the open space. It looked set for a news conference. Journalists grabbed chairs at vantage points but realized quickly this was only a 'holding area' where, over the next eight hours, each of us would be put through a security routine so gruelling and meticulous that it would put any post-9/11 airport check to shame. It left me amazed, angry, fatigued, frustrated and humiliated, all at the same time.

Through the day, several Tigers—mid-level functionaries in the organization's elaborate hierarchy—watched over us but could not tell us what time the press conference might be held.

'It could be at any time,' was the only reply to repeated queries.

But they cranked out what would be the longest security procedure most of us had ever experienced, starting with the announcement that satellite equipment would not be allowed at the press conference. Journalists used to prevailing in similar situations elsewhere, usually by shouting their way through, found that did not work here.

'But I am from the BBC, I have to have my phone,' said one reporter, who had flown to Sri Lanka for the press conference.

The Tigers remained unmoved by this and by the loud protests from other journalists that they would miss deadlines if they could not phone in reports from the press conference.

'Nothing is more important than our leader's security,' one Tiger said.

Ahmed Shah Masood, the commander of the Northern Alliance in Afghanistan, had been killed only a few months before by a suicide bomber posing as a journalist. Prabhakaran was taking no chances. He had killed many people, starting with the mayor of Jaffna in 1975, and had powerful adversaries. Four governments had tagged him as terrorist, he was on Interpol's most-wanted list, intelligence agencies worldwide were interested in him. Signals from a satellite phone could tell the outside world the exact location of the press conference. Therefore, no satellite phones. They also advised us to leave behind every other non-essential personal belonging—the more we carried, the longer it would take to process us.

Only experts in the art of evading security, like the Tigers, could have mounted a security drill so thorough. Their suicide bombers had slipped past security checks so many times, concealing lethal explosives on their bodies, they knew all the possibilities. The women cadres who checked me looked inside my nostrils, under my tongue, in gaps between my teeth, behind and inside my ears. They ran expert fingers over the hemline and buttons of my shirt and pants. They examined my hair through to the scalp, virtually going through every strand. They checked my watch and my earrings. They tapped the heels of my shoes to check for hollowed-out hiding places. One journalist had to watch the insoles of his shoes being ripped out. Men were asked to take off their shirts. Everyone was photographed, profile and face front. Cameras were taken apart and weighed, piece by piece. I left my bag in the van and carried only a notebook, two pens and a tape recorder. They checked the notebook, page by empty page. They sniffed at the pens to make sure there was only ink in them. And then they took those away, put them in a plastic bag with my name tag on it, and gave it to me only as I got into the bus taking us to the real venue of the press conference. It was almost 4 p.m. All along the route, were women cadres silhouetted against the low sun, standing guard with assault rifles in their hands.

*

The venue of the press conference was a long meeting hall with a fresh coat of paint. It had a low wall on three sides, and was covered on top with corrugated metal sheets. As we packed into the hall, and fought with each other for vantage positions, an elderly man, who introduced himself as George and a senior member of the Tigers, made an announcement that stunned us into silence and orderly behaviour.

'Please understand the circumstances in which this press conference is being held. The security arrangements of our leader are of the utmost importance to us. Please remember we have armed guards here who have come to safeguard the security of our leader, so we must not create a situation of panic,' he said in his gravelly voice.

Uniformed LTTE cadres armed with assault rifles were standing all around the building. Some wore earpieces with an attached mike through which they communicated with one another. Cadres wielding still and video cameras recorded our faces in close up as we trooped in. At the front end of the hall, a long table was set up on a raised platform. A gap of about 20 feet separated the platform from the first row of chairs. Fencing off the chairs was a sleek chain-link cordon.

*

In A. Sivanandan's novel *When Memory Dies*, Yogi, the militant, is telling his friend Vijay about the 'Commander'.

> Vijay saw the reverence on Yogi's face and wondered how such a level-headed chap could be so wrapped up in one man.
>
> 'I know what you are thinking,' said Yogi, 'but there is something about him.'
>
> He went on hesitantly looking for words. 'A presence you could say. Yes a presence, quiet, aloof. But commanding of attention, of devotion even, there is that glow of certainty about him, you know what I mean. I don't know how to say it, but you could see straightaway that he is never going to lose. You can follow a man like that.'[2]

Prabhakaran finally appeared at the press conference only as the light began fading. It was 5.30 p.m., more than ten hours since we had set out that morning. He walked in surrounded by tall guards, their guns concealed under loose shirts. Even though it was growing dark, the guards wore Ray Ban shades. They took up positions around him in the manner of the US presidential security service bodyguards.

Dressed in a blue-grey safari suit, Prabhakaran appeared much chunkier than in his photographs and the bulletproof vest under the tunic did not help trim his frame. Here finally was the man who masterminded terrorist attacks and suicide bombings, who killed off all his rivals, and was described as a military genius who commanded the undying fealty of his cadres. In his outdated chic, he looked like a small-town businessman from India.

It had been more than a decade since Prabhakaran had addressed a news conference. The last time was in 1990 when he met a group of seven or eight journalists in Jaffna. But on this occasion, he faced forty times as many reporters. Before the conference, there was an expectation that Prabhakaran might make a path-breaking announcement in order to move forward the peace process that had begun with the formal ceasefire agreement in February. But when the conference ended, we realized he had not said anything new: he remained committed to his goal of Eelam, he did not think the time was yet right to give up the armed struggle, and he still wanted a negotiated political settlement to the conflict.

One of the interesting moments in the press conference came when an Indian journalist asked Prabhakaran if he regretted killing Rajiv Gandhi. At first, Prabhakaran was at a loss for words. He and Balasingham conferred for what seemed like ages, before he came up with a reply that made me wonder whether he had failed to anticipate this, the most obvious of all questions.

'It is a tragic incident that happened more than ten years ago,' he said, and Balasingham duly translated this for the audience that had been waiting for the reply in total silence. That only provoked more questions on the subject from the scores of Indian journalists present, bringing forth similarly brief and unrevealing answers, until eventually, Balasingham declared the subject closed.

Prabhakaran had arrived for the press conference with his military and political aides, looking tense and ill at ease. He did not acknowledge the waiting journalists. His chief aide, Anton Balasingham, who called himself the LTTE's 'theoretician', did most of the talking during the press conference, translating question and answers for Prabhakaran. Sometimes, he took it upon himself to answer questions while Prabhakaran looked on. When the press conference ended, Prabhakaran rose with a smile at his aides that spoke of relief more than anything else. He had no parting niceties for the journalists.

As his motorcade left in a swirl of dust, the generators that had powered the lights at the venue were switched off and everything plunged into darkness. We searched in confusion for the buses that would take us back to where we had left our computers, phones and other belongings. Suddenly panicky, I held on to the shirt of a reporter in front of me for fear I would be left behind.

The press conference had lasted 135 minutes, a record of sorts. We had waited ten hours for it to begin and had assembled for it more than twenty-four hours ahead, travelling a long distance to be there on time. We were virtually Prabhakaran's prisoners for that period. Finally, his words had revealed little.

Regardless of what he said or did not say, I learnt much about Prabhakaran that day. Many described the press conference as Prabhakaran's coming-out party, the evidence that he was throwing off his 'bunker mentality' and transforming himself into a political leader.

For me, the most important takeaway from the press conference was this: Prabhakaran is a prisoner for life, a Tiger locked in a cage of his own making. In order to embrace normal life and democratic politics, Prabhakaran had to leave the cage first. He could never do that.

As I finished writing up my report and dictating it laboriously over the three-dollar-a-minute satellite phone to the office of the *Hindu* back in Chennai, India, I was reminded of what Varatharaja Perumal, one of the people on Prabhakaran's hit list, had once told me. I had met Perumal many years ago in Ajmer, a small town in Rajasthan in northern India.

Perumal heads the EPRLF, a militant group-turned political party. His organization incurred Prabhakaran's wrath by supporting the 1987 Indo-Sri Lanka Accord. Following the Accord, the EPRLF declared it was renouncing the armed struggle to join the democratic mainstream of Sri Lankan politics. The Tigers had rejected the concessions in the Accord as inadequate and Perumal became a 'traitor' for participating in its implementation. The EPRLF was the main backer of the Accord, setting up a provincial administration in north-east Sri Lanka following regional elections. Perumal was its chief minister. Behind the EPRLF was the IPKF, sent by New Delhi to assist in the implementation of the agreement. But it ended up fighting the Tigers instead. Protecting Perumal from the

Tigers became one of its main tasks.

The north-east provincial government experiment was short-lived because the Sri Lankan government failed to live up to its side of the bargain in devolving powers to Perumal's administration. Instead, it began peace talks with the Tigers and asked the Indian army, which was fighting the Tigers, to leave. Perumal fled Sri Lanka when the Indian army withdrew in 1990. The Indian government gave him safe haven, arranging for him to live under tight security in Ajmer.

This is what he told me that afternoon I met him at his high-security home in Ajmer in 1995:

> One day, after Prabhakaran dies, I will be able to come out of this jail that I have to live in now. I can go back to Jaffna a free man. I will be able to contest an election or make a speech in public without fear of being killed. But can Prabhakaran do that? Never. Forget about hiding from the Sri Lankan government or the Indians or the Americans. He has so much Tamil blood on his hands, he can never move freely even among the people he claims to lead. One of his own people will get him. Prabhakaran knows that better than anyone else.

Notes:

1.   There is also an intelligence wing, a women's wing, a sea wing known as the Sea Tigers and there have even been references to an air wing, though no one has seen Tiger planes yet.
2.   A. Sivanandan, *When Memory Dies*, London: Arcadia, 1997.

13

Trouble in Trincomalee

Had it not been for the conflict, Trincomalee, a town of exceptional picture-postcard beauty on Sri Lanka's east coast, 260 km from Colombo, would have been an exotic tourist destination. But for nearly twenty years, until the February 2002 ceasefire, Trincomalee lay abandoned by all except those who had to live there. When I returned to Sri Lanka for a short visit between July and September 2003, the ceasefire was nearly eighteen months old, and Trincomalee suddenly found itself under siege by tourists. Resort hotels that had closed in the 1980s were back in business and Sri Lanka's large population of expatriate aid workers and international bureaucrats was pouring in. The conflict had preserved Trincomalee's coastline and coral reef in pristine condition. Now those seemed certain to go the way of the tired beaches of Sri Lanka's southern coast. Some hotels were booked every weekend until the New Year's Day of 2004 at room rates three times those of pre-truce days.

I went to Trincomalee too, to visit a fishing hamlet called Mutur. In Mutur, the ceasefire had split wide open a side to the conflict everyone knew existed but one that the ceasefire planners inexplicably seemed not to have taken into account.

*

Nearly half the 60,000 people in Mutur are Muslims. The Tigers hate the Muslims. The Muslims are the third party in Sri Lanka's ethnic conflict after the Sinhalese and Tamils. They form about

8 per cent[1] of the country's total population, and are most numerous in the three eastern districts of Trincomalee, Batticaloa and Amparai.

Sri Lanka conducted its last official census in the north-east in 1981, before the conflict began. But according to unofficial estimates collected from the region during the census of 2001, Muslims form more than one-third of the total population in these three eastern districts, even more than Tamils. The area is also home to a small number of Sinhalese. The presence of such a large number of Muslims, and to a lesser extent, the Sinhalese, in the east challenges the Tigers' claim of the entire north-east as an unbroken Tamil homeland.

Mutur, with its Muslims, was the embodiment of that challenge. In the days before the ceasefire, Mutur, located on the southern tip of Trincomalee Bay, was in the grey zone between government-controlled and LTTE-controlled Trincomalee.

The Tigers controlled Sampur, a village at the extreme southern tip of the bay, next to Mutur. At the top of the bay, in Trincomalee town, was the Sri Lankan military's most important naval station.

When not out at sea, gunships and troop carriers of the Sri Lankan navy anchored in Trincomalee's China Bay naval harbour. This was where, despite the saturation security, the Tigers bombed two navy gunships to announce they were pulling out of the 1994–5 ceasefire. A team of the Sea Tigers, the naval wing of the Tigers, swam underwater to escape detection and carried out the bombing.

The strong military presence in Trincomalee did not extend as far as Mutur, even though it was in the area controlled by the government.

A ferry was virtually the only connection between the hamlet and Trincomalee town. From my hotel on Orr's Hill in the town, with its spectacular view of Trincomalee Bay, I could see the ferry tooting off on the one-hour journey to Mutur four times a day.

Government employees commuting to their jobs in Mutur packed into the ferry every morning. On its return journey across the wide bay, it brought students and other commuters from Mutur.

A few weeks after the ceasefire came into effect in 2002, the Tigers were allowed to set up 'political offices' in areas under government control in the north-east. Mutur was one of the first places where they opened shop.

Troubles began almost immediately, said Mohammed Jaseem, an employee of the Sri Lankan government in Mutur. He was also associated with the Muslim Information Centre (MIC), a Colombo-based group that documented events relating to Muslims. We had arranged to meet at the jetty where I got off the early morning ferry to Mutur.

Jaseem said first someone destroyed one of the fourteen heavy concrete crosses on top of Third Mile Post Hill outside Mutur. That was in June 2002, four months after the ceasefire. The crosses were a year old then, planted there by Roman Catholic Tamils living in the area.

Other than 33,000 Muslims, Mutur has about 25,000 Tamils, both Hindu and Christian, and a sprinkling of mostly Buddhist Sinhalese. The Muslims live in the main town—also called Mutur—while the Tamils live in surrounding villages.

'A rumour spread that we Muslims had destroyed the cross,' Jaseem said.

The same evening, a gang of Tamils beat up a Muslim youth as he was returning from the outskirts back to his home in town. An hour later, the newly set up office of the Tigers in Mutur came in for some stone-throwing. The stones damaged the board with the Tiger insignia and broke the windows.

Five days later, the Tigers called a general strike in Trincomalee to protest against the attack on their office. The morning of the strike, a Tamil newspaper ran a statement from the Tigers saying the attack on their office struck at 'the soul of the Tamil nation', and asked Muslim leaders to keep 'their people' in check.

The soft-spoken Jaseem said that virtually amounted to an accusation against the entire Muslim community of Mutur for the attack on the office even though it was the work of just one or two people angry at the attack on the young man.

Muslims all over Trincomalee, fearing retribution from the Tigers if they ignored the strike call, shut their shops, businesses and schools. But in Mutur, even such obedience proved futile. That evening, a large mob of Tamils from the surrounding villages stormed into Mutur town. When the Muslims blocked their way, the two groups clashed, throwing stones at each other in the town's narrow lanes.

The mob retreated, damaging shops and breaking windows and fences on the way.

'When they were going back, the attackers covered the Jabal Nagar mosque with filth,' Jaseem said, referring to obscene graffiti the retreating mob scrawled on the mosque's walls.

*

Sri Lanka's conflict is between people claiming separate national identities on the basis of their different languages, the Sinhalese and the Tamil. It is not a conflict of two religions. True, the Sinhalese are mainly Buddhists but there are some Christians among them, just as there are Christians among the mainly Hindu Tamils. So where do Muslims come into this? Muslims are also mainly Tamil-speakers, but they do not view themselves as Tamil. They consider themselves a separate ethnic group identified by their religion. From the earliest census conducted by British rulers in colonial Sri Lanka, Muslims were classified as Moors. And they seriously began nurturing a religion-based political identity in the late 1980s.

At first, many eminent Muslims identified with the Tamil cause. Hundreds of Muslim youth joined Tamil militant groups that sprang up in the early 1980s. Then, the Tigers turned on the Muslims, accusing them of being informers of the Indian army and the Sri Lankan security forces, and began killing them.[2]

Two big incidents marked the final separation of ways between Muslims and Tamils. One was in Kattankudy, an all-Muslim coastal village a few kilometres outside Batticaloa town, where I went on my first visit to the east in 1995. The town leaders took me to two mosques where in August 1990 the Tigers had carried out simultaneous attacks at prayer time, killing more than a hundred men. In the prayer hall of one of the mosques, the priest silently pointed out the holes the automatic rifles had made in the light-green tiled walls. The community had not repaired the wall, letting the holes serve as reminders of why the Muslims should never trust the Tigers.

The second incident was in October the same year. The Tigers, newly in control of Jaffna after the departure of the Indian army's peacekeeping force, ordered 80,000 to 100,000 Muslims who had been living in the peninsula for generations to leave. They were given forty-eight hours to vacate their ancestral homes and lands. Most did not wait that long, fleeing with whatever possessions they could carry. Many of them still live in bleak refugee camps in Puttalam, a town on the western coast of Sri Lanka, 100 km north of Colombo. When I visited the camps in 2000, exactly a decade after their arrival, their conversations revolved around dreams of one day returning to the houses, land, shops and businesses they had left behind.

Those two events in 1990 convinced Muslims they could not hitch their fortunes to the Tamils. They formed the SLMC, a party that grew up demanding a separate solution to the political aspirations of Muslims, independent of the Tamils.

In the mid-1990s, the Muslim Congress even called for a separate region for Muslims in the east made up of three Muslim-majority electorates. The formation of the South-Eastern Council, as the Muslims called it, was one of the conditions on which the Muslim Congress gave its support to the first government of President Chandrika Kumaratunga in 1994. But Kumaratunga later persuaded the party to drop the demand, saying that any settlement she negotiated with the Tamils would also provide adequate safeguards for Muslims living in the north-east.[3]

When the Muslim Congress won seats in parliament and played kingmaker in Colombo, it gave Sri Lanka's Muslims a feeling of being empowered. It brought development to Muslim enclaves in the east. Kattankudy, for instance, was smaller than Batticaloa town, but in 1995 it had more telephones than Batticaloa because the minister of communications was a Muslim Congress leader from Kattankudy, M.L.A.M. Hisbullah. The connection to government also gave Muslims a feeling of security in the Tamil-dominated north-east.

Despite the undercurrent of hostility between Muslims and Tamils arising from the actions of the Tigers, the two communities had by and large lived in peace in the east since 1990. On the Batticaloa coast, Muslim and Tamil villages alternate in a knit–purl pattern. The villages have been linked for centuries through farming, fishing and trade—the Muslims are mostly traders, the Tamils sell produce to them and buy goods from them.

But after the February 2002 ceasefire, that peace between the two communities became fragile. The Muslims realized that their political clout in Colombo counted for little with the Tigers, who were fast on their way to establishing themselves as the de facto rulers of the north-east.

Even before the ceasefire, the Tigers ran a parallel administration in areas under their control with a reach that extended to people living in government-controlled areas of the north-east. The ceasefire agreement gave the Tigers a freedom of movement in the government-controlled parts of the north-east they had not had before, making it much easier for their police to 'arrest' people living in these areas, hand down to them punishments ordered by their courts and to collect 'taxes'.

The ceasefire agreement virtually bestowed on the Tigers the status of 'sole representative' of the Tamil people by ensuring that all other political parties except those that had the approval of the Tigers would have to stop functioning in the entire north-east. This the ceasefire agreement did by requiring the government to disarm all the political parties that carried arms for self-protection against the Tigers.[4] Fearing for their lives after being stripped of their weapons, most of these political parties withdrew from the region. Most Tamils in the north-east accepted the Tigers as their leaders, either out of fear or out of genuine conviction that only the Tigers represented their best interests.

But not the Muslims. The Tigers said they were the 'sole representative' of not just Tamils, but all 'Tamil-speaking' people. The Muslims rejected that interpretation. The Tigers responded by destroying the boats of Muslim fishermen and the paddy fields of Muslim farmers. They got Tamil people to boycott Muslim shops.

They kidnapped Muslim traders, fishermen and farmers for ransom. The repeated confrontations between the Tigers and the Muslims had the effect of setting Tamils against Muslims. Mutur was a regular flashpoint.

*

In an extremely poor corner of Mutur, I met Manzoora. She lived in a hovel by the edge of the sea. Six months before, in March 2003, her husband Abdur Razak Jabir, a fisherman, disappeared after putting out to sea with his friend Maqbool Naim.

'The Tigers arrested them, that's all I know,' the twenty-four-year old Manzoora said.

She pointed to where the water splashed up in small waves behind her house. 'That's where he climbed into the boat with his friend. That was the last time I saw him,' she said.

In the days following their disappearance, said Manzoora, Tamil traders coming from Tiger-controlled Sampur to stock up on their supplies had said the Tigers had detained the two fishermen for dealing in drugs. In Tiger territory, that is close to a capital offence. Another story doing the rounds was that the two had wandered too close to a Tiger military installation on the Sampur shoreline.

Accompanied by Jabir's mother, Manzoora went several times to the office of the Tigers in Sampur to plead for her husband's release.

'They would not tell us anything,' she said.

Fifteen days later, Jabir's mother committed suicide by drinking poison. Angered by the conduct of the Tigers, the Muslims of Mutur called a general strike. Shops, schools, government offices, banks and other establishments in Mutur remained shut for three days.

On the third day of the strike, a gang of Tamils stopped two Muslim men on a bicycle at a village outside Mutur and beat them up. The men then climbed back on the bicycle, and on their way home, beat up two Tamils. Within hours, the tit-for-tat incidents erupted into a full-scale riot with Muslims and Tamils fighting each other on the streets.

The Tigers then issued a denial saying the fishermen were not in their custody. By then, three people had died in the violence, houses and other property burnt and destroyed, and the divide between the Muslims and Tamils of Mutur complete.

The Tigers denied any role in the riots, but Mohammed Jaseem said no one believed that.

'They rule this area. This is their turf. If they did not want the riots, they had the power to stop the violence but they did not. That can only mean they were behind it,' he said.

No mob of armed Tamil men could have gathered anywhere in Trincomalee without the Tigers getting to know of it first, especially in areas under their control, he said.

Tamil raiders burnt paddy harvests, and took away tractors and other valuables in Muslim areas. Muslim gangs burnt Tamil homes. It seemed the violence would never end. The police and the security forces appeared powerless to stop it. According to Jaseem, they did not intervene because they were afraid it might lead to a confrontation with the Tigers and a breakdown of the ceasefire.

Finally, four days after the troubles began, the Sri Lanka Monitoring Mission (SLMM), an international committee supervising the ceasefire, stepped in. They arranged a meeting between Tamils and representatives from all the mosques in Trincomalee. The Tigers had denied their role in the riots and did nothing to stop them. But they represented the Tamils at the meeting and signed an agreement with the Muslim representatives that the two communities would live in peace from then on.[5]

That did not bring back Jabir. By the time of my visit, the community had given up both him and Naim for dead. Manzoora had even observed the traditional Muslim mourning period for widows.

'But I don't know if he's really dead or if the Tigers are still holding him alive,' she said.

She and Jabir had been married nine years. They had four children, the youngest just seven months old.

The violence too continued. Two Muslims were killed immediately after the signing of the agreement. And on 3 August, exactly a month before my visit to Trincomalee, a Muslim man was shot dead in Mutur as he was cycling to the restaurant that he ran. He had once worked in the police intelligence-gathering unit in Trincomalee, tracking Tiger activities in the area. Naturally, everyone suspected the Tigers had killed him.

The next day, a twenty-one-year-old Tamil boy was shot dead. Ten days later, on 13 August, two Muslim men riding on a motorcycle on the outskirts of Trincomalee town were shot dead. Two hours later, a Tamil boy left his home in Mutur on an errand and did not return.

*

Joseph Erington Sellar was at his desk when I walked into his office in Mutur at the local cooperative society where he worked as a manager. He readily closed the files in front of him when I approached and asked if we could talk about his twenty-two-year-old son Adrian, the Tamil boy who had disappeared three weeks before on 13 August. Sellar looked considerably older than his fifty-nine years. His eyes were red and his complexion was florid, like that of a man who had been drinking too much.

Adrian was the youngest of his four sons. The war had not spared any of them. His eldest son Jesuntreepan was among the twenty boys taken away by the army in August 1990. He never came back and is believed to have been among the hundreds of suspected Tiger supporters killed at the Plantation Point army camp in Trincomalee. His second son Presley Stephen, who had joined the Tigers, was killed in fighting a month before that, in July 1990. His third son John Stewart was arrested on suspicion of being a Tiger in the mid-1990s. He jumped out of a train when he was being taken to attend court in Colombo and was killed. That was in March 2000.

'I know Adrian is also out,' he said. By 'out', he meant dead.

His voice was a mumble that I strained to hear as he told me the circumstances around Adrian's disappearance the same evening two Muslim men were killed in Trincomalee town. Adrian had booked a van to take his family and their friends on a pilgrimage to a famous Roman Catholic shrine in Madhu, across the island in the Mannar district of north-western Sri Lanka.

But the van was late. All the people going on the trip were assembled and waiting at the Sellars' home. At about 9.45 p.m., they saw a van stop at the tea shop down the road. As usual, lots of people were standing around the shop.

Sellar took me to his home, behind the Mutur church and a short walk from his workplace, to show me how clearly he could see the tea shop from his doorway. His wife showed me faded photographs of her three older boys and a recent one of Adrian.

'Adrian took his bicycle to check if it was the van he'd arranged. As he got there, we saw the shop shutting down. The lights went off, the people moved away quickly and the van reversed out and drove off,' Sellar said.

When Adrian did not return immediately, Sellar thought nothing of it. He did not link the sudden happenings down the road with Adrian not coming back home.

'The police came fifteen minutes later. They asked me if my son was missing. Until then I did not know that he was missing. But someone who had seen everything had obviously informed them. That is why they came,' he said.

Sellar now believes someone in the van grabbed Adrian and took him away in revenge for the killings of the two Muslim men in Trincomalee town that evening. In the days that followed, he received two anonymous letters, one in Sinhalese and the other in Tamil, telling him he could perform his son's last rites. Both letters gave names and addresses of the people they said were behind the killing. Sellar also got an anonymous telephone call telling him his son was murdered at a particular address.

'I have told the police but nothing has come out of my complaints,' Sellar said.

Sellar's was one of the few non-Muslim families in Mutur. He had lived in and around Mutur for thirty-five years. His son Adrian had plenty of Muslim friends. He was the only person in the family who kept contact with his sister Anita, who had married a Muslim against her parents' wishes.

'I am a very popular man in Mutur. So was Adrian. I never thought they would do this to us,' he said.

*

Mohammed Jaseem said the problems were not between Muslims and Tamils.

'The problem is only between Muslims and the Tigers, and it has caused an artificial separation between the people,' he said.

At the heart of the problem, as Jaseem saw it, was that the Tigers simply wanted Muslims out of the east. They saw Muslims as an obstacle to becoming absolute rulers of the north-east. Instead of crudely asking Muslims to leave as they had done in Jaffna in 1990, the Tigers—now under closer international scrutiny—had adopted a subtler tactic.

'This time, they are trying to drive us out by targeting our economy,' Jaseem said.

After so many violent incidents, Muslim fishermen were scared to put out to sea. Muslim farmers had abandoned their fields because they felt unsafe going to work. In the rioting, the worst violence was directed at boats, fishing nets, paddy stocks and shops belonging to Muslims. Jaseem said some families had already moved out of Trincomalee to live in the relative safety of southern Sri Lanka.

Before the April 2003 troubles, Tamil fishermen and farmers would come from Sampur to sell their produce to Muslims traders in Mutur. But after the riots, the Tigers banned Tamils from doing business with Muslims.

In Mutur, bands of vigilantes kept Tamils away from Muslim shops. At their checkpoints, Tigers confiscated anything that had been bought from Muslim shops. Or they imposed heavy fines on the purchases.

It hurt Mutur's small economy. Some shops had shut down; their Muslim owners had packed up and left for areas outside Trincomalee. But it also caused hardship to Tamils who had to travel to the nearest Sinhalese village to trade. Only two weeks before I visited Mutur, the Tigers had lifted the ban, evidently under pressure from the Tamil people.

After the ceasefire in February 2002, the SLMC leader, Rauff Hakeem, met Velupillai Prabhakaran, the leader of the Tigers. Prabhakaran told Hakeem—they signed an agreement as well—that Muslims could return to the lands and properties they had abandoned in the Jaffna peninsula in 1990, and elsewhere in the north-east during the long years of the conflict.

Immediately, Muslims in Trincomalee tried to reclaim their long-lost villages, properties and fields. But in all cases, the Tigers found reasons to prevent their return, in some instances telling the claimants it was unsafe to move back because the area was strewn with landmines.

Around the time of my visit to Trincomalee, the hot issue was a camp that the Tigers had set up south of Mutur, at a place alternately called Kurangupachchan and Manirasankulam. Setting up camps across the boundaries that separated government-controlled areas from those under the Tigers was against the ceasefire rules. But the Tigers could not be bothered. They refused to dismantle the camp they had set up in government territory despite the ceasefire monitors directing that they must. The newspapers were full of the story, with dire warnings that the Tigers were positioning themselves once again to break the truce with an attack on the naval harbour at China Bay, as they had done in 1995.

For Muslims, there was another issue at stake. They said the land under the new camp belonged to them.

At a girls' school in Mutur, I ran into Mohammed Jawad, a small-built man who was an official in the federation of local mosques. He had dropped by to see the headmaster who was his friend. I was there to meet the headmaster too, but he seemed relieved when Jawad walked in, and took the chance to escape to a teachers' meeting in the school. After that, the articulate Jawad did all the talking.

Jawad said the area where the Tigers had set up their camp was earlier known as Majeedpura.

'It was a Muslim area until 1990. The Tigers have put up the camp on the ruins of a mosque and a Muslim school,' Jawad said.

Following the ceasefire, the Muslims had started venturing back to the area to check on their lands and fields. But now they feared confrontations with the Tigers at the camp so they did not go there any more, he said.

Some of the classes at the school were being held outdoors. We walked past a science class. The teacher was speaking to his students in Tamil, the language of instruction at the school.

'We cannot be treated as Tamils just because we speak Tamil. We Muslims are different from Tamils, we have our own culture and our own aspirations,' Jawad said.

The main aspiration for Muslims, he said, was to rule themselves within Sri Lanka. Muslims did not want to be ruled over by the Tamils, and certainly not by the Tigers.

He said the Tigers were treating Muslims with the same contempt with which Sinhalese leaders had once treated Tamils.

'The Tamils know what it is to suffer as a minority. The Tigers should not subject us to the same suffering,' Jawad said.

The Muslim fear, Jawad said, was that the peace process might end with the Tigers being given sole charge of the north-east.

'They are treating us like dirt already. Imagine if the Tigers were to assume 100 per cent control!'

I asked Jawad the same question that I had asked others I met in Mutur during the one day I spent there: was it true, as some of the Colombo newspapers were reporting, that Muslims were arming themselves for protection against the Tigers? The reports had even mentioned an armed group called Osama.

Mohammed Jaseem had burst into laughter when I asked him this question but could not hide a trace of irritation in his reply.

'Has any Tamil been abducted or detained for ransom? Has any Tamil been beheaded? Has any Tamil been shot dead?' he asked. 'But Muslims keep disappearing and getting killed even though this is supposed to be a ceasefire. And they talk about Osama and arms. I'll tell you what. In every incident in Mutur, something has happened to a Tamil only after something happens to a Muslim.'

Jawad had very nearly the same reply. Community leaders were trying to channel Muslim discontent into a democratic response. But, he said, everything depended on how quickly their grievances could be addressed.

'We have no arms now. That is the truth. But we do not want a situation where our youth are forced to take to arms. That is why we are saying, resolve our problems now.'

Otherwise, he said, Muslim youngsters might take a leaf out of the Tamil book and do what Tamil youth did in the 1980s: turn militant. Then, Jawad said, the moderates would be swept aside. The extremists would take over.

Notes:

1.   *Statistical Pocket Book—2002*, Department of Census and Statistics, Ministry of Interior, Sri Lanka.
2.   Rajan Hoole, Massacres of Muslims and What it Means for the Tamils (www.uthr.org/publications.htm).
3.   The draft constitution of 2000, which Kumaratunga had to abandon for want of support to ensure its passage through parliament, included such safeguards for the Muslim community in the east.
4.   Ceasfire Agreement, 21 February 2002, Article 1.8.
5.   MIC, Sri Lanka, 'April 2003 Attacks on Muttur and Thoppur Muslims'.

Afterword

Returning to Sri Lanka in July 2003 after having been away a year was like coming back home and finding someone had rearranged the furniture. The ceasefire between the government and the Tigers was then eighteen months old. The two sides had held six rounds of face-to-face talks with Norway's help. But the peace process itself had stalled in April 2003. The Tigers refused to attend a seventh round of negotiations unless Sri Lanka withdrew its armed forces from the north-east.

The government had nearly 30,000 troops in Jaffna and smaller numbers in other parts of the north-east. The Tigers said the soldiers were occupying lands and houses of the Tamil people, and public buildings such as schools and temples. Pending a final political settlement, the Tigers also wanted to set up an 'interim administration' in the north-east that they would run virtually independently of the government in Colombo.

The government did not meet either demand, and the Tigers did not attend the talks. But the ceasefire continued to hold. In Colombo, people believed the peace process was a success, even though this was a truce and permanent peace was nowhere in sight. For them, it was enough that the monthly suicide bombings had stopped and that there were no longer military checkpoints on the roads.

The Central Bank, where Vasumathy had been killed, was now fully rebuilt at its old location at one end of the Galle Face Green oceanfront. In all the years I lived in Colombo, I had never been on the road where its bombed out remains stood. Immediately after the bombing in February 1996, the road had been cordoned off at both ends, guarded by tough-looking naval sentries. That was my memory of the bank.

But now, that road was mostly open except for a portion next to President's House, the official home of Chandrika Kumaratunga. The hotels on the road, which were also damaged in the bombing, had been renovated in the hope that the trickle of tourists coming to Sri Lanka with the ceasefire would soon turn into a flood. Dining in a new restaurant in one of the hotels, directly in the shadow of the newly rebuilt bank, I noticed that it had nine floors, one more than the number in the old building.

'That's a message to the Tigers that we can do one better,' joked the friend accompanying me.

As for the other places and people in this book . . .

Vavuniya, the one-time town of multicoloured passes on the boundary of northern and southern Sri Lanka, was now the frontier of the ceasefire. The opening of the A9 highway into northern Sri Lanka, even before the truce, had turned Vavuniya into a boom town of sorts. People still streamed into the town but no more as refugees escaping the war. These were people living in the south going on a visit north to Kilinochchi or Jaffna. Or they were Tamils living in the north headed for a visit to Colombo or to Batticaloa or Trincomalee. In Vavuniya, they changed buses or rested overnight in the several new hotels that the town now boasted, before proceeding onward.

Permitted by the ceasefire, the Tigers set up two offices on Station Road. They were not allowed to wear military uniforms but their civvies for both men and women—pleated black trousers with tapered legs and loose greyish-blue shirts with tiny checks and the sleeves rolled up—marked them out as cadres of the LTTE.

Ganesh was still the government agent. He should have retired but his years of experience walking the three-way tightrope between the government, the Tigers and the security forces—and the fair amount of trust all three placed in him—made him indispensable.

He said the government had asked him to continue in the job for a while longer till the ceasefire took root. Without the tension of a raging war just north of the boundaries of his district, and free of the responsibility for feeding and finding shelter for all the people who arrived in Vavuniya fleeing the fighting in the north, he looked like a man from whose shoulders a huge weight had been taken off. He was still the tight-lipped bureaucrat I knew from before but he was more relaxed than at any other time I had met him.

Travelling to Jaffna was much easier now. For one, the ceasefire cut out the rigmarole of writing to the ministry of defence for permission to travel to the peninsula and the subsequent scramble for a seat on a Sri Lankan air force-operated charter flight. Now, with the A9 open, Jaffna was linked by road to the rest of the country. I could have driven there on the bus or in a hired car. Much as a separate country would, the Tigers had set up a border control regime that screened travellers and imposed taxes on vehicles passing through and on the things that people carried with them, describing these as 'customs' procedures.

But I did not get to see this for myself because I flew to Jaffna on one of the new commercial flights. The plane still landed at Palaly, the military airbase. At Rs 7000 (about $70) for a return trip, it was not cheap for the average Sri Lankan, but even so, it was tough to find a seat.

The ceasefire had brought back hundreds of Sri Lankan Tamils who had fled Jaffna years earlier to live abroad. They came back to check out the homes they had left behind, and to visit ageing relatives or friends who either could not get out all these years or had simply decided to stay.

They brought their children, either born abroad or too young when they left to remember anything, to show them what Jaffna looked like. The place was full of Tamil teenagers wearing cosmopolitan clothes and hairstyles, with pierced bodies and accents from England, Europe and North America.

Even Sinhalese curious to see Jaffna were going up there. There were several new hotels and guest houses but they were all packed and the demand had sent the room tariffs rocketing. Jaffna looked and felt better than it had done on any of my previous visits. A Colombo supermarket had opened shop in Jaffna. People were finally repairing their war-damaged roofs and walls. The Jaffna Library, its building and its treasure of Tamil literature burnt by Sinhalese rioters in 1982, was standing again after a seven-year-long reconstruction effort. Best of all, with security restrictions easing up, mobile phones finally worked up there. A year earlier I had struggled to find one of the sixty landline connections that could call out of the peninsula of 500,000 people. For me, that was the most amazing change.

The Kugharajans had moved out of the Reconstruction and Rehabilitation Authority for the North (RRAN) guest house where I first met them in 2000. They now lived in the home of a relative who had emigrated to the West.

I was at their home for dinner when an Indian man walked in carrying a huge bundle of saris. He was a travelling salesman from Karaikudi in Tamil Nadu. Kugharajan's wife Usha haggled with him over the price. He told me that since August 2002, he had been spending fifteen days a month in Jaffna selling Indian saris.

Each time, he flew from Chennai to Colombo where he hired a van to travel north, stopping first at Vavuniya and then driving up the A9. He was matter-of-fact about the taxes he had to pay to the Tigers to get his saris across the border at Omanthai. It was just like a customs post, he said and told us the story of two other Indians whose entire consignment of saris the Tigers had confiscated because they suspected the salesmen of undervaluing.

'We have to be careful how we conduct ourselves here because the Tigers suspect us of being Indian intelligence agents,' he said.

The Tigers had a political office in the town, which carried out intensive propaganda in the peninsula, mainly against the Sri Lankan military which they wanted out of Jaffna. They also campaigned against rival Tamil political parties in the peninsula. The Tigers could at a moment's notice mobilize large crowds for a demonstration. On several occasions, they brought life in the entire peninsula to a halt by ordering a general strike.

Some months before, the political unit had successfully mobilized support against the inauguration of the rebuilt Jaffna Library. The Sri Lankan government, from the time President

Kumaratunga came to power, had financed the rebuilding as a symbolic gesture of reconciliation with the Tamil people. The Tigers would have preferred the library to remain as it had lain for two decades, a charred-out shell that—through the war—Tamils saw as the symbol of Sinhalese hatred towards them. The Tigers could not undo the new building but they certainly made sure it would lie unused.

The Tigers also had a 'taxation' unit whose job was to keep the Tiger treasury full. Traders were their particular targets. They had to pay 'tax' on everything they sold. The traders in turn passed it on to customers. Kugharajan said people were unhappy but realized there was nothing they could do about it.

'It does seems to be a small price to pay for peace,' he said.

But Jaffna was not entirely peaceful either. Early one morning in June 2003, a few weeks before I visited Jaffna, a sniper killed Robert, the leader of the EPRLF, one of the few anti-Tiger politicians who had dared remain in the peninsula. A single shot felled him as he exercised on the terrace of his office where I used to meet him every time I was in Jaffna. No one doubted it was the Tigers who killed him. His colleagues showed me the exact spot where he had fallen on the terrace. The bullet had come from the direction of a girls' school across the EPRLF office. Robert's grief-stricken comrades guessed the sniper had most likely lain in wait in the empty classroom directly across.

Chavakachcheri, the town that was destroyed in the fighting in 2000 and was little more than a heap of concrete rubble when I last saw it, was being rebuilt. The poster town for the devastation the war had caused, Chavakachcheri had turned into a 'must-see' destination for every dignitary—Sri Lankan and international—who visited the peninsula. Days after signing the ceasefire, Prime Minister Ranil Wickremesinghe visited the peninsula, the first time in several years that a top Sri Lankan leader had made the trip. Media in tow, Wickremesinghe went walkabout in the ruined town. After that, every visiting dignitary, including scores of diplomats, especially from countries that were offering aid to Sri Lanka, made the pilgrimage. An enterprising Englishman, who ran an adventure tour company in Sri Lanka and usually took people mountain biking and river-rafting, began marketing Jaffna soon after the ceasefire, and put the 'ruins of Chavakachcheri' on his itinerary.

But by mid-2003, the main market that had been levelled in the fighting was almost fully rebuilt, filled with jewellery stores and even a shop selling new Indian motorcycles.

But in many other ways, Jaffna was unchanged. I met Paramanathan Selvarajah, who had founded the JGAFD and whom I had last met during the excavations of the skeletons at Chemmani in 1999. He was seated at the counter of the hardware store where he worked near the main Jaffna bus stop. His eyes filled with tears as we talked about his son Prabhakaran, still untraced after all these years.

'Until the government tells me what happened to my son, I am going to keep the issue alive, no matter how many more years it takes,' he said.

Shanthini, whose husband Rasiah Satheeshkumar was identified as one of the two skeletons excavated at Chemmani, now lives at her mother's home in Meesalai with her three children. She had been pregnant with the last child when her husband disappeared.

Shanthini was not at home but I met her mother and two of her four sisters. In 2001, her brother Chenthuran had stepped on a mine near their home and had had to have his leg amputated below the knee. She had taken him to Chennai in south India so he could be fitted with an artificial leg.

In December 2002, the Human Rights Commission of Sri Lanka (HRCSL) carried out an investigation into the alleged mass grave at Chemmani, and appointed a panel to inquire into the disappearances of 296 people in Jaffna peninsula. The three-member panel met six times in Jaffna to interview family members of the disappeared, policemen, soldiers and even Tigers. A commission official said they were doing this to establish the 'respondents' for the disappearances.

In southern Sri Lanka, the ceasefire should have improved the economy and eased the unemployment in the countryside. The economy did register spectacular growth after its worst period in

2001, the year the Tigers bombed the Katunayake International Airport and sent the country tumbling below the red line. But the improvement was visible only in Colombo, where the country's trade-based economy was concentrated. Businessmen in the capital had prospered from the ceasefire. The capital had new international food chains, coffee shops and restaurants. Rich youngsters lounged at new night spots. Flash new imported cars—Sri Lanka does not have an auto industry—crowded Colombo's narrow roads. Property developers were demolishing old houses in the nice areas and putting up luxury high-rise apartments with a view of the ocean to die for.

But the wealth did not trickle very much out of Colombo, not even as far as Kalutara, a seaside town 50 km outside the capital. There I tracked down Lekha Fernando, whom I met first when she was setting off for Lebanon to work as a housemaid and earn herself a dowry. Lekha said she had returned penniless to Sri Lanka within a year after being cheated out of her salary by her Lebanese employer.

After coming back, Lekha married Sujith, a commando in the Sri Lankan army and a family friend who, fortunately for her, did not demand a dowry. They had three children.

The newspapers were still full of horror stories about women who went abroad to work and returned after enduring physical and mental abuse, and torture, by their employers. But undeterred by all that, Lekha was once again considering going abroad to work. Her husband's salary was grossly inadequate to bring up three children, she said. They lived in an unfinished house. It was their own but they had no money to complete it. She used to borrow money from one of her better-off sisters to supplement her husband's income, but they had recently fallen out.

I also revisited Veyangoda where I met Leticia and Lester de Vas Goonewardene, whose son Harshana had gone missing in action in the Mullaithivu battle. The couple said they were now reconciled to the death of their son. They had even started placing a death anniversary remembrance message, with his picture, in the *Daily News*. But the heart refused to accept what the mind had made peace with, and they still clung to the slender hope of their son being alive. They asked me if there was a chance that the ceasefire and the peace talks between the government and the Tigers would lead to the release of any prisoners from Mullaithivu the Tigers might be holding.

Their neighbour, Dayani Gamlath, whose husband was missing in action in the same battle, still believed her husband was alive, Leticia said. She had not remarried and was actively involved in efforts to force the government to trace soldiers missing in action. Leticia's voice held admiration for the young woman's dedication to her husband.

Curious to know if Saman Suresh Kumara, the little boy I met during his ordination as a Buddhist monk in 2001, was still a monk, I went back to the Dimbulagala temple in Polonnaruwa. Contrary to my expectations, he was at the temple. He had grown a little taller and wore his orange robes with a little more confidence than two years earlier. He nodded when I asked if he still missed his mother.

'But I want to be a monk, I don't want to leave the sangha,' he said.

He visited his home twice a year, staying for a week or so each time.

'I play with my old friends,' he said.

I went further east, to Batticaloa, to meet Dharmalingam Sritharan, the boy I had met after his escape from a Tiger camp. He was not at home. His mother, who was returning from the market with a bag of vegetables on her head as I got to their place, said she had sent him to live with her sister in another part of Batticaloa.

'For his safety,' she said.

His brother Jayakanthan said they were waiting for him to turn eighteen.

'Then we can try and fix him a job abroad, maybe in the Middle East,' he said.

A few weeks after his brother's escape from the camp, Jayakanthan said, two men, evidently Tigers, came knocking at their door.

'They wanted the bicycle that Sritharan stole from the camp,' Jayakanthan said.

'I had seen Sritharan's bicycle at their office when I went looking for him, so I told them, bike for bike, we are even,' he said.

The men left but warned they would be back soon.

'That is why we did not want Sritharan here,' he said.

Chitravel Nishanthan, the other boy who had had a close encounter with the Tigers, was living in Switzerland with his brother and sister. Their mother had remarried and emigrated there and had recently sent for her children.

On that memorable day of the news conference by the leader of the Tigers, Velupillai Prabhakaran, he promised he would be more accessible to journalists than he had been until then. But he went back into hiding immediately, emerging only to meet a high-ranking international visitor, such as a foreign minister or a special envoy from abroad. He was not meeting any journalists, and certainly never any of the people whose 'sole representative' he claimed to be. He remains where he was when I saw him in April 2002—a prisoner for life, confined to a cage of his own making, one that he never dare leave.

Timeline

1815   British establish control over the entire island of Ceylon.

1948   Ceylon gains full independence from Britain.

1949   Government disenfranchises Indian Tamil plantation workers.

1956   Solomon West Ridgeway Dias Bandaranaike elected prime minister; brings in the Official Language Act, also known as the Sinhala Only Act.

1959   S.W.R.D. Bandaranaike assassinated by a Buddhist monk.

1960   His wife, Sirimavo, becomes the world's first woman prime minister after winning the elections that year on a sympathy wave.

1970   After losing an election in between to the United National Party (UNP), Sirimavo returns to power.

1971   Janatha Vimukthi Peramuna (JVP), a radical leftist party of Sinhalese students, launches an armed uprising; India and Pakistan help Ceylon crush the revolt.

1972   Sirimavo brings in a new constitution; Ceylon becomes Sri Lanka; Buddhism becomes the country's foremost religion; Tamil resentment grows.

1976   Liberation Tigers of Tamil Eelam (LTTE) formed in Jaffna, northern Sri Lanka.

1977   UNP trounces Sirimavo in the elections; J.R. Jayewardene becomes prime minister; replaces Sirimavo's socialist policies with free-market capitalism.

1978   J.R. Jayewardene introduces a new constitution; the president replaces the prime minister as head of government; J.R. Jayewardene becomes president.

1982   J.R. Jayewardene extends term of parliament, giving his government another six years in office.

1983   Anti-Tamil riots sweep through Colombo, the capital of Sri Lanka, following the killings of thirteen soldiers in an LTTE ambush in Jaffna; India begins covert training of Tamil militants.

1986   LTTE crushes rival militant groups in internecine wars.

1987   Sri Lanka intensifies war against Tamil militancy; India steps in to sign the Indo-Sri Lanka Accord to stop militancy and give Tamils limited political autonomy; India sends its army to disarm militants; LTTE refuses to disarm; begins fighting the Indian soldiers, known as the Indian Peace Keeping Force (IPKF).

1988   JVP, protesting against the presence of Indian soldiers in the north-east, launches an armed insurrection in southern Sri Lanka; UNP wins the parliamentary elections and another term in government; J.R. Jayewardene steps down as president after completing two terms in office; his prime minister, Ranasinghe Premadasa, defeats Sirimavo in the presidential elections; government responds to JVP insurrection with military action; tens of thousands of Sinhalese go missing.

1989   LTTE makes overtures to the Sri Lankan government; peace talks commence between LTTE and the government; Sri Lanka asks IPKF to leave.

1990   India withdraws soldiers; peace talks between the Sri Lankan government and LTTE collapse; war breaks out once again between the LTTE and Sri Lanka.

1991   LTTE assassinates former Indian prime minister, Rajiv Gandhi, one of the architects of the Indo-Sri Lanka Accord.

1993   LTTE suicide bomber kills President Premadasa at May Day rally; Vice-President Dingri Banda Wijetunga takes over as president.

1994   Chandrika Kumaratunga, leader of the Sri Lanka Freedom Party (SLFP) and of the People's Alliance (PA) coalition, wins the parliamentary elections, becomes prime minister; begins peace process with LTTE; LTTE kills Gamini Dissanayake, the UNP candidate in the presidential elections, two weeks before the election; Kumaratunga wins the presidential elections; appoints her mother Sirimavo as prime minister.

1995   LTTE bombs two Sri Lankan navy ships in Trincomalee harbour to announce withdrawal from the ceasefire and peace talks; war breaks out once again; LTTE begins terror strikes in Colombo; Kumaratunga calls it 'war for peace' and announces proposals for a new constitution with a federal-style arrangement for power-sharing with Tamils; Sri Lankan military launches operation to wrest Jaffna peninsula from the LTTE; LTTE withdraws from the peninsula and engineers an exodus of civilians from Jaffna, triggering a massive humanitarian crisis.

1996   LTTE bombs Sri Lanka Central Bank; Sri Lankan military establishes control over Jaffna peninsula; more than 600 Tamil civilians in the north disappear as the military tries to prevent LTTE infiltration into the peninsula.

1997   Government consolidates hold over Jaffna; LTTE hits back with terror in the capital; government responds by imposing restrictions on the movement of Tamils.

1998   Sri Lanka celebrates fifty years of independence in the shadow of the LTTE bomb attack on the Temple of the Tooth, a venerated Buddhist shrine in Kandy, central Sri Lanka; military launches Operation Jaya Sekurui to secure highway to Jaffna peninsula through LTTE-controlled northern Sri Lanka; LTTE launches counter-attacks.

1999   Military calls off Operation Jaya Sekurui; LTTE suicide bomber attempts to kill President Kumaratunga at a public meeting days before the presidential elections, which she is contesting for the second term; blinded in one eye by the attack, Kumaratunga wins the elections but the results show a considerable erosion in support since 1994; discloses after victory that she has invited Norway to help facilitate peace talks with the LTTE.

2000 Kumaratunga intensifies efforts to build consensus with all parties, especially the Opposition UNP, on her constitutional proposals; LTTE attacks and takes over Elephant Pass, the biggest army camp in the north and gateway to Jaffna peninsula; military manages to stave off the LTTE from the peninsula; Kumaratunga introduces a new constitution in parliament for mandatory approval by two-third majority despite opposition from Sinhalese nationalists; withdraws it to avoid defeat when Opposition UNP refuses support to it; in the parliamentary elections, the PA wins; LTTE leader Velupillai Prabhakaran emerges to meet Norwegian special envoy Erik Solheim, signalling the start of the peace process.

2001 Government refuses to lift the ban on the LTTE, a precondition set by the group for negotiations; government's position in parliament shaky after Sri Lanka Muslim Congress (SLMC) pulls outs from PA coalition; LTTE attacks Sri Lanka's only international airport; Sri Lankan economy nosedives; minority PA government enters into a survival pact with the JVP; Kumaratunga decides to call a fresh election; PA loses; Ranil Wickremesinghe becomes prime minister following UNP victory; begins a government of cohabitation with Kumaratunga; LTTE announces ceasefire; new government responds with its own.

2002 UNP government enters into a formal ceasefire agreement with the LTTE; Prabhakaran meets journalists at a press conference for the first time in a decade; peace talks begin between the government and the LTTE.

List of Acronyms

AFSMIA : Association of the Families of Soldiers Missing in Action

BTA : Batticaloa Traders Association

EPRLF : Eelam People's Revolutionary Liberation Front

EROS : Eelam Revolutionary Organisation of Students

FP : Federal Party

GUES : General Union of Eelam Students

HRCSL : Human Rights Commission of Sri Lanka

ICES : International Centre for Ethnic Studies

ICRC : International Committee of the Red Cross

IPKF : Indian Peace Keeping Force

JGAFD : Jaffna Guardian Association for Families of the Disappeared

JVP : Janatha Vimukthi Peramuna

LTTE : Liberation Tigers of Tamil Eelam

MBRL : Multi-Barrel Rocket Launcher

MIA : Missing in Action

MIC : Muslim Information Centre

NIB : National Intelligence Bureau

NSC : National Sangha Council

PA	:	People's Alliance
PLOTE	:	People's Liberation Organisation of Tamil Eelam
PTA	:	Prevention of Terrorism Act
RRAN	:	Reconstruction and Rehabilitation Authority for the North
SLFP	:	Sri Lanka Freedom Party
SLMC	:	Sri Lanka Muslim Congress
SLMM	:	Sri Lanka Monitoring Mission
SOFE	:	Solidarity Organization for the Foreign Employed
TELO	:	Tamil Eelam Liberation Organization
TNA	:	Tamil National Army
TULF	:	Tamil United Liberation Front
UNHCR	:	United Nations High Commissioner for Refugees
UNP	:	United National Party
UTHR	:	University Teachers for Human Rights

Bibliography

Here is a list of books that enriched my understanding of Sri Lanka. They present diverse viewpoints of the country, its history, society, politics and the conflict.

Non-fiction

Balasingham, Adele A. *Women Fighters of Liberation Tigers*. London: Liberation Tigers of Tamil Eelam International Secretariat, 1993.

Chandraprema, C.A. *The Years of Terror: The JVP Insurrection 1987–1989*. Colombo: Lake House, 1991.

de Silva, K.M. *A History of Sri Lanka*. Delhi: Oxford University Press, 1981.

Dissanayake, T.D.S.A. *The Agony of Sri Lanka: An In-Depth Account of the Racial Riots of July 1983*. Colombo: Swastika Pvt. Ltd, 1983.

Dixit, J.N. *Assignment Colombo*. Delhi: Konark, 1998.

Geiger, Wihelm (trans). *The Mahavamsa or The Great Chronicle of Ceylon*. Colombo: Department of Information, Government of Sri Lanka, 1950.

Gunaratna, Rohan. *Indian Intervention in Sri Lanka: The Role of India's Intelligence Agencies*. Colombo: South Asian Network on Conflict Research, 1993.

Hoole, Rajan. *Sri Lanka: The Arrogance of Power—Myths, Decadence and Murder*. Colombo: University Teachers' Human Rights

(Jaffna), 2001.

Jayewardene, Kumari. *Nobodies to Somebodies: The Rise of the Colonial Bourgeoisie in Sri Lanka*. Colombo: Social Scientists Association, 2000.

Loganathan, Ketheeswaran. *Sri Lanka: Lost Opportunities*. Colombo: Centre for Policy Research and Analysis, University of Colombo, 1996.

Manor, James. *The Expedient Utopian: Bandaranaike and Ceylon*. Cambridge, Cambridge University Press, 1989.

McGowan, William. *Only Man is Vile: The Tragedy of Sri Lanka*. London: Picador, 1992.

Narayan Swamy, M.R. *Tigers of Lanka: From Boys to Guerillas*. Delhi: Konark, 1994.

Pratap, Anita. *Island of Blood: Frontline Reports from Sri Lanka, Afghanistan and Other South Asian Flashpoints*. New Delhi: Viking, 2001.

Rahula, Walpola. *History of Buddhism in Ceylon*. Dehiwala (Sri Lanka): Buddhist Cultural Centre, 1956.

Rasanyagam, Mudaliyar C. *Ancient Jaffna*. Delhi: Asian Educational Services, 1984.

Ratnatunga, Sinha. *Politics of Terrorism: The Sri Lanka Experience*. Canberra: International Fellowship for Social and Economic Development, 1988.

Seneviratne, H.L. *The Work of Kings*. Chicago: University of Chicago Press, 2000.

Somasundaram, Daya. *Scarred Minds*. New Delhi: Sage, 1998.

Thambiah, Stanley J. *Buddhism Betrayed?: Religion, Politics and Violence in Sri Lanka*. Chicago: University of Chicago Press, 1992.

Thiranagama, Rajini, Rajan Hoole, Sritharan, and Daya Somasundaram. *Broken Palmyrah: The Tamil Crisis in Sri Lanka, An Inside Account*. California, The Sri Lanka Studies Institute, 1990.

Wilson, A. Jeyaratnam. *S.J.V. Chelvanayakam and the Crisis of Sri Lankan Tamil Nationalism 1947–1977: A Political Biography*. Honolulu: University of Hawaii Press, 1994.

Memoirs

Gooneratne, Yasmin. *Relative Merits.* New York: St. Martin's Press, 1986.

Ondaatje, Michael. *Running in the Family.* New York: Vintage International, 1993.

Fiction

Gunasekera, Romesh. *Monkfish Moon.* New Delhi: Penguin India, 1992

———. *Reef.* New Delhi: Penguin India, 1994.

Muller, Carl. *The Jam Fruit Tree.* New Delhi: Penguin India, 1993.

———. *Yakkada Yaka.* New Delhi: Penguin India, 1994.

Ondaatje, Michael. *Anil's Ghost.* London: Bloomsbury, 2000.

Selvadurai, Shyam. *Funny Boy.* New Delhi: Penguin India, 1994.

———. *Cinnamon Gardens.* New Delhi: Penguin India, 1998.

Sivanandan, A. *When Memory Dies.* London: Arcadia Books, 1997.

Woolf, Leonard. *Village in the Jungle.* Oxford: Oxford University Press, 1981.